ABOVE FLANDERS' FIELDS

ABOVE FLANDERS' FIELDS

A COMPLETE RECORD OF THE BELGIAN FIGHTER
PILOTS AND THEIR UNITS DURING
THE GREAT WAR, 1914-1918

WALTER M PIETERS

GRUB STREET · LONDON

Published by
Grub Street
The Basement
10 Chivalry Road
London SW11 1HT

Map by Walter M Pieters

A complete record for this book is available from the British Library

ISBN 1 898697 83 3

Typeset by Pearl Graphics, Hemel Hempstead
Printed and bound by Biddles Ltd, Guildford and Ling's Lynn

Contents

Foreword

Walter Pieters contacted me a couple of years ago when I was just starting to research Volume 4 of Grub Street's WWI aces series, *Above the War Fronts*. I was delighted because Belgium was one of the countries my co-authors and I were covering and I hoped that Walter would be able to fill many gaps in my information. I was not to be disappointed.

Very generously he supplied me with a vast amount of information on the handful of Belgian aces from the 1914-18 conflict — far more than I needed in fact, which led me to ask what else he knew of these and other Belgian fighter pilots of World War One. What I discovered was that he had a vast knowledge of these men, and his research into them was on-going. I immediately told him I thought this project should be made available in book form, and felt certain that Grub Street would take an interest. Again I was not disappointed.

I was fortunate in Walter asking me to edit what he had written. Not that I was able to add anything to his manuscript, his requirement was simply to put his Belgian-English into English-English. This I was pleased to do, but it led me to learn quickly just how much information Walter had on his fellow countrymen who had fought in the skies over Flanders in the First World War.

By contrast to the major belligerents Belgium's contribution had to be small, in direct comparison to their military as well as geographical size. Nevertheless, in like proportion, the Belgian fighter pilots were no less dedicated in their task and with due pride and expertise, took their place alongside British and French airmen who fought the German army and marine aircraft on the northern end of the lines, next to the Channel Coast.

The reader will find a mass of interesting information in these pages, made all the more intriguing because we know so little about these men and their fighting force. Therefore, this history fills a definite gap in our knowledge and will also fascinate those who take only a general interest in war flying. Being such a small fighting force, Walter is able to encompass every Belgian fighter pilot who saw active service, thus the book covers not just the aces or the well known, but every one who flew a fighter 'plane in Belgian service.

If this is not enough, then the sheer mass of photographic coverage will surely overwhelm the reader. That so much exists shouldn't really surprise me I suppose, but it is nevertheless amazing what has survived over so many years. The vast majority of these images come from private albums, but in any event, my guess would be that historian and enthusiast alike will never have seen coverage of the Belgian fighter pilots in such profusion. With well over one hundred such pictures, none of us will be disappointed.

Grub Street Publishers are to be commended in grasping the opportunity of publishing in recent years a number of books on WWI aviation subjects, which I know include my own, and my own along with co-authors. These, and two or three others which will be following shortly, will soon enable the historian and enthusiast alike to have such a range of informative books on WWI fighter aviation, that he or she will be able to study or play for hours, referencing and cross referencing all this data. Walter Pieters' book can only add to that data base of information.

You will not be disappointed either.

Norman Franks

Introduction

One fine day I was shopping and looking for a record of my favourite rock band. Finding the record shop closed I wandered through the city when suddenly a corner of my eye spotted a book called *Above the Trenches, a complete record of the fighter aces and units of the British Empire Air Forces 1915-1920* by Christopher Shores, Norman Franks and Russell Guest. I went into the bookshop and turned over the leaves. I was flabbergasted by the way the authors had brought everything so clearly together. The only thing that bothered me at the time was the price, so I walked back to the recordshop. That evening at home I was again turning over the leaves of the book, for I did not buy the record, but had bought the book!

Whilst reading it, my mind wandered off in the direction of our Belgian airmen. Our pilots were there also, although not so numerous. They played their part in the Great War Air Battle, but their stories are not well known by the public, especially abroad. Some time ago I read an article about their victories and it fascinated me. Linking all these thoughts an idea was born — to write a book about our Belgian fighter pilots!

I started with visiting the Brussels Air Museum several times, where I found evidence of some 25 victories by our pilots. Not satisfied with the result I took the opportunity of reaching the Belgian population by means of the National Broadcasting Institution (BRT 2), where people who are looking for some special item can make a request over the air. I was invited for an interview and only a few minutes after this, I received a phone call from Lieutenant-Colonel SBH M.Emonts-Gast, a modern fighter pilot, stationed at Evere, who opened the most important door to me. This door was none other than the one at the Centre de Documentation Historique de l'Armée Belge (CDH) at Evere, Brussels. Here I had the opportunity to consult the *Ordres Journalières de l'Aviation Militaire Belge*.

Regretfully the 'Ordres' were not complete, ranging only from 3 February 1915 till 26 June 1918. Luckily other sources at the CDH, like combat orders of Divisional Intelligence Reports (2me Section), completed the missing days somewhat. Another important source was a legacy of the Groupe de Chasse, which kept a diary (*carnet de vols*) and it registered everything till 11 November 1918. All this information gave me a good start for my enterprise. However, some former or later fighter pilots, mentioned in this book, who flew with the recce-units after 26 June 1918, have no exact number of offensive patrols (OP) or combats against their names in their description (e.g. Lieutenant Louis Robin who at the time was a recce-pilot, or Adjudant Charles Gordinne who in May left the 9me Escadrille de Chasse for the 5me Escadrille d'Observation). Therefore, I was also given the opportunity to consult nearly all the pilots' surviving service records.

A third great help came in the person of Mr. Norman Franks, one of the outstanding historians on the Air War 1914-18. Somehow I managed to get his address, made contact and he was willing to help me. He compared Belgian claims and losses with all German claims and losses, so we could trace who-got-who up along the North Sea coast. He encouraged me to try an English version and he put my English into English English!

Yet another great help was Baron de Chestret de Haneffe. His father was the brother of two of our fighter pilots and he was kind enough to give me more details concerning his uncles and gave me some addresses of other pilots' descendants. They all kindly helped me to obtain some personal notes of their fathers and loaned me some photographs which are very rare and of course have never been published before. Indeed, all these personal notes increase our knowledge of what really happened and give the book a more 'personal' touch.

Mrs. Maggie Olieslagers, the pilot's only daughter, was also kind enough to lend me some photographs together with two of the most interesting books concerning the history of the Aviation Militaire Belge: *Reclassements, hélice en croix and vue cavalière*, edited by our most famous fighter pilot, Baron Willy Coppens de Houthulst. The fact that Coppens resided the last five years of his life at Mrs. Olieslagers' home gave me a great deal of information about Coppens as well. Another source appeared to be Mr. Georges Lecomte. He possesses a remarkable collection of WWI photographs in his private collection.

Last but not least I found an address at Deurne Airport where an extremely rare collection of photographs was donated by the late Mr. Eddie Rerren. Somehow he managed to obtain many pilots' addresses and from most of them, Mr. Rerren was able to add photographs. Not only of the Great War pilots, but even pre-war and post-war pilots, so his collection is probably the most important one of all concerning the Belgian Air Service's pilots. So, with these photographs added to the others, I succeeded in finding pictures of nearly all our fighter pilots. In the book the highest rank reached during the War will be shown under the pilot's picture, as it was very difficult to find out when the photograph was taken. You will notice that some NCO's reverted to soldier at their own request (Adjt G.Coppens d'Eeckenbrugge, S/Lt Pierre de Chestret de Haneffe, ...), prior to being posted to the Aviation Militaire. This was, however, no necessity, but sometimes it occurred for some unknown reason.

I tried to find as much information as possible about our pilots although, even if their service records were found, the dates of their subsequent death were not always easy to find. Honours and awards won during the years are strictly the Military Medals found in the service records, and in most cases tracing relatives of the pilots was very difficult. Therefore civil honours and awards were harder to trace. The aircraft used by most of our pilots are extremely difficult to puzzle out as well: the most easy way would have been to say that all Hanriots were flown by the 9me Escadrille, all Spads by the 10me and all Sopwith Camels by the 11me Escadrille pilots, but photographs show that every unit used any scout available: even a Sopwith Pup (#SB4) carried 10me Escadrille's Comet on its fuselage. It was also possible that a pilot took to the air in someone else's aircraft, possibly from one of the other units, for they were all based at the same airfield! It all depended on serviceability.

Also bear in mind that at the time I was born, in 1960, only 26 out of the 80 fighter pilots were still alive and from those who died during the years, I only knew the name of Willy Coppens, although I was never given the chance to meet him. This was due to the fact that hardly anyone ever wrote anything concerning the Aviation Militaire Belge, e.g. Louis Robin, successful gunner/observer to Fernand Jacquet, with four victories was a complete unknown to me until only three years ago! Up till then, to me, Jacquet was a single-seater Spad pilot (I have a picture of him standing in front of his Spad). I knew of the existence of Louis Wouters, renowned observer to Jules Jaumotte, a very successful team for aerial photographical work, but it was only a few weeks prior to writing this introduction that I learnt he was also known as Emile Wouters, the fighter pilot.

Therefore I cannot claim this is a *complete* record of our fighter pilots and their units, but it is as complete as possible and I hope you will enjoy it.

This book is dedicated to our brave Belgian Airmen, that their memory may not be forgotten !

The Aviation Militaire Belge

King Albert was one of the first to realize the benefit of an Aviation Militaire, although General Hellebaut, at the time the Minister of War, was the first military man to fly, in July 1910. It happened at Kiewit near Hasselt and he was flown in the aircraft of civilian pilot, Chevalier Jules de Laminne. Chevalier de Laminne was the proud owner of a new French Henri Farman airplane, stationed at Kiewit and General Hellebaut was invited on a flight by the former. General Hellebaut saw the benefits in using aircraft and gave the order to introduce the aircraft into an Aviation Militaire, which up till then only consisted of observation balloons. De Laminne in turn was asked by the General if he was willing to teach the first officers appointed by the War Ministry to undergo flying training. The commanding officer of the Aviation Militaire, Commandant Le Clement de Saint-Marcq, was assigned to appoint an officer as the first military man to obtain a brevet. The choice made was Lieutenant Georges Nelis who received his brevet (nr. 28) on 21 December 1910 and for whom personally an aircraft was purchased. The previous brevet holders were all civilians, except two. These two officers were Lieutenants Baudouin de Montens d'Oosterwyck and Alfred Sarteel. Both men were artillery officers who received their brevets on 30 September (nr.19) and 10 November (nr.23) 1910 respectively. They had learned to fly at their own expense and initiative in a private school, run by Baron Pierre de Caters. The latter was the first Belgian to receive a civil brevet, in 1909. The school was situated at Sint-Job-in-'t-Goor, near Antwerp.

Commandant Le Clement de Saint-Marcq, not at all convinced, was meanwhile instructed to establish a training programme. This, however, took too much time and the War Ministry decided that officers were to be trained in the way adopted in French civilian flying schools, thus they should first receive a civilian brevet before being sent to the Military Aviation School. During the War, Lt Nelis, although still a very young officer, became adjutant to the Commanding Officer of the Aviation Militaire (Commandant Emile Mathieu) and afterwards, from 1915 onwards, the Commanding Officer of the technical service in Calais-Beaumarais, a post he held till the end of the war, thus never seeing action over the front.

In the spring of 1911 the Military Aviation School was established, but it did not have any aircraft! The Aviation Militaire's personnel tables proudly showed the existence of five pilots (Lieutenants Nelis, Dhanis, Bronne, Sarteel and Lebon), two mechanics and one carpenter. The school became operational after it received an aircraft donated by King Albert, that had been presented to his Majesty by Baron de Caters. The King, himself not being a pilot, turned this unusual present over to the School.

The strength of the Aviation Militaire Belge (AMB) in 1914 was four squadrons, with four Henri Farman 80HP aircraft each. The flying personnel consisted of a Commanding Officer (CO), five pilots and six observers. The four CO's were Capitaine-Commandant Theo Wahis (Infantry), Capitaine Francois Deschamps (Engineer), Lieutenant Jules Soumoy (Infantry) and Lieutenant Arsène Demanet (Artillery). The AMB, being a very young service, detached all the men serving in it, from other services, such as the Artillery and Engineers. It was actually a bit of an élite-corps to the two services mentioned. The ground equipment could boast five lorries, (one used as workshop and one luggage-van for each squadron). This meant that our small Aviation Militaire was at least very mobile.

Belgium's incidental involvement in World War I

Belgium, at the outbreak of hostilities, was a neutral country (Treaty of 19 April 1839) and was violated by Germany, as part of the famous Schlieffen-plan. A sweep through Belgium was necessary to outmanoeuvre the French troops fighting on their frontier with the German Army. This turn through Belgium would mean a direct threat to Paris, and the capture of the French capital surely would result in the surrender of its Army. A march-through was 'politely' requested by Kaiser Wilhelm, through Mr. Von Below-Saleske to the Belgian Minister of Foreign Affairs, but refused by King Albert. Thereupon Germany declared war on Belgium on 3 August 1914.

On August 4th, the first German troops violated the frontier. At this stage the strength of the Belgian Army consisted of 188,000 soldiers serving in the Field Army and 88,000 at the garrisons. Another 40,000 young men enlisted as volunteers in those early days. The Belgian Field Army consisted of six Infantry Divisions (DA), one Cavalry Division (DC) and three garrison brigades (Liège, Namur and Antwerp).

The brunt of the attack in the opening days fell upon Liège and its fortresses under the command of General Leman. These fortresses were supposed to be the best ones built in the 19th Century. The last fortress, however, surrendered on 16 August, at least one week later than the German Army had reckoned with. In fact the German Oberst Heeresleitung did not anticipate strong Belgian resistance and heavily underestimated the obstinacy of the small Belgian Army. Aggression towards the population and its towns began to occur almost daily as a result of the Belgian opposition.

The Belgian Army, more or less left alone because of the German push against the French troops and the battles on the frontier (Franco-Belgian border in Belgian Luxembourg), became isolated in the direction of Antwerp (Antwerpen). A first attempt to break through the German defences was carried out, without success, between August 24th-26th. The British Naval Division was hastily embarked to Ostende in the direction of Antwerpen and during the Battle of the Marne, Belgian troops, together with the Naval Division, made a second attempt to break through the side-wing of the German 4.Armee between 9 and 13 September. After the failure of the Battle of the Marne, the German 4.Armee again turned its attention to the Belgian front. A third attack of the Belgian Army was launched on 25 September, but also failed. The first German attacks in the direction of Antwerpen began on the 28th and after increasing their efforts, the situation of the besieged Army became untenable. Antwerp surrendered on 10 October (signed at Kontich) and the Belgian Army withdrew through a narrow corridor to the Yser river. Because the gap was so narrow, a part of the Army had to retreat into Holland and 33,471 Officers, NCO's and men were interned.

The next battle, at the Yser river, began on 16 October (thus hardly leaving any time for the hard-pressed, poorly equipped Belgians to recover). After many days of heavy fighting at the Yser river, the situation became critical. A few hamlets on the western side of the river had already fallen into German hands. Therefore it was decided that the locks at Nieuport needed to be opened (a tactic already used in the middle ages) to stop the German Army in their advance to the Channel ports. The fields between the river and the railway line, connecting Nieuport with Dixmude, were slowly flooded and after several attempts, the desired result was achieved on 1 November. The German troops on the western riverbed withdrew hastily to the other side, only occupying a few isolated 'islands'.

The last piece of Belgium was thus saved. Apart from the capture of Dixmude on 10 November no changes worth mentioning appeared on the Belgian front line. Casualties from 4 August until 1 November were 11,657.

Mobilisation of the Aviation Militaire Belge

On 1 August 1914, when mobilisation was ordered, Escadrilles I and II were fully operational units. Escadrilles III and IV were not yet completely established. Escadrille I (CO Lieutenant Demanet) was stationed at Ans near Liège, Escadrille II (Lieutenant

Soumoy) at Belgrade near Namur. Escadrille III (Capitaine Deschamps) was stationed at Louvain and Escadrille IV (Capitaine-Commandant Wahis) was based at Wilryck (now Wilrijk), near Antwerp. On August 11th eight more Farman 80HP aircraft were delivered by the French Government to keep our AMB operational, for many aircraft were already unserviceable. A fifth Escadrille (Escadrille V) was formed and equipped with four Blériot monoplanes flown by civilian pilots who had been called to military service. Temporary command was given to Sous-Lieutenant Henri Crombez who flew his personal Deperdussin monoplane. The unit was based at Wilryck and Crombez was soon replaced by Lieutenant Louis Stellingwerff. The Aviation School was based at Sing-Agatha-Berchem, near Brussels, but sent to Wilryck, together with its, by now, eight Maurice Farman aircraft.

After the fall of Liège and Namur, all the escadrilles moved to Wilryck, except Escadrille II, which moved to Chimay near Amiens, France, where its CO, Lieutenant Soumoy, was killed in an accident. Lieutenant Felix Isserentant then took command and moved the Escadrille to the Wellington hippodrome at Ostende. While the other escadrilles were still based at Antwerpen, a British Royal Naval Air Service Squadron and a French Escadrille were sent to help the AMB for it had lost most of its aircraft in a furious gale on 13 September. Two aircraft were demolished and many others were made unserviceable.

On 4 October, the Bollekens factory moved from Antwerpen to Ostende. This factory built Farman aircraft under license and was the workshop for the entire AMB (when it later moved to Calais, the factory was closed and Lieutenant Nelis took command of the Military Workshop).

The four escadrilles based at Wilryck all left that same evening for Ostende. On 11 October, Escadrilles II and III moved to Saint-Pol-sur-Mer in France, soon followed by the other escadrilles, but Escadrille I left Saint-Pol-sur-Mer for Coxyde on the 17th. In March 1915, Commandant Theo Wahis became the new CO of the AMB which was reorganised after the total destruction of our aircraft, again due to a hurricane on 28 December 1914. There is no exact number of aircraft destroyed during this massive storm, but the French Government again provided the AMB, this time completely, with new aircraft.

The First Fighter Pilots

As there were no dedicated fighter aircraft at the beginning of the war there were obviously no fighter squadrons in any of the countries engaged in the Great War. Before the war, however, Belgium was the first European country to experiment with a machine gun on board an aircraft. This occured on 12 September 1912 when an aircraft flown by Lieutenant Nelis with Sous-Lieutenant Stellingwerff as observer fired a few rounds at a ground target (sheet) from a low altitude. Our army was persuaded to give it a try by Lieutenant Lewis, an American, who had invented the Lewis machine gun.

Ironically our Aviation Militaire did not have any machine guns at the outbreak of the war. On the contrary, the two airmen who demolished the sheet were punished for doing so!! British Air Services, however, did have machine guns. In November 1913, Capitaine-Commandant Mathieu and Lieutenant Stellingwerff went over to England and gave demonstrations of the machine gun, first at Hendon, then at Aldershot, with the result that the weapon was adopted by the British. I doubt that the two Belgians were punished for demolishing some items of equipment over there!

During the first months of hostilities, aircraft were only used for reconnaissance, but their information was not always believed by the various Headquarters of the besieged armies. The first aircraft lost was a Farman two-seater (#22), flown by Lts De Bueger and Schmidt. They landed at Roosteren (Holland) and were kept on the ground until the afternoon. Both men were then liberated and sent to Belgium, crossing the Meuse river by boat. The aircraft was to be left in Dutch hands. Most of the opposing airmen who met each other in the air simply waved to one another, but there were actually a few pilots who were not so friendly to the enemy. Sous-Lieutenant Crombez was such a man for he had a few early airfights in August. On 25 September the airmen Carbury/Prince de Ligne were forced to land after an airfight over Kontich near Antwerp, but the force-landing was not the work of the German opponent. Carbury, an English pilot from the Royal Naval Air Service Squadron, was obliged to crash his aircraft when his motor stalled. On the same day two other airmen (Sous-Lieutenant de Petrowski/Sergent Benselin) forced a German Taube to land on the airfield of Sint-Agatha-Berchem. The German pilot was mortally wounded during the fight by a rifle bullet fired from either de Petrowski or Benselin. This, however, was never an official claim, but if it had been, it would have been the first aerial victory in history, for it happened two weeks before the first official victory by the French crew Frantz/Quenault .

On 3 January 1915 two Lewis machine guns were delivered through the English aviation park at St Pol-sur-Mer. These were fitted on two aircraft, thus creating the first two fighter aircraft. This also meant that, when a Belgian front line Division signalled the approach of hostile aircraft to the Centre d'Aviation at Furnes, this centre could then order two airmen to take off in pursuit.

In February the AMB came under the command of the 1ère Section, Grand Quartier General (GQG). The base of the 1ère Section was at Houthem, near the GQG. That same month, 28 offensive patrols were flown by 13 different airmen. Fourteen airfights were made in which one Farman (Lieutenants Hedo and Declercq) was forced to land due to a fight between ten Albatros two-seaters and three Farman two-seaters. This happened on 26 February and it became the first 'dogfight' in which Belgian aircraft were involved.

The first possible victory was claimed on 26 March. Lieutenant De Bueger with his observer Sous-Lieutenant Boschmans were flying a patrol over the Yser river at 600 metres, when they spotted an Albatros two-seater over Woumen. After a burst of Boschmans' Lewis gun, the German two-seater went into a steep dive, with the pilot apparently hit, because he supported his head with both hands. Whether the plane crashed or simply landed was not witnessed.

When in April the great French pre-war pilot Roland Garros equipped his Morane monoplane with a machine gun that fired through the propeller, the blades of which had metal strips attached to deflect bullets, we can speak of the first real fighter.

Inspired by Garros' victories that month, Lieutenant Fernand Jacquet fitted a machine gun on his own Farman. Garros, of course, had a propeller in front of him, whereas Jacquet's Farman was a 'pusher' - the propeller being behind him. Therefore Jacquet could fire ahead without worrying about bullets hitting the propeller. Unfortunately, Garros eventually damaged his blades which forced him down inside German lines to become a prisoner. Jacquet, in turn, started to chase every German plane he saw, and on 17 April the first German aircraft officially fell to the guns of a Belgian aircraft. The first men to attack an observation balloon were Adjudant José Orta with his observer Sous-Lieutenant Louis de Burlet, who threw three bombs on the balloon over Houthulst. Fortunately they missed their target, otherwise the two would have been on their last patrol, had the balloon exploded.

In June 1915 the first Nieuport N10 *Bébés* began to arrive and in July the following fighter pilots were to be found in the Aviation Militaire's personnel roster:

Escadrille I		(CO Capitaine A.Demanet)	
Capt	A.Demanet	pilot	Nieuport N10
Lt	F.Jacquet	pilot	Farman
Lt	H.Vindevoghel	observer	

Escadrille II		(CO Lieutenant F.Isserentant)	
Adjt Lt	R.Castiau L.Robin	pilot observer	Nieuport N10
S/Lt	J.Olieslagers	pilot	Nieuport N10 scout

Escadrille III	(CO Commandant R.Dhanis)
None out of six Voisin two-seaters, although Adjt J.Orta/S/Lt L.de Burlet flew quite a few offensive patrols on their own initiative.	

Escadrille IV		(CO Capitaine Hagemans)	
S/Lt Lt	H.Crombez L.Stellingwerff	pilot observer	Nieuport N10

Escadrille V		(CO Lieutenant E.Moulin)	
Lt S/Lt	J.Dony C.Dumont	pilot observer	H.Farman

Escadrille hydravions
Only one Farman Seaplane was flown by Capitaine A.De Bueger with his observer Lieutenant Ruysschaert.

Both Sous-Lieutenants Jules Tyck and Robert Lagrange were at the time at Villacoublay to collect two Nieuports. Sous-Lieutenant Lagrange's aircraft crashed while taking off on 2 July and he was killed.

From 1 July 1915 a daily program was started for the fighter pilots who were, as listed above, not operating in just one escadrille. Nevertheless the readiness state on July 4th was:

Mission de chasse:	S/Lt J. Olieslagers	readiness	3 am -12 noon
	Capt A. Demanet	readiness	12 noon -9 pm
	Adjt A. Behaeghe	reserve	—

The first fighter pilot to fly a war mission in a Nieuport N10 monoplane was Sous-Lieutenant Crombez on 26 August. A few days later Adjudant Behaeghe followed his example and he became the first man to have an aerial combat in a scout. Sous-Lieutenant J.Olieslagers flew his first scout mission on 6 September and had his first combat the same day. Six days later he was the first Belgian fighter pilot to down an aircraft.

October 1915 was the month that the tally of fighter pilots was doubled to six, being: Capitaine A.Demanet, Sous-Lieutenants R.Castiau, H.Crombez, J.Olieslagers, J.Tyck and Adjudant A.Behaeghe. Commandant Wahis, CO of the Aviation Militaire, was caught that month bringing his wife into the trenches on 15 October which led to his removal in 1916. Command was then given to Major Roland Van Crombrugghe, an Artillery Officer, who had never flown in an aircraft and, in fact, never did.

With six pilots on strength, the structure of availability for offensive patrols was changed as follows (e.g. 5 December 1915):

Mission de chasse:	S/Lt J.Tyck	6 am - noon
	Capt A.Demanet	reserve
	S/Lt A.Behaeghe	noon -6 pm
	S/Lt P.Hanciau	reserve
	S/Lt J.Olieslagers	overall reserve

Creation of the Fighter Units

The decision for the creation of a fighter unit was made on 18 January 1916. Escadrille I was finally transformed to the 1ère Escadrille de Chasse on 22 February. The CO was Capitaine Demanet, who stayed at the post he already occupied. In June, however, he was replaced by Capitaine Jacquet and the Escadrille changed its base from Coxyde to Les Moeres. The Escadrille consisted of the following pilots: Capitaine Jacquet, Lieutenant Louis Robin (observer to Jacquet), Sous-Lieutenant Olieslagers, Adjudant Egide Roobaert, 1ers Sergent-Majors Louis de Chestret de Haneffe, Charles de Munck, Maurice Franchomme, Albert Van Cotthem and Sergent Robert De Leener. The aircraft were still Nieuport N10 *Bébés*, except for Jacquet's obsolete Farman two-seater. In August 1916 these Nieuports were replaced by the 'newer' Nieuport N11, and a second fighter unit was formed.

The Escadrille V became the 5me Escadrille de Chasse and Capitaine Jules Dony was appointed CO. The unit consisted of Sous-Lieutenants Pierre Braun, Alexandre de Petrowski, Adjudants Charles Ciselet, Edmond Desclée, Jacques Goethals, Max Orban, 1ers Sergent-Majors Pierre de Chestret de Haneffe and Ernest Lambert. The base for this unit remained the airfield of Coxyde and transfer to Les Moeres did not take place before the summer of 1917.

The 5me Escadrille was the first to have more than two pilots in the air at the same time: on 15 February 1917 seven pilots took the air together for an offensive patrol. At this stage of the war the number of single-seaters in the Aviation Militaire was 21 out of a total of 44 aircraft. During this time, no unit markings existed and most pilots carried just a personal marking, such as a 'sparrow-hawk' on Adjt Goethals' Nieuport, the word 'Fox-Trot' on Adjt Roobaert's N11, blue, red and white chequered wheel coverings on Adjt Franchomme's Nieuports or the word 'Vampire' on S/Lt Crombez' various single-seaters.

In the early days of the Escadrilles de Chasse the pattern to secure the sky over the Belgian lines was as mentioned in October 1916:

| Mission de chasse: | 1ère Escadrille de Chasse from 1 Oct, noon to noon 2 Oct |
| | 5me Escadrille de Chasse from 2 Oct, noon to noon 3 Oct |

Official victories, however, remained a rarity. This was not due to lack of heroism. There were other reasons: the two great battles of the Somme and Verdun took most German Staffeln into France during 1916. Another reason was the lack of good aircraft. There was also the wind which always came from the West, thus from the sea. This meant that every combat, although started above the Belgian lines, always ended on the other side of the lines. To break off a combat was extremely difficult for the same reason: they had to be flown against the wind and there were always German scouts on the look-out for such planes to intercept. All these reasons make it clear that confirmed victories were very hard to achieve, for nearly all the downed German aircraft fell behind their own lines.

To confirm a victory, beyond doubt, the aircraft had to be destroyed within Allied lines or it had to be seen to fall, close enough to the German front lines in order for it to be confirmed by Allied ground troops. Confirmation by other pilots sharing in the combat or witnessing it, was not sufficient. Besides the AMB could not permit heavy losses to its own aircraft/airmen, so prolonged combat was not encouraged.

The total number of aircraft in the AMB available on 1 January 1917 was a mere 39: six at Hondschoote, six (fighters) at Les Moeres, twelve (including the 5me Escadrille de Chasse) at Coxyde and fifteen at Houthem. The 1916 plan to secure the sky over our Front was kept well into 1917. The number of fighters increased to 30 during the year (fifteen to each squadron) and from July onwards no lone sorties were allowed anymore. Pilots had to fly with at least one companion. The time of the lone wolf on the prowl was over. Even the great French ace, Capitaine Georges Guynemer fell in combat whilst flying alone, although he had started out with a companion who had become separated and the demise of Werner Voss, shot down in a heroic fight with SE5s from both 60 and 56 Squadron (RFC) is also known to all air enthusiasts. With this new situation, the escadrilles de chasse received the following schedule on 13 July 1917:

Mission de chasse:	chasse:	am	1ère Escadrille de Chasse
		pm	5me Escadrille de Chasse
	protection:	am	5me Escadrille de Chasse
		pm	1ère Escadrille de Chasse

Armament and Equipment

The lack of worthy, adequate equipment played a great role. Belgium itself was robbed of nearly all its resources following the retreat and, anyway, from the very beginning she wasn't equipped to fight a war, being initially a neutral state country. France, however, was happy to equip the Aviation Militaire Belge from time to time with aeroplanes and later 'updated' aircraft, so the AMB could be kept operational. Belgium remained the 'little brother' for the rest of the war.

There were no great pushes against or by Belgian troop positions. The front line hardly changed and this was experienced through all aspects of the war. In other ways the Belgian Army could not afford great losses in strength nor did it have the necessary financial resources, so always stayed the poor 'relation' to the other Allies.

When, for instance, in France the Nieuport N17 was replaced by the far better Spad S7, the AMB still flew with Nieuports N10, N11, N12 and N16, forerunners of the Nieuport N17! The French Escadrille N57 was equipped with the Nieuport N17 as early as June 1916. These aircraft were delivered in small numbers to the Belgian Army, but instead the Nieuport 23 was purchased from June 1917. With these aircraft, the first Flights came into existence: four flights equipped with three scouts each (the word 'Flight' became the only English word used in the Francophobe AMB). The newly equipped 1ère Escadrille de Chasse took the *Thistle* as its insignia, suggested by Adjudant Andre de Meulemeester. Almost at the same time, the 5me Escadrille de Chasse was also given the N17 and N23; here Adjudant Franchomme created the *Comet* as the squadron's insignia. The N17 was powered with a le Rhône 9y 120 HP engine or a Clerget 9b 130 HP engine.

Another Nieuport used was the N10 'mono' of which four were ordered in 1915. The first was wrecked when Sous-Lieutenant R.Lagrange crashed to his death on 1 July 1915. Of the remaining three, 1ère Escadrille, 2me Escadrille and 4me Escadrille each received one. The N10 was powered with a le Rhône 9c 80 HP engine and armed with one Lewis machine gun on top of the upper wing, set to fire over the propeller arc.

The Nieuport N11 C1 'Bébé' was first delivered to the 1ère Escadrille in February 1916 and stayed at the front until June 1917. The N11 had a le Rhône 9c 80 HP rotary engine and like the N10 was armed with a Lewis gun on top of the upper wing.

The Nieuport N16 with a le Rhône 110 HP engine became operational at the end of 1916 and also stayed at the front until June 1917. It could be also armed with four le Prieur rockets for attacking German observation balloons.

A Ponnier M1 scout was tested during the summer of 1916, but was not considered good enough and it never flew in any of the belligerent countries, although photographs show that at least ten Ponniers were purchased: Sous-Lieutenants Crombez, Braun and Adjudants De Neef, Franchomme, de Munck and Roobaert were all photographed with a Ponnier bearing their personal marking. Sous-Lieutenant Jan Olieslagers, however, convinced Belgian Headquarters to abandon its purchase and all Ponniers went to the Pilot School at Etampes where it served as 'Penguins' (the student pilots could run the machine up and down the airfield, though not fast enough to give flying speed). Thus from the 30 Ponniers ordered, only ten were actually delivered, but after a fortnight they were all sent to Etampes. The Ponnier had a le Rhône 9y engine and was armed with one Lewis 7.7 mm machine gun on the upper wing.

In September 1917 the 5me Escadrille de Chasse received the Spad S7 of which a mere 15 were delivered during the war. Like before, this single-seater was delivered one year after it had been to other Allied squadrons. By that time the improved Spad S13 had already made its appearance. The Spad S7 used a Hispano-Suiza 8Aa 150 HP engine and was armed with a single Vickers 7.65 mm synchronized machine gun, firing through the propeller. The first Spad S7 was bought by Prince de Caraman et de Chimay for the price of 525.000 franks and donated to the Aviation Militaire Belge!

The 1ère Escadrille de Chasse began to receive the Hanriot Dupont HD1 (a 1916 designed aircraft) in September 1917, of which some 125 were purchased by the Belgian Government throughout the war. The first HD delivered to the Escadrille was given to S/Lt J.Olieslagers on 22 August. He passed it over to Adjt A.de Meulemeester, the other ace of the unit. The latter, however, was not keen to receive an aircraft which was cast off by a man like Olieslagers. Therefore 1Sgt W.Coppens became the man to change his antiquated Nieuport N11 for the 'new' aircraft. He took this chance with both hands and became the most successful exponent of this aircraft. The Hanriot remained the standard fighter for the 1ère Escadrille and later for the newly formed 11me Escadrille de Chasse. It was, however, an aircraft with but one Lewis machine gun and it did not fly over 180 km/h with its le Rhône 9Yb 120 HP rotary engine, but in the hands of Belgian (and Italian) pilots it turned out to be a good single-seater. By August 1917 the total number of aircraft of the AMB had increased to 81, of which 28 were scout aeroplanes.

Another scout which appeared on the scene, but mainly as a protection aircraft with the 3me Escadrille de Reconnaissance, was the Sopwith Pup. Six of these aircraft bearing the Belgian cockades flew during the Great War. At least one carried 5me/10me Escadrille's *Comet* on its fuselage. The Pup used a le Rhône 9c 90 HP rotary engine and was armed with a single 7.7 mm Vickers synchronized machine gun.

In 1918 the first of 37 Spad S13 C1s began to arrive, together with some 50 British Sopwith Camels. At first the latter was refused by our pilots, but then a few preferred it to the Hanriot. The first Camel on trial was sent on 29 November 1917 and by March, when the Groupe de Chasse was formed, eight Camels were flying alongside the Spads and Hanriots. The Camel, however, was a difficult aeroplane for the novice pilot with its powerful rotary engine (Clerget 9B 130 HP), but once mastered, was a good 'dogfighter'. The newly formed 11me Escadrille de Chasse took most of the Camels onto its inventory, together with two of the observation units, the 4me and 6me Escadrille d'Observation, which used the Camel to protect their two-seaters. Quite a few of the observation pilots were killed or injured in flying accidents with the Camel, one of them being Lieutenant Léon Colignon who, in 1915, had been observer to Lieutenant Jacquet and who had scored two probable victories with him. Two of the Camels were used aircraft: C164 was first assigned to the American 17th Aero Squadron, and E7309 was an American 148th Aero Squadron original. Two Sopwith Snipes (#E6317 and E6319) were also delivered on trial, late October

1918. The Spad XIII was equipped with the standard Hispano-Suiza 8BEc 235 HP engine. Both the Spad and Camel were armed with two synchronized Vickers machine guns, fitted on the engine cowling.

It is interesting to note that for most of the war (except for 1914-1915) the Belgians were flying generally inferior equipment against a well-equipped enemy. Therefore the exploits of our fighter pilots must be looked at in this light. When it is understood that even the armament was inferior to that of our Allies (i.e. the Hanriot with only one 7 mm Vickers machine gun in 1918), it may be considered that our aces, although rather small in number, were in fact excellent fighter pilots.

Task of the Fighter Pilots

It was not until the reorganisation of the Aviation Militaire in March 1918 that the fighter units operated solely as a fighter unit. Most of the flights made were protection sorties for our two-seaters or the observation balloons. The offensive patrols were either 'on call' from one of the front line Regiments, or at the pilot's initiative. This does not mean that few offensive patrols were flown, for most of the fighter pilots had the aggressive spirit needed to fulfil their task. It was not until the summer of 1917 that the AMB received any recognition however, by being allotted an active part in helping the British and French troops in the Third Ypres Offensive. When dogfights of 50 or more planes began to occur, there could always have been a few Belgians who joined these fights. During 'Third Ypres', a few Belgians shot down more than one aircraft: Sous-Lieutenant Edmond Thieffry and Adjudant Andre de Meulemeester each downed four, while Adjudants Georges Kervyn de Lettenhove and Maurice Medaets each claimed two during this period.

The 2me and 6me Escadrilles d'Observation (artillery observation) were very active in their British Sopwith 1½ Strutters and RE 8's as well.

Groupe de Chasse

In March 1918 the Groupe de Chasse was formed, and King Albert insisted that Capitaine Jacquet was made the CO. The 1ère Escadrille de Chasse became the 9me and Capitaine Walter Gallez (CO of the 1ère Esc. since December 1917) stayed at his post, and the *Thistle* remained its symbol; the 5me Escadrille de Chasse was renamed the 10me Escadrille de Chasse with Capitaine-Commandant Dony remaining CO. The *Comet* was kept as its sign.

A new escadrille, the 11me Escadrille de Chasse, came into existence under the command of Capitaine Paul Hiernaux, although the unit did not become operational until May 28th. It flew mainly Sopwith Camels from the former 1ère Escadrille, together with a few Hanriots. Its insignia was the former personal marking of the renowned Adjudant Willy Coppens: the *Cocotte*, a folded piece of paper in the shape of a chicken. Adjudant James Lamarche asked the permission of Coppens to use it. The airfield of the Groupe de Chasse remained the main fighter base at Les Moeres, until it moved closer to the advanced frontline at Moerkerke at the end of October 1918.

Pilots of other units (such as Adjudants Jacques Ledure and Robert Rondeau) were persuaded to join the Groupe de Chasse, while others (like the Gordinne brothers and Adjudant Alfred Mouton) were transferred to the observation units. Other pilots (e.g. Sous-Lieutenant Jules Goossens, DCM) were posted to the observation units at their own request.

Capt Jacquet showed his skill as CO and moulded the Groupe de Chasse into a real fighting unit, although limited by strength in numbers and still inferior to its adversaries in equipment.

At the start of the final Flanders Offensive in September 1918, the Groupe de Chasse was incorporated with the Allied Air Services and could send its 40-odd aircraft in the air at the same time. This occurred, in co-operation with the Allied Forces, for instance, on

29 September:

6 to 8 am	low altitude OP	11me Esc	incl. 2 a/c for balloon-strafing
	high altitude OP	9me Esc	
7.30 to 9.30 am	low altitude OP	11me Esc	incl. 1 a/c for balloon-strafing
	high altitude OP	10me Esc	
12.30 to 14.30 pm	low altitude OP	9me Esc	
	high altitude OP	10me Esc	
14.00 to 16.00 pm	low altitude OP	9me Esc	
	high altitude OP	10me Esc	

or on 2 November:

from 6.30 to 8.10 am	10me Esc
from 8.30 to 10.00 am	11me Esc
from 11.30 to 13.00 pm	9me Esc
from 14.00 to 15.30 pm	11me Esc

By this time the French Groupe de Combat 23, the last GC to be formed in August 1918, under the command of Capitaine Paul Gastin, was flying alongside its Belgian Allies. By mid October, 61 Wing, RAF under the command of Colonel Osmond and based at the former German airfield at Varssenaere, also secured the Belgian skies.

During the days of the Groupe de Chasse, 4,424 offensive patrols were flown during which 732 aerial combats were fought and 71 official and 50 probable victories were claimed, for the loss of six pilots either killed or taken prisoner.

Scout Pilots of the Recce Units

From March 1918 a small number of recce pilots started to fly their own unit's protection and from 1 May onwards, 22 scouts were at the disposal of these recce units. The 7me Escadrille d'Observation Photographique, by that time, consisted of but one observation two-seater and eight scouts! These recce pilots, some from the former Escadrilles de Chasse, flew protection flights and even offensive patrols and flew in Flights of three aircraft as well. The most active of these scout pilots were Lieutenant Robin, the former observer to Capt Jacquet and 1ers Sergents Paul de Liedekerke de Pailhe and Jules Holbrechts, who were often seen flying together in a Flight doing some ground-strafing and OP's in their Hanriots.

This ground-strafing took place between April 17-18 in particular, when the Battle of Merckem was going on. The battle, Operation Tannenberg, only took one day (17 April) and is still underestimated by most historians, but if the German Army had broken through the Belgian defences, together with the breakthrough south of Ypres when they captured Mont Kemmel, Ypres would have certainly been lost, together with a whole British Army, to the Germans. On the other hand, the Belgian Army would have become isolated and surrounded, leading to its capitulation. Nevertheless, it withstood the German attacks which were launched at dawn, after a very short preliminary bombardment. The 23-battalion-strong German force had hoped to take the Belgian trenches, defended by regiments of both 3me and 4me Division d'Armée, with a bayonet-charge, supported by trench mortar fire and 'minenwerfer'. Two divisions were in close support to expand the expected success. After a day of bitter fighting and a counterattack of the seven defending Belgian regiments, the

Germans withdrew at 21.30 leaving 779 prisoners, 60 machine guns and numerous dead.

Unfortunately, further daily reports of the recce-units were lost or were not sent to the GQG at Houthem, so from July until the end of the war no such missions or combats can be traced, but it is understood that these escadrilles were again very active during the final liberation offensive. The first of its four stages was fought between September 28th-30th during the Battle of the 'Flanders Heights'. The next assault was launched as the Battle of Thourout-Thielt between October 14th-30th. Because of the quick advance of the Army, supply of the assault troops became difficult. In the first days of October especially, the troops were supplied by the recce units who dropped all sorts of packets, from cigarettes and food to ammunition.

The third phase was the Battle of the Lys river and its Diversion Canal, followed by the Battle of the Scheldt river and the Canal de Terneuzen during the last days of the War. Belgian casualties during the Liberation Offensive were 30,067 of whom 3,338 died.

Unconfirmed/probable Victories

These victories are, as they are presented in the pilot's biography, often shared between more than two pilots. It was indeed difficult to say which pilot should receive the credit when it was not specified who of the two or three pilots involved really fired the 'fatal' shots at the opponent. The 'out of control' claims are also difficult to interpret. Some aircraft which were forced to land are listed in the pilot victory lists, simply because some of them were made official claims. Unlike the British system of victories, the Belgian victory credits were more on the lines of the French. If they had mirrored the British, individual scores would have been higher.

Terror of the Kite Balloons

As you will also see in the following chapter concerning the biographies, Lieutenant Willy Coppens was not only by far the highest scoring Belgian pilot, he also was the greatest balloon-buster. In 1918 especially, balloon strafing became a very dangerous task and many of these men were killed during such attacks.

Throughout the belligerent countries the balloon-busters were famous for their fearlessness. The top British balloon-buster was Major Anthony Beauchamp-Proctor who downed 16, the most successful American was Lieutenant Frank Luke Jr. (killed in action) who claimed 14. In France Lieutenant Léon Bourjade shot down 27 while Lieutenant Michel Coiffard (kia) downed 24 and Lieutenant Maurice Boyau (kia) 21. The most successful German was Oberleutnant Fritz von Roth with 20, closely followed by Leutnant Heinrich Gontermann (kia) with 17 and Vizefeldwebel Karl Schleger with 14.

Lieutenant Coppens surpassed them all in downing 35 of these drachens. It is known that Coppens always celebrated his victories with an outstanding performance of aerobatics. This was not only due to the oncoming AA fire, but he seemed to like performing for the infantry soldiers who, no doubt, saw the attacked balloon burning.

One reason why Coppens stood out from his fellow countrymen could be found in the following: General Cabra, a GQG Officer was his uncle and some sources say that Coppens, through his uncle, was the only Belgian to receive the ammunition needed to burn these 'gasbags'. Whether this story is true or not, Coppens stayed an outstanding pilot and was indeed the highest scoring balloon-buster.

Our Fighter Pilots' Adversaries

The first German unit to fly against Belgian aircraft was the Brieftauben-Abteilung Ostende (BAO), based at Steene-Ostende. It was actually the forerunner of the Marine Feldflieger Abteilungen and later the Marinefeld Jagdstaffeln, based at or close to the coast. In 1915 the

Marine Feldflieger Abteilung (MFA) 2 was based at Zeebrugge, equipped with four Friedrichshafen seaplanes. The Feldflieger Abteilung (FA) 40 too was based in Flanders. In 1916, FA6 was based at Roulers, together with FA33, and Jagdstaffel (Jasta) 8. This Jasta thus became the first scout unit to operate up along the North Sea coast. During 1917 many more Jasta's moved to the 4.Armee front, which was not only fighting at Ypres, but also at the Yser Front where the Belgian Army held the lines. On 20 October Jagdgruppe Dixmuiden was formed under the command of Leutnant Harold Auffarth. It was linked up with Jastas 7, 29, 33 and 35b. On 7 February 1918 these changed into Jastas 7, 16b and 51 under the command of Oberleutnant Hans Gandert. Jagdgruppe Dixmuiden changed into Jagdgruppe nr.6 on 1 March. Oberleutnant Gandert stayed at his post, but the Jastas changed: 7, 28w and 51. On the 9th Jasta 47 was added but it moved again on the 29th. Jasta 56 became its successor on 12 April. On 5 May Jastas 7, 40s, 51 and 56 were the units belonging to Jagdgruppe nr.6. Jasta 16b returned on 11 May and Jasta 20 was added to the Jagdgruppe on 6 June. On 1 October, after the capture of Oblt Gandert, Hauptmann Erhard Milch became the CO of Jastas 7, 20, 40s and 51. Milch had been a two-seater pilot since August 1915 and had worked his way up to a commander of a Jagdgruppe due to his remarkable leadership. He later rose to the rank of Generalfeldmarshall during WWII.

The other 'Wing' to fly against our gallant airmen was of course the Marine Jagdgruppe. From 1917 there were two Seefrontstaffeln I and II. They were formed at Nieuwmunster in October 1917 to maintain security for the MFA 2 seaplanes. The Albatros DIII and Pfalz DIII scouts they originally flew were replaced by Fokker DVII aircraft in 1918. Resulting from the Seefrontstaffeln, the Marinefeld Jasta (MFJ) I was formed in February 1917 at Nieuwmunster, flying Albatros DIIIs. This unit later moved to Aertrycke. MFJ II was formed in October 1917 at Coolkerke, flying Pfalz scouts. In April 1918 the unit changed base to Jabbeke, receiving Albatros DV and later Fokker DVII scouts. MFJ III was formed at Jabbeke in June 1918 from personnel of MFJ I & II. The original Pfalz Scouts were soon replaced by the better Fokker DVII. The Marine Jagdgruppe was thus formed on 17 October 1917. In September 1918 two more MFJ's (IV and V) were formed, also in Jabbeke and flying Fokker DVII. These units were all placed under the command of Leutnant zur See Gotthard Sachsenberg, and renamed the Royal Prussian Marine Jagdgeschwader. The Jagdgruppe claimed 206 aircraft for the loss of 35 pilots. It is known that not only the Belgians were fighting against this Marine Jagdgruppe, for the British Naval Squadrons fought, together with their Belgian Allies, a sort of private war against their German opponents up along the North Sea coast.

There were, of course, other Jastas who encountered Belgian aircraft. Jasta 2 with Leutnant Erwin Böhme (1er Sergent Robert Ciselet) and Jasta 56 with Leutnant Franz Piechulek (Sergent Max Martin) were units to claim Belgian fighter pilots. Both Belgians were killed in action. Jasta 56 was a unit belonging to Jagdgruppe nr.3 (Jastas 14, 16b, 29 & 56) under the command of Leutnant Harold Auffarth.

Two-seater units operating on the 4.Armee Front in January 1918 were Schutzstaffeln 11, 18, 23, 26, 29 & 33; Feldflieger Abteilungen der Artillerie 19, 204, 213, 224, 231, 233, 238, 256 & 293; Feldflieger Abteilungen 8, 48 & 65; Kampfgeschwaders 15, 16 & 17 and two Riesenflugzeug-geschwadern 501 & 502.

The most active unit in Flanders must have been 4 (N) Squadron (RNAS) which became 204 Sqn (RAF) on 1 April 1918, for they not only attacked the invader, but also the defender. More than one Belgian was forced to land after an attack from the over-active Sopwith scouts from this particular English unit. Fortunately no fighter pilot was seriously wounded during such encounters.

Weather Conditions

With the sort of aircraft flying at the time it is obvious that there wasn't activity on every single day. The wind coming off the sea blew harder than anywhere else on the Western Front. In 1915, 105 days of enforced inactivity were counted. 1916 was no better with 146 days of inactivity with no fewer than 21 days in December alone. It is therefore evident that few victories were claimed on either side of the lines in those early days. The following January was no better with sixteen days of inactivity. 1917 counted some 113 days when the fighter pilots could not fly, but 1918 counted only 66 days. From February 1915 until November 1918, 432 out of 1,380 days were so bad that no fighter pilot took to the air, which means that there was no action during one third of the war up along the North Sea coast. This inactivity, of course, was practically the same for the German opponents.

King Albert and Queen Elisabeth over the Front

The King of the Belgians is believed to have flown on several occasions over the front lines to overlook the general situation. The first time he went over the lines was on 18 March 1917, at Dixmude, between 17.30 and 18.15 hrs. The flight occurred in Capitaine Jacquet's Henri Farman, escort was given by four Nieuport Bébés, flown by Lieutenant A.De Neef, 1er Sergent A.de Meulemeester, Sergents G.de Mevius and F.de Woot de Trixhe. On one of the other flights King Albert made (6 July), Queen Elisabeth was in Italy at the time. She had, however, knitted a warm cap which the King insisted on wearing during his flight. Capitaine Jacquet tried to suggest that this wouldn't be a good idea for it was far too cold in the air. King Albert, however, insisted stubbornly and had to hold his cap with both hands during the entire flight, resulting in him getting a bad cold. On this flight, he asked the pilot, Sous-Lieutenant Jacques de Meeus (4me Escadrille, in the first Sopwith 1½ Strutter of the Aviation Militaire) to fly to Thourout to overlook the German defences. The latter, however, realizing the dangers his 'observer' might meet, pretended that he didn't understand what his King wanted and turned back to the Belgian side of the lines. On another occasion, again flying with Capitaine Jacquet, the latter pointed to a certain part of the German front lines. King Albert, however, not knowing what Jacquet was pointing at, immediately took his gun and started to aim at an enemy aircraft which wasn't there!

Even Queen Elisabeth flew close to the Belgian front lines and on one such occasion, on Armistice Day, in the Spad XI flown by Lieutenant Henri Crombez, they got into a spin over Oostcamp airfield, only to come out of it close to the ground. After the aircraft had landed, and with everyone anxious to know what had happened, the Queen said laughingly that she had asked Crombez to show her what a spin was like.

It is obvious that King Albert was very much interested in flight. One day he was invited to France to join a war flight in a Handley-Page bomber. The entire Headquarters of the Aviation Militaire Belge was invited. The King of the Belgians flew to his destination, but the CO of the AMB, Maj Roland Van Crombrugghe and his Adjutant Maj Jules Smeyers (nicknamed the *Elephant*), went by car, for they did not dare to fly. On arrival they told King Albert of the dangers he might meet in the air and their influence on the King must have been overwhelming, because he abandoned the chance given to him, although the King had flown twice in a Handley-Page bomber previously. On 5 and 6 June 1917, he was flown by 7 Squadron's (Royal Naval Air Service) CO J.T. Babington from Coudekerque. On the second flight, Queen Elisabeth joined him. Again in 1917 King Albert was flown twice by 48 Squadron's (Royal Flying Corps) CO Maj H.S.Shields, MC. On one of these occasions the King was even flown over Ostende ! In September 1917 he joined a war flight in a Morane, belonging to Capitaine Brocard's French Escadrille Spa.3, of the famous Stork group, which counted Capitaine Georges Guynemer amongst its pilots.

On 5 July 1918 a trip was made to Folkestone, from Calais in two Belgian seaplanes.

King Albert was flown in the FBA 1, piloted by Sous-Lieutenant Tony Orta and the Queen flew in another FBA 1, piloted by Sous-Lieutenant Victor Boin. Yet in 1918 many more flights were made by the King on board Lieutenant Crombez's Spad XI. During October, while 4me Escadrille was based at Oostcamp, Lieutenant Crombez flew almost daily to La Panne, where he landed as close as he could to the Royal villa to pick up his Majesty. They then flew to Oostcamp or just surveyed the front as the King was very anxious about the way the Offensive was going. Probably he was the only Commanding Officer of an Army to do such exploits, albeit ... a King !

Fighter Unit Histories

At the end of each unit history a list is given of the pilots who gained victories for the unit. The figure between brackets is the number of probable victories scored whilst flying with the unit.

1ère Escadrille de Chasse

Formed in February 1916 flying Nieuport N10 Bébé, its Commanding Officer was Capitaine Arsène Demanet. He was succeeded in December 1916 by Capitaine Fernand Jacquet, who was replaced by Capitaine Walter Gallez, when the former was charged to take command of the Groupe de Chasse in December 1917. By this time the unit was flying Nieuport Scouts, as well as the first Hanriot Dupont HD1 and Sopwith Camel scouts. Its first base was at Coxyde until it moved to Les Moeres in June 1916, where it stayed until the reorganisation. The unit took the Thistle as its insignia and was credited with 15 official victories, but claimed 52, for the loss of six pilots killed. Capt Jacquet with his observer Lieutenant Louis Robin had scored the unit's first victory on 20 May 1916. Adjudant Egide Roobaert was the first to be killed (by accident) on 19 December 1916.

Adjt	A.de Meulemeester	7(12)	Adjt	C.de Munck	- (1)
Capt	F. Jacquet	4(6)	S/Lt	A.De Neef	- (1)
Lt	L.Robin	4(6)	1Sgt	F.de Woot	- (1)
Lt	J.Olieslagers	3(13)	1Sgt Maj	P.Dubois	- (1)
Adjt	G.Kervyn	2(6)	Adjt	J.Goethals	- (1)
Adjt	W.Coppens	-(2)	Adjt	J.Goossens	- (1)
Adjt	G.de Mevius	-(1)	Adjt	E.Roobaert	- (1)
			Sgt	C.Verbessem	- (1)

5me Escadrille de Chasse

Formed in August 1916 with the arrival of the Nieuport 11 scouts, the unit became operational in September. The Commanding Officer was Capitaine J.Dony. The base was the former 5me Escadrille's one at La Panne. This did not change until the summer of 1917, when the unit moved to Les Moeres, which was to become the main fighter base. Together with the move to the new airfield, the Nieuport N17 and N23 arrived and the Comet was adopted as the squadron's insignia. In the autumn of that year the Spad VII was purchased and became the main fighter for the unit. The 5me Escadrille de Chasse claimed 15 victories and 12 probables, for the loss of two pilots being killed and one unfit for further service. Adjudant Louis de Chestret was the first to be credited with a victory on 17 November 1916 and Sous-Lieutenant Charles Ciselet was the first casualty on 23 September 1917 when he was severely wounded during an evening combat.

S/Lt	E.Thieffry	10(5)	Adjt	L.de Chestret	1
S/Lt	P.Braun	21)	S/Lt	J.Goethals	- (2)
Adjt	M.Medaets	2	1Sgt	G.Medaets	- (1)
Adjt	P.de Chestret	1(2)	S/Lt	M.Orban	- (1)
S/Lt	C.Ciselet	1	1SgtMaj	E.Weekers	- (1)

9me Escadrille de Chasse

Formed in March 1918, the former 1ère Escadrille being renumbered to become the 9me. Capitaine W.Gallez stayed at his post of Commanding Officer and the Hanriot scouts remained the standard scout for the unit, although a small number of Sopwith Camels were also used. The unit stayed at the airfield of Les Moeres, which became the base for the newly formed Groupe de Chasse. Its first victory was claimed on 12 March by Sous-Lieutenant Pierre Dubois. Adjudant Maurice Jamar was the first casualty, captured after being shot down by AA fire on 3 October. On the evening of 13 June, six Hanriots were destroyed during a German bombing mission on the airfield. The Escadrille was grounded for seven days, until the first camouflaged Hanriots began to arrive (camouflage colours were light and dark brown, dark green and dark grey surface and light blue underside). At the end of October the unit, together with the two other Groupe de Chasse units, moved to Moerkerke airfield, closer to the front after the Belgian Army advance. The 9me Escadrille de Chasse 'les chardons' (the *Thistle*) was credited with 51 official victories (41 balloons) for the loss of three pilots taken prisoner or severely wounded.

Lt	W.Coppens	37(3)	S/Lt	P.Dubois	1 (1)
S/Lt	A.de Meulemeester	4(5)	Cdt	W.Gallez	1 (3)
Sgt	E.Hage	3(3)	Adjt	M.Jamar	1 (1)
Lt	M.de Crombrugghe	2(1)	Adjt	G.Ory	- (2)
Cdt	F.Jacquet	2(1)	S/Lt	P.de Chestret	- (1)
S/Lt	G.Kervyn de Lettenhove	2(3)	S/Lt	J.Goossens	- (1)
Lt	J.Olieslagers	2(2)	Adjt	G.Kervyn de Meerendre	- (1)
S/Lt	G.de Mevius	1(5)	Sgt	J. Lemaire	- (1)

10me Escadrille de Chasse
The 5me Escadrille was renumbered 10me Escadrille de Chasse in March 1918. Capitaine J.Dony remained its Commanding Officer, until his death on 1 October. Lieutenant F.de Woelmont then took command for four days, being replaced by Lieutenant L.Robin on 6 October. Both men were observers until 1917. Les Moeres stayed the base, the Comet was held as its insignia, but the Spad VII was replaced by the more powerful Spad XIII, although some of the former remained in the unit. It also flew a Hanriot and even a few Nieuports stayed in active service. The 10me Escadrille produced no aces, but claimed 22 victories of which only 10 were officially credited. The first victory was claimed on 8 May by Adjudant Maurice Siraut, and Sous-Lieutenant Louis de Chestret was the unit's first loss, when he did not return from an offensive patrol on 12 June, being captured when he crash-landed close to his second victory (which was not confirmed). Six pilots were casualties: three killed, two taken prisoner and one wounded. A move to Moerkerke occurred at the end of October 1918.

Adjt	C.de Montigny	2(3)	Adjt	M.Siraut	1 (2)
S/Lt	J.Goethals	2(2)	Adjt	E.Weekers	- (2)
Adjt	J.Ledure	2	S/Lt	L.de Chestret	- (1)
Adjt	G.Medaets	2	Lt	E.Desclée	- (1)
S/Lt	R.De Leener	1(1)	Lt	L.Robin	- (1)

11me Escadrille de Chasse
Formed in March 1918, although the unit did not become operational until the end of May, Capitaine Paul Hiernaux took command of the unit. This post he held till the end of the war, although shot down on 15 October by Obltn z S. Gotthardt Sachsenberg of Marinefeldjasta I (unconfirmed victory). The escadrille took most of the Sopwith Camels from the 1/9me Escadrille de Chasse as its main fighter scout, but a few Hanriots were flown

as well by some pilots (e.g. Capitaine Hiernaux). The *Cocotte* was chosen as its insignia and the escadrille was based at Les Moeres, together with the two other units of the Groupe de Chasse. Adjudant Robert Rondeau claimed the first victory on 27 September and Sergent Max Martin (Ltn Franz Piechulek's 14th and final victory) was the unit's first loss on 4 October. Together with the other fighter units, the 11me moved to Moerkerke airfield at the end of October. The 11me Escadrille de Chasse was credited with only seven victories, although 12 were claimed by its pilots. Three of its pilots became casualties: two killed and one wounded.

Sgt	L.Guillon	2	Adjt	J. van der Voordt	1 (1)
Adjt	R.Rondeau	2(1)	1SgtMaj	J.Vuylsteke	1
1SgtMaj	R.Declercq	1	Adjt	J.Lamarche	- (2)
			Sgt	M.Martin	- (1)

Spelling of the Belgian Towns and Villages

Although the brunt of the War was fought on Flemish soil, all the names of places were spelt in French, for the Belgian Establishment was strictly Francophile. In this book the places are written in the way they were written in the war days, so if the reader takes a modern map of Belgium and looks up the places mentioned in the book, he will experience some difficulty in finding them, for nowadays the places have been changed from their former French spelling into the Flemish names. An alphabetic list therefore follows with the place's old and new name.

Old	New	Old	New
Alveringhem	Alveringem	Lys (river)	Leie
Asseneede	Assenede	Menin	Menen
Avecapelle	Avekapelle	Merckem	Merkem
Bixschoote	Bikschote	Nieuport	Nieuwpoort
Boitshoucke	Booitshoeke	Nieuwcapelle	Nieuwkapelle
Bruges	Brugge	Ostende	Oostende
Caeskerke	Kaaskerke	Oudecapelle	Oudekapelle
Caprijcke	Kaprijke	Passchendaele	Passendale
Clercken	Klerken	Pervyse	Pervijze
Comines	Komen	Poperinghe	Poperinge
Couckelaere	Koekelare	Praat Bosch	Praatbos
Coxyde	Koksijde	Pypegaele	Pijpegale
Cruypenaerde	Kruipenaarde	Ramscapelle	Ramskapelle
Dixmude	Diksmuide	Roulers	Roeselare
Eecloo	Eeklo	Schoore	Schore
Eesen	Esen	Selzaete	Zelzate
Fort Knocke	Knokkebrug	Sleijhage	Sleihage
Furnes	Veurne	Slype	Slijpe
Gheluvelt	Geluveld	St-Georges	St-Joris
Gheluwe	Geluwe	St-Jacques-Capelle	St-Jacobs-Kapelle
Ghent	Gent	St-Pierre Capelle	St-Pieters-Kapelle
Ghistelles	Gistel	Stuyvekenskerke	Stuivekenskerke
Handzaeme	Handzame	Tervaete	Tervate
Hoogstaede	Hoogstade	Thourout	Torhout

Houthem	Houtem	Vladsloo	Vladslo
Keyem	Keiem	Wercken	Werken
La Panne	De Panne	Wervicq	Wervik
Leffinghe	Leffinge	Wulveringhem	Wulveringem
Lendeleede	Lendelede	Ypres	Ieper
Lombartzyde	Lombardsijde	Yser (river)	IJzer

Aircraft Used by the Fighter Pilots

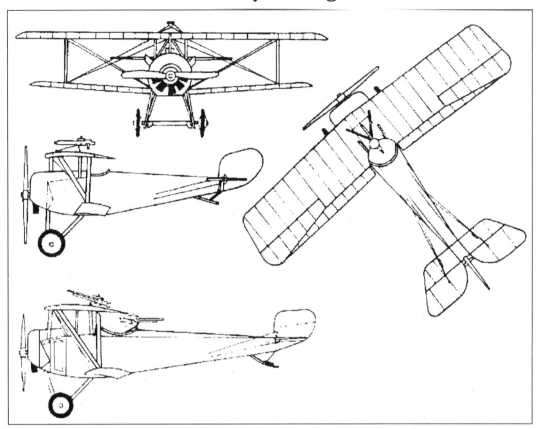

Nieuport N10 Bébé and two-seater

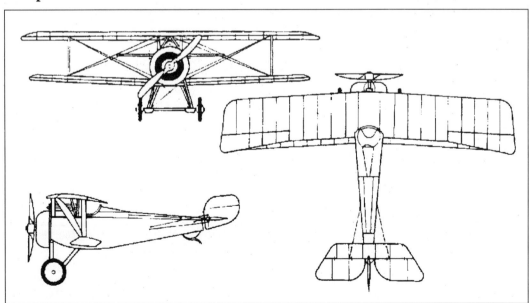

Nieuport N16, N17, N23

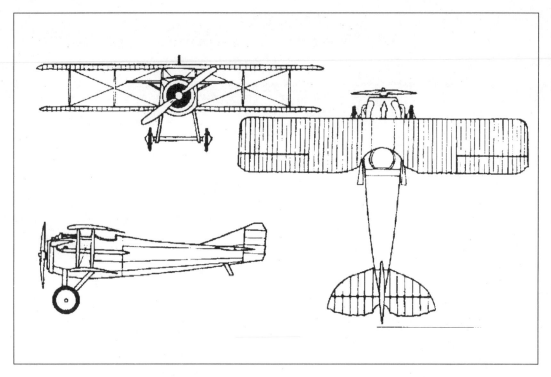

Spad S7

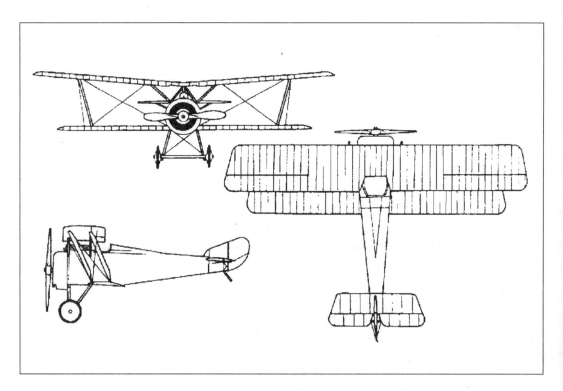

Hanriot-Dupont HD1

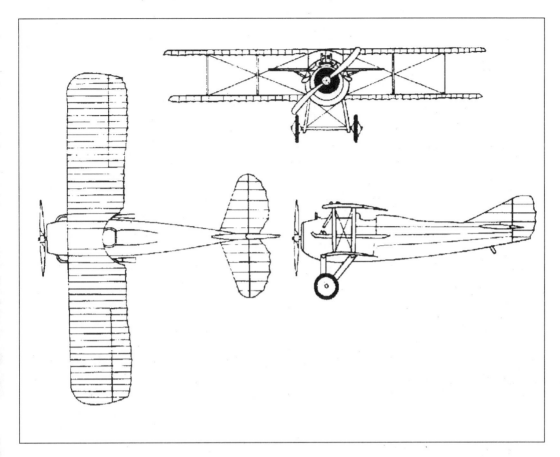

Spad S13

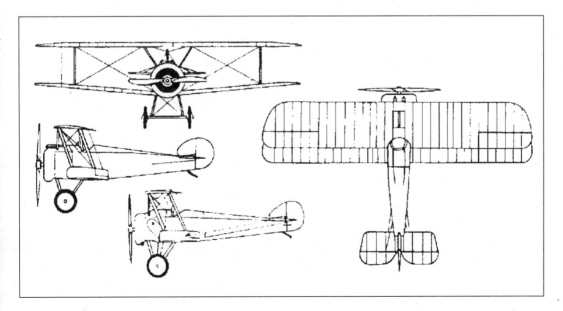

Sopwith Camel

Battle Area over Flooded Flanders

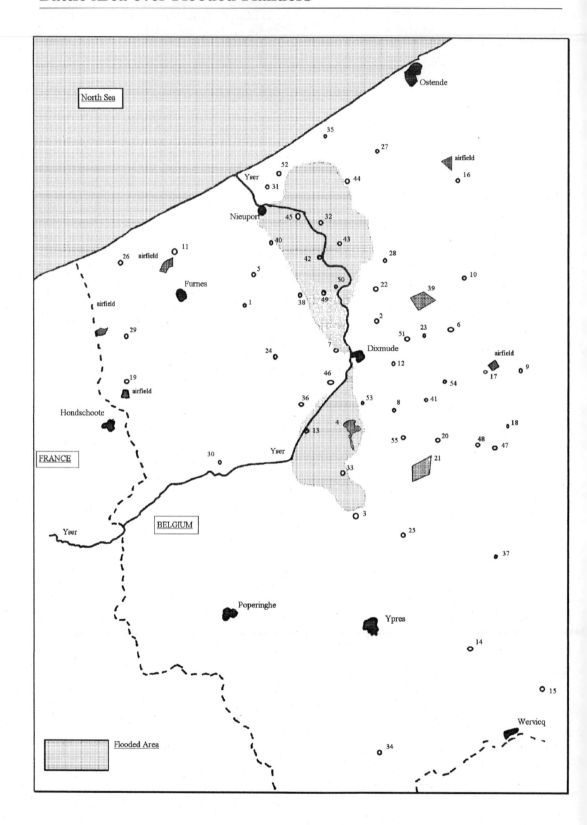

North Sea

Ostende

35

27

52   airfield
Yser   16
31   44

Nieuport   45   32

40   43

26   airfield   11   28

5   50   10
42   22

Furnes   38   49   39

1   7   2

airfield   23   6

29   51

24   Dixmude   airfield

12   17   9

19   46   54

airfield   36   53   8   41

Hondschoote   13   4   18

55   20   48   47

30   Yser   21

33

FRANCE   3

BELGIUM   25

Yser   37

Poperinghe   Ypres

14

15

Wervicq

Flooded Area   34

KEY

1	Avecapelle	29	Les Moeres
2	Beerst	30	Linde
3	Bixschoote	31	Lombartzyde
4	Blankaert lake	32	Mannekensvere
5	Boitshoucke	33	Merckem
6	Bovekerke	34	Messines
7	Caeskerke	35	Middelkerke
8	Clercken	36	Nieuwcapelle
9	Cortemarck	37	Passchendaele
10	Couckelaere	38	Pervyse
11	Coxyde	39	Praat Bosch
12	Eesen	40	Ramscapelle
13	Fort Knocke	41	Ruiterhoek
14	Gheluvelt	42	Schoorbakke
15	Gheluwe	43	Schoore
16	Ghistelles	44	Slype
17	Handzaeme	45	St-Georges
18	Hazewind	46	St-Jacques-Capelle
19	Houthem	47	Staden
20	Houthulst	48	Stampkot
21	Houthulst Forest	49	Stuyvekenskerke
22	Keyem	50	Tervaete
23	Kortewilde	51	Vladsloo
24	Lampernisse	52	Westende
25	Langemarck	53	Woumen
26	La Panne	54	Zarren
27	Leffinghe	55	Zwartegat
28	Leke		

Introduction to the Next Chapter

All the Belgian fighter pilots are enumerated in the next chapter, containing as much information as possible for each man. The eventual claims are registered in columns with all the information found, such as: the number of victories, date, which aircraft was downed, the aircraft flown, the escadrille, place, time and result. The abbreviations made in the following chapter are listed below:

German aircraft	EA	enemy aircraft
	D	enemy scout
	Alb	Albatros (DII, DIII, DV, DVa, C)
	Fok	Fokker (EI, DII, DrI, DVII)
	Halb C	Halberstadt two-seater
	Hydr	Seaplane
Belgian aircraft	N—	Nieuport (N10, N11, N12, N16, N17, N23)
	Nieup	Nieuport of unknown type
	HD	Hanriot Dupont HD1
	Camel	Sopwith Camel

	Spad	Spad VII or XIII
	Strut	Sopwith 1½ Strutter
	MF	Maurice Farman (MF20,30,40,60)
Claims	DES	destroyed
	DES(f)	destroyed and burning
	CAPT	captured
	OOC	out of control
	FTL	forced to land
German ranks	Flg	Flieger
	Gefr	Gefreiter
	Flgm	Flugmaat
	Flgmstr	Flugmeister
	Flgobmt	Flugobermaat
	Fw	Feldwebel
	Vfw	Vizefeldwebel
	OfStv	Offizierstellvertreter
	Ltn (zS)	Leutnant (zur See)
	Ltn d R	Leutnant de Reserve (Army)
	Obltn(zS)	Oberleutnant (zur See)
	Obltn d R	Oberleutnant de Reserve (Army)
Belgian ranks	Cpl/Brig	Caporal/Brigadier
	Sgt/MdL	Sergent/Maréchal des Logis
	1 Sgt	1er Sergent
	1 Sgt Maj	1er Sergent Major
	Adjt	Adjudant
	S/Lt	Sous-Lieutenant
	Lt	Lieutenant
	Capt	Capitaine
	Cdt	Capitaine-Commandant
	Maj	Major
	Lt-Col	Lieutenant- Colonel
	Col	Colonel

The

Fighter Pilots:

Biographical

Notes

BEHAEGHE Aimé Lieutenant 1, ESC HYDRAVIONS

Born 17 November 1890 at Kachtem (West-Flanders), Behaeghe volunteered for the Aviation Militaire Belge on 29 October 1914, where he was made a Caporal one month later. He left the Pilot School early in April 1915 and was promoted to Sergent on the 17th. Promotion to Adjudant occurred on 30 May. On 16 June, he and his observer, Lt R.Verhaegen, in company with Lt F.Jacquet/Lt L.Colignon, tried to intercept a Zeppelin, but to no avail. When Behaeghe returned to the front on 29 July 1915 with a Nieuport 10, purchased at Calais, he became the very first Belgian fighter pilot to fly a single-seater. He flew his first offensive patrol on 30 August and on 9 September he attacked a German anti-aircraft artillery position with 1,500 fléchettes over Eesen. He repeated this feat four times and altogether dropped 6,000 of these pointed dart-like missiles. In those early days he participated in 14 combats during 92 offensive patrols, but only one of these combats was fought in a single-seater: the N10 (#N8517).

He was posted to the Belgian Congo on 12 December 1915 on the formation of a seaplane squadron in the colony. Behaeghe, commissioned on 22 November 1915, had a very active time there, including many bombing missions. On 10 June he sank the German torpedo-boat *Graf von Götzen* in his Short bomber, flying with Lt L.Colignon as his observer. Besides Flemish and French, Lt Behaeghe also spoke, wrote and read Italian, Spanish and Portuguese. During the year he became ill and, exhausted by war strain and climatological conditions died on 4 December 1916 in Dumbo, in the Belgian Congo.

Behaeghe was made a Chevalier de l'Ordre de l'Etoile Africaine and decorated with the Croix de Guerre with two citations.

	1916						
_*	10 Jun	torpedo-boat	Short	—	Kigoma	—	SUNK

* obs. Lt L.Colignon, the boat was the *Graf von Götzen*.

BENOIDT Victor Octave Georges 1er Sergent 9

Born at Watermaal-Bosvoorde, Brussels, on 5 November 1895. He managed to cross the North Sea to Folkestone on 25 April 1915, the date he volunteered for the duration of the war. He was sent to the 1ère Division de Cavalerie on 30 July and stayed there until 1 September. On this date Benoidt transferred to the Balloon company (Compagnie des Aérostiers) belonging to the Corps of Engineers. Here he was made a Caporal on 10 September and a Sergent on 12 November. On 1 October 1916 he lost his stripes at his own request and on the same day went to the Artillerie à Cheval of the 1ère Division de Cavalerie. One year later, 29 June 1917, he passed to the 6me Régt d'Artillerie. Again he did not stay long at his new unit, for he transferred to the Aviation Militaire on 28 January 1918. He qualified as a pilot in April and regained his Sergent's stripes on 25 August. Posted to the 9me Escadrille de Chasse, Sgt V.Benoidt made his first war flight on 24 September 1918, together with Capt W.Gallez and S/Lt P.de Chestret de Haneffe. He flew only 23 patrols during which he was involved in three combats. On 3 October his flight (Gallez and de Chestret de Haneffe) attacked and drove off a Fokker which was attacking a Spad of 10me Escadrille, flown by Adjt R.de Leener. On 5 October he attacked a two-seater together with S/Lt A.de Meulemeester, S/Lt G.de Mevius, S/Lt G.Kervyn de Lettenhove and Sgt E.Hage, without success and on 14 October he fired some shots at two scouts attacking S/Lt de Meulemeester.

After 18 October Sgt V.Benoidt disappears from the patrol list of the Groupe de Chasse, but was made a 1er Sergent on 27 October. For his feats he was awarded with the Croix de Guerre with two Palmes, Médaille de la Victoire, Médaille Commémorative 1914-18 and five Chevrons de front. Afterwards he gained the following medals: Officier de l'Ordre de la Couronne, Officier de l'Ordre de Leopold II, Chevalier de l'Ordre de Leopold, Croix du Feu, Croix Civique 1ère classe, Médaille du Volontaire Combattant 1914-18 and Médaille Commémorative du Centenaire.

After the war he was promoted to 1er Sergent Major on 2 March 1919 and on 7 April 1920, Benoidt engaged himself for yet another year of military service. He was commissioned on 22 June. He was discharged, at his own request, and joined the Reserve list on 27 April 1923 and became a Lieutenant de Réserve on 26 June. In the Réserve he attained the rank of Capitaine on 22 July 1931.

After the capitulation of the Belgian Army on 28 May 1940, Benoidt was arrested. He was deported to Germany on 19 August 1941, where he remained until repatriated on 28 April 1945. He received a three months convalescence period and was recalled to duty on 12 June 1945. Again he was promoted, to Major de Réserve, on 13 October and was finally pensioned out of the service on 31 December 1945. Mentally affected by all kinds of hardship endured in prison camp from which he never really recovered, Victor Benoidt died on 23 June 1975 at Klemskerke, West-Flanders.

BRAUN (ter Meeren) Pierre Louis Marie   Sous-Lieutenant   5,1,5

Pierre Braun was born 6 October 1897 at Sterrebeek, Brussels, and joined the Aviation Militaire at the age of 16½ years, which earned him the nickname 'Bambino'. He volunteered on 20 August 1914 and became a lorry driver at the Aviation Militaire until December. Transferred to the Pilot School he gained his civil flying brevet on 5 February 1915 in Etampes being promoted a Caporal eight days later. One month later (20/3/1915) he joined the 5me Escadrille together with a new observer, S/Lt F.de Woelmont. Promotion to Sergent occurred on 23 March and on 30 May he was promoted to Adjudant. In the beginning of his flying career he was a pilot in the observation units, doing also artillery spotting missions for which he and his observer S/Lt de Woelmont received their first citation on 15 October 1915. A week later Braun was sent to the Parc d'Aviation in Calais for one month (advanced pilot training) and returned to his front-line unit on 24 November. On 28 December he flew from Calais to Houthem in a Nieuport N10, and began his fighter pilot career just one day later, whilst S/Lt F.de Woelmont stayed his observer for a period. The first combat occurred on 9 January 1916 south-east of Dixmude. On 13 February he was posted to the 1ère Escadrille de Chasse, but two months later returned to the 5me Escadrille. On 11 May 1916 Pierre Braun was commissioned, and on 14 February 1917 was awarded the Croix de Guerre. The first days of December 1917 were very bad and cold. The fifth day however was bright and Braun started twice for an offensive patrol. When he flew off in the afternoon for his 173rd offensive patrol, he gained his second official victory. Returning over the sea, he started to roll close to the surface. One wing touched the water and Braun crashed to his death. He had engaged in 19 aerial combats altogether.

He was decorated with the Chevalier de l'Ordre Leopold (18/12/17), Chevalier de l'Ordre de la Couronne (15/11/17), Croix de Guerre (14/2/17) and received seven citations. In three different official sources, Braun has been respectively credited with one, two and three official victories.

	1917						
_*	27 Jul	EA	Nieup	5s	Clercken	14.55-15.40	DES
1**	20 Aug	D	Nieup	5	Vladsloo	08.05	DES
2***	5 Dec	DFW C	Spad	5	Nieuport	13.45	DES

* together with 1Sgt G.Medaets, possibly Jasta 29 who had two pilots wounded, one seriously. ** was this Flgmstr Grosch, MFJ I, wia ? *** as he was killed returning from this combat, the claim was only made official on 12 December. (On 5 December, 16.00 hrs a phone call from the 'Mission Brittanique' to the Belgian GQG said that at 13.45 hrs a Belgian Spad had downed a DFW C-type over Nieuport. As no combat report existed, the French 1ère Armée was asked if there was a combat between a French Spad and a DFW. The French Army too told GQG that it concerned a Belgian Spad. Since Braun was the only Spad pilot in the air at the time, it was confirmed that Braun must have shot down the two-seater.)

CASTIAU Roger Celestin Lucien Aimé   Lieutenant   1,2,Esc Hydravions,7

Born at Ronse (East-Flanders) on 26 May 1889, Castiau was a pre-war pilot receiving brevet nr.89 on 18 November 1913. He volunteered at the Aviation Militaire on 6 August 1914 and became a Caporal on the same day. Castiau left for the front and joined Escadrille I on 15 March 1915 still as a Caporal, arriving in a new Blériot monoplane from Calais. Six days later he was promoted to Sergent; promotion to Adjudant occurred on 30 May. He turned out to be one of the very first fighter pilots on 26 June when he arrived at La Panne in a new Nieuport 10 two-seater. By then there were but two other fighter pilots (Capt A.Demanet and S/Lt J.Olieslagers). S/Lt L.Robin joined Castiau on most of his offensive patrols, and on one such outing (19 September 1915), Castiau and Robin decided to fly over occupied Brussels. During the night of 25-26 September both men undertook five consecutive night bombing missions. At this time Castiau had already been commissioned on 10 September 1915. The next feat occurred on 10 October when he, again with S/Lt Robin, flew over occupied Ghent and Antwerp. At 16.00, 125 newspapers were thrown over Antwerp, together with a large Belgian flag and six streamers. At 16.27 they flew over Ghent throwing the remaining 25 newspapers and yet another Belgian flag. All the way they were fired upon by German AA-units, inflicting minor damage to the aircraft. During 1915 Castiau flew 68 sorties, took part in 12 aerial combats, including an attack on a Zeppelin on 31 May, but without result. He was assigned to the Escadrille d'Hydravions and sent to the Belgian Congo on 21 December 1915. Here he was made a Chevalier de l'Ordre de l'Etoile Africaine in September and decorated with the Croix de Guerre in March 1916. Returning to Belgium, he was promoted to Lieutenant on 30 June 1917 and left for the Military Pilot School at Etampes on 11 August 1917. There he stayed until 17 March 1918 when he was transferred to the newly formed 7me Escadrille d'Observation. With this unit on 16 April 1918 he was made a Chevalier de l'Ordre de la Couronne for his work as a reconnaissance pilot and flying bombing missions.

Other honours and awards were the Chevalier de l'Ordre Leopold II with Palme, Médaille de la Victoire, Médaille Commémorative 1914-18, Médaille Commémorative d'Argent des Campagnes d'Afrique and he received eight Chevrons de front. Castiau was demobilized on 29 September 1919, but died at Ixelles on 7 May 1926, aged only 36.

CISELET Charles Eduard Louis   Sous-Lieutenant   4,5

'Sidi' Ciselet was born 3 October 1894 in Hove, Antwerp and was one of four brothers who all entered the Aviation Militaire. Two of them were killed in action: Robert (see below) and Marcel, a 6me Escadrille pilot, on 18 May 1918 over Zwartegat, Houthulst Forest. Maurice, the third brother, was severely injured during the war and was invalided out of the Aviation Militaire, only to die shortly after the armistice as a consequence of the wounds sustained in active service.

Charles, however, volunteered on 23 May 1915 and asked to be posted to the Aviation Militaire immediately. On 1 August he was promoted to Caporal and finally joined the 4me Escadrille on 30 December 1915. Promotions in 1916 followed quickly; to Sergent on 9 January, 1er Sergent on 21 February and to 1er Sergent Major on 30 April. By then he was an artillery-observation pilot working with a wireless telegraphic installation on board of his Farman two-seater. He was severely wounded whilst crash-landing into the sea on 13 March 1916. During this crash his observer, Lt Robert Smits was killed. The next forced landing occurred at Houthem on 5 May when he had been hit by AA fire. Again his Farman was a write-off. May was also the month Ciselet started to fly some protection flights. During one of these patrols, on 25 May, he became involved in a fight with a German two-seater. Ciselet's Farman was hit several times, but the German certainly was hit by Ciselet's observer, S/Lt Alberic Rolin. Ciselet, teamed up with another Farman, flown by 1Sgt Maj John de Roest d'Alkemade/Capt Roger d'Hendecourt, pursued the German well over the latter's own lines, where the pursuit finally ended. This could, however, mean that on his very first combat a possible victory was claimed. From June he started to fly more and more offensive patrols, mostly with S/Lt A.Rolin as his observer. The second time Sidi Ciselet was severely wounded occurred on 2 July when he received a direct hit from AA fire. This time observer Lt Joseph Gilles was killed. For a few days Ciselet hovered between life and death, but survived, coming out of hospital after eight months. During his time in hospital he was promoted Adjudant on 20 August. Commission was finally given on 19 May 1917. On 9 June, he claimed his only official victory over Bixschoote whilst engaged in a fight with two scouts, whilst two other ones attacked a Farman two-seater which was out on a photo-mission. During this time his Nieuport scout was baptised *Flo-Flo*. He received his third wound, flying a Spad VII (# Sp2) during an evening combat on 23 September and these injuries meant the end of his flying days. Ciselet had flown on 98 offensive patrols during which some 17 combats were fought. Promotion to Lieutenant occurred on 18 December 1918. S/Lt C.Ciselet was made a Chevalier de l'Ordre Leopold with Palme, Chevalier de l'Ordre de la Couronne, Chevalier de l'Ordre Leopold II with Palme and received the Croix de Guerre, Médaille de la Victoire, Médaille Commémorative 1914-18, eight Chevrons de front and two Chevrons de blessure.

After the armistice, he started a garage, but stayed in close contact with flying, and was finally discharged on 16 August 1922. In 1923 he started his own airline company at the newly opened airport of Deurne, Antwerp. He met his death on 1 April 1931 over Mortsel, Antwerp when his aeroplane crashed shortly after taking off. Ciselet, the only surviving son of four children, was then only 35 years old.

	1916						
_*	25 May	LVG C	MF	4	Dixmude	—	OOC
	1917						
1**	9 Jun	D	Nieup	5	Bixschoote	12.45	DES

* obs S/Lt A.Rolin, together with 1Sgt Maj J.de Roest d'Alkemade/Capt R.d'Hendecourt . ** shared with Adjt P. de Chestret de Haneffe.

CISELET Leon Andre Robert   1er Sergent   5
Robert as he was known, was born at Antwerp on 23 May 1892 and was one of the above mentioned four brothers. He too was a volunteer in the early days of the war and made his way to the Aviation Militaire in 1916. On 24 July 1917 he arrived at the front where he was promoted to Sergent three days later. Promotion to 1er Sergent occurred on 24 September.

On 20 November 1917 at 09.35 he was attacked by five Albatros scouts from Jasta 2. With two bullets in the head and another three in the heart, he fell victim to the fire of Jasta 2's CO, Ltn E. Böhme for the latter's 23rd victory of an eventual 24. The Nieuport fell between Caeskerke & Oudecapelle, near Dixmude. Ciselet flew 55 OP's and only took part in two combats, the second being fatal. 1Sgt Ciselet was made, like every killed soldier, posthumously a Chevalier de l'Ordre de Leopold and was decorated with the Croix de Guerre.

COLIGNON Leon François Joseph   Capitaine   1, ESC HYDRAVION,6
Leon Colignon was born 13 December 1891 at Bonines, Namur, although another official source states Colignon was born at Antwerp, 7 April 1894. He joined the army on 30 April 1908 and was made a Maréchal-des-Logis on 4 December 1911 with the 4me Régtd'Artillerie. He was commissioned on 31 July 1912 and when war broke out, he was with this Regiment at Antwerp. After the surrender of this city, he went to the Aviation School on 18 September, leaving the next day for a French escadrille. Here his pilot was killed in a crash on 4 November 1914, while Colignon was injured. At the end of the month he returned to the Aviation Militaire Belge for a short period, but returned to a French escadrille until 2 March 1915. On this date he finally came back to the Aviation Militaire Belge in which he stayed. His first patrol was made in May. In those early days he mainly flew with either S/Lt P.Hanciau or Lt F.Jacquet. With the latter he had an aerial combat over Westende on 26 July, at 18.20. The German two-seater pilot they attacked immediately turned his aircraft and force landed at Gits. Gits, however, was well behind the German lines, so an official claim could not be made. On 8 October 1915, Colignon was promoted to Lieutenant. The last two months of 1915, he mainly flew as the observer in S/Lt Hanciau's Nieuport, during some offensive patrols. A total of 22 OP's was reached in which ten aerial combats were fought.

On 25 December he joined a unit in the Belgian Congo, flying on many bombing raids over Tanganyika Lake. Two of the most spectacular feats were first the sinking of the torpedo-boat *Graf von Götzen* on 10 June and secondly the burning of a German petrol dump on 17 and 18 July.

Colignon returned to Belgium on 24 March 1917, and two days later joined the 6me Escadrille d'Observation. Here, impressed by the African jungle, he painted a big roaring Gorilla face on both sides of the fuselage of every aircraft he flew. He was again wounded on 15 April

1917, and later went to the Pilot School on 24 March 1918. Back at the front, he was killed in a Sopwith Camel during a test flight on 14 September 1918 when he suddenly spun into the ground.

Capt L.Colignon was made a Chevalier de l'Ordre de Leopold, Chevalier de l'Ordre de l'Etoile Africaine, Chevalier de l'Ordre de la Couronne for flying over 400 hours at the front, and was also decorated with the Croix de Guerre and five citations, and with the French Légion d'Honneur.

	1915						
_*	20 Jun	EA	MF	1	—	—	OOC
_*	26 Jul	Aviatik C	MF	1	Gits	18.20	FTL
	1916						
_**	10 Jun	torpedo-boat	Short	—	Kigoma	—	SUNK

* pilot Lt F.Jacquet . ** pilot Lt A.Behaeghe, this was the *Graf von Götzen*.

COPPENS (de HOUTHULST Baron) Willy Omer François Jean
Lieutenant 6,4,1,9

Born at Watermaal-Bosvoorde near Brussels on 6 July 1892, he entered the war with the 1er Régt Grenadiers. In September 1915 he learned to fly in the UK (RAC 2140 on 9/12/15) and went to France to the Belgian Aviation School in Etampes. It took Coppens almost a year to get to the front, which actually happened in April 1917 when he went to the 6me Escadrille d'Observation on BE2c's. 1 May 1917 saw his first airfight for which he got his first citation on the 2nd day of the month for bringing his aircraft home! (After the war Coppens, somewhat astounded, admitted that he needed that b... aircraft to bring himself home!!) The next transfer happened on 17 June 1917 when he went to the 4me Escadrille d'Observation on Strutters. A month later (14/7/17) he managed a transfer to the 1ère Escadrille de Chasse, which was really what he wanted. Here he had his first fight in a Nieuport N11(!) on 21 July 1917. On 17 August, Coppens was attacked twice by two French Spad VII scouts between 11.55 am and 00.15 pm. On the 19th he became Adjudant. Three days later he was the first Belgian to fly a Hanriot on a war mission.

He got his commission to Sous-Lieutenant in June 1918. After his second triple on 22 July 1918 he was decorated with the British MC by General Plumer himself, although punished by the Belgian Army; the victories being made within five minutes over the British front near 'Plugstreet' and Belgian aircraft were not allowed to fly over this front. On 22 August he became a Flight Commander (only three planes in a Belgian Flight). His last (228th) OP occurred on 14 October: at 05.40 he started with Sergent Etienne Hage for what was to become both pilot's last combat. The object was to destroy the balloon over Praat Bosch (Vladsloo). The victory he scored at 06.00 was Coppens' 36th and on they went for the next target, being the balloon over Thourout. At 500 m distance from the balloon, Coppens received a direct hit from an AA unit and was seriously wounded in the left tibia. He continued with his attack and shot down the balloon (confirmation for his 37th victory was only made in the late 1930's). Coppens, however, managed to land quite safe behind the Belgian lines, became unconscious and was hastily transferred to the closest Military Hospital. More dead than alive, King Albert insisted that his left leg should be amputated to save Coppens' life. Coppens had been engaged in 94 aerial combats during his sorties. Rumour has it that one of Coppens' victories was made over a 'trap' kite balloon. A 'drachen' armed with a basket full of explosives instead of an observer hung silently waiting for the balloon-strafer to arrive. As Coppens' Hanriot was pure cobalt-blue, it was easily recognised and when he arrived to attack that particular balloon, it should have been exploded from the ground. When Coppens attacked the balloon however, its Ballonzug-crew was having a meeting and there was no-one on the look-out. The 'drachen' was downed and the basket exploded in the midst of the ones who had set the trap.

He was made an Officier de l'Ordre de Leopold, Officier de l'Ordre de la Couronne and decorated with the Croix de Guerre with 27 Palmes & 13 Lion Vermeils and 28 citations. By the Allied countries he was decorated with, apart from the British MC, the DSO and the Serbian

Order of the White Eagle.

Coppens became Baron Willy Coppens after the war and was honoured with the addition of 'de Houthulst' to his name and stayed in the Army despite having only one leg. It was King Albert himself who persuaded Coppens to stay. Coppens deeply regretted this as the years wore on because he didn't get the promotions which he thought he deserved. He finally left the army in 1940, still only a Major, having spent most of his years as a Military attaché in Italy, Switzerland, France and Great Britain. During World War II he resided in Switzerland organising some resistance work and marrying there. In the late sixties he went back to Belgium and lived the last five years with Jan Olieslagers' only daughter until his sudden death on 21 December 1986. His famous book *Days on the Wing* was published in 1934.

	1917						
_#	7 Jul	C	Strut	4	Middelkerke	15.55	OOC
_##	30 Sep	C	HD#1	1	Roulers	10.40	FTL
_###	1 Oct	C	HD#1	1	Beerst	15.45	OOC
	1918						
_*	12 Mar	C	HD	9	St-Georges	09.10	DES
1**	25 Apr	D	HD	9	St-Georges	12.20	DES
2	8 May	balloon	HD	9	Zarren	07.10	DES
3	8 May	balloon	HD	9	Houthulst	09.55	DES
4***	15 May	balloon	HD	9	Houthulst	08.07	DES
5 †	19 May	balloon	HD	9	Houthulst	09.45	DES
6	5 Jun	balloon	HD	9	Houthulst	06.40	DES
7	9 Jun	balloon	HD	9	Zonnebeke	09.22	DES
8	10 Jun	balloon	HD	9	Ploegsteert	07.47	DES
9	24 Jun	balloon	HD	9	Warneton	06.45	DES
10	24 Jun	Hannover C	HD	9	Ploegsteert	06.46	DES
11	30 Jun	balloon	HD	9	Bovekerke	06.30	DES
12	30 Jun	balloon	HD	9	Gheluvelt	08.30	DES
13	30 Jun	balloon	HD	9	Passchendaele	08.34	DES
14	14 Jul	balloon	HD	9	Passchendaele	09.30	DES
15	16 Jul	balloon	HD	9	Bovekerke	18.55	DES
16	19 Jul	balloon	HD	9	Ruiterhoek	19.20	DES
17	20 Jul	balloon	HD	9	Houthulst	05.57	DES
18	22 Jul	balloon	HD	9	Gheluwe	07.30	DES
19	22 Jul	balloon	HD	9	Wervicq	07.31	DES
20	22 Jul	balloon	HD	9	Comines	07.34	DES
21	24 Jul	balloon	HD	9	Ruiterhoek	19.20	DES
22	3 Aug	balloon	HD	9	Reutel	07.50	DES
23	10 Aug	balloon	HD	9	Leffinghe	06.05	DES
24	10 Aug	balloon	HD	9	Ruiterhoek	06.25	DES
25	10 Aug	balloon	HD	9	Leffinghe	07.45	DES
26	24 Aug	balloon	HD	9	Ploegsteert	14.55	DES
27	24 Aug	balloon	HD	9	Warneton	14.57	DES
28	3 Sep	balloon	HD	9	Ten Brielen	11.02	DES
29	4 Sep	balloon	HD	9	Wercken	09.23	DES
30	27 Sep	balloon	HD	9	Leffinghe	11.05	DES
31	27 Sep	balloon	HD	9	Leffinghe	11.05	DES
32	29 Sep	balloon	HD	9	Leffinghe	10.05	DES
_ ††	2 Oct	C	HD	9	Handzaeme	12.45	OOC
_ ††	3 Oct	C	HD	9	Menin	07.10	DES
33	3 Oct	balloon	HD	9	Leffinghe	15.20	DES
34	5 Oct	balloon	HD	9	Lendeleede	08.14	DES
35	5 Oct	balloon	HD	9	Cruypenaerde	08.20	DES
36 †††	14 Oct	balloon	HD	9	Praat Bosch	06.00	DES
37 †††	14 Oct	balloon ·	HD	9	Thourout	06.05	DES

observer Capt G.Declercq. ## shared with Adjt A.de Meulemeester. Possibly a Kasta 18 aircraft which lost Gefr Friedrich Egner, kia. ### shared with S/Lt J.Olieslagers, Adjts A.de Meulemeester & J.Goossens-Bara. * shared with Capt W.Gallez and Adjt P.Dubois, the latter being credited. ** shared with Capt W.Gallez (1). This was one of a formation of 25, possibly Jasta 36. *** Coppens rammed this balloon with the wheels of his Hanriot, the ammunition being insufficient † Lt J.Olieslagers flew

protection to this attack and later that day got his 5th confirmed victory as well. - †† shared with Sgt E.Hage, these victories where not found in the daily reports of the Groupe de Chasse and were only mentioned in Coppens' *Jours Envolés*. ††† Bz 153.

COPPENS d'EECKENBRUGGE (Baron) Gabriel Virgile Auguste Marie Joseph
Adjudant   5,10

This lesser known Coppens was born 17 January 1890 at Chailly-en-Biere (Seine et Marne), France. He went to the Military Academy in November 1908 and on 30 September 1912 was assigned as a Maréchal-des-Logis to the 7me Régtd'Artillerie. On 30 July 1914 he was recalled to duty and went to war with the 12me Régtd'Artillerie, 107me Batterie. He went to the balloon section on 9 March 1917, and was made a Sergent. He was allotted to the balloon nr.3. On 29 June, however, he was made a private at his own request, to receive a transfer to the Aviation Militaire. Coppens d'E (as he was known in the diaries) received his civil brevet at Etampes on 27 July 1917 and his wings on 21 September. Transfer to the 5me Escadrille de Chasse occurred on 12 December 1917, together with Cpl C.de Montigny. On 23 December he was made a Sergent, in February a 1er Sergent and on 21 April 1918 he became a 1er Sergent Major. Two days later, he was on a ground-strafing mission, together with his CO Cdt J.Dony and Adjt C.Wouters. This was an ordinary duty, of course, but it was Coppens d'Eeckenbrugge's first exploit. On 23 June he was promoted to Adjudant.

Coppens d'E never was a very aggressive pilot, for his first combat did not occur until 29 September 1918, almost a year after arriving at the front. It was the first of four combats in 104 offensive patrols. That day, in a Flight with S/Lt M.Orban and Adjt J.Ledure, they were pursued by twelve enemy scouts over Passchendaele. A few minutes later, he and Ledure were attacked by three of them. The only attack he himself made was on 2 October when he, together with S/Lt J.Goethals, opened fire on a two-seater over Roulers. On October 15, Coppens d'E was involved in a dogfight against fifteen scouts over Roulers. In this fight three Germans were claimed and one Belgian had to force land after being severely wounded (Adjt de Montigny who afterwards died of his wounds).

Coppens d'E seemed to suffer quite a lot from engine trouble during his patrols. For instance when he returned from Calais in a brand new Spad XIII (# Sp22) on 1 November 1918. When he started for his afternoon patrol, the engine failed yet again! Adjt G.Coppens d'Eeckenbrugge was made a Chevalier de l'Ordre de la Couronne and decorated with the Croix de Guerre, Médaille de l'Yser, Médaille de la Victoire, Médaille Commémorative 1914-18. After the war, on 10 October 1919, he was engaged for yet another year which allowed him to be commissioned. This happened on 22 June 1920; he was made a Lieutenant on 26 June 1923 and finally reached the rank of Capitaine-Honoraire on 26 June 1931. At that time he had already retired, on 4 June 1928. Coppens d'Eeckenbrugge died on 4 January 1957.

CREMERS Leon Benoit   Adjudant   11

Leon Cremers was born 7 May 1897 at Zwijnaarde near Ghent. On 17 August 1914 he volunteered into the 1ère Division d'Armée and on 15 October was posted to the 2me Division d'Armée. He managed a transfer to the Pilot School on 2 August 1917 and was sent to the Parc d'Aviation in Calais and from there to Etampes, where he qualified as a pilot on 25 September 1917 and received his wings on 6 December 1917. Managing to get a transfer to a front-line unit, he arrived at the new 11me Escadrille de Chasse on 12 May 1918. His first war flight was flown on 20 May under the sharp eye of Adjt R.Rondeau, with whom he flew nearly all his missions. He turned out to be a daring pilot who flew some 120 offensive patrols during which he was involved in 17 combats, although all without result. On two occasions he had to crash-land due to engine trouble. On 17 October 1918 he was one of the first Belgian fighter pilots to land on the beach of Ostende. On 30 October he was promoted to Adjudant.

Adjt Cremers was made a Chevalier de l'Ordre de Leopold and decorated with the Croix de Guerre, Médaille de l'Yser and Silver Medal of Merit (Serbia). After the war he went with the Inter-Allied forces to occupied Germany and was stationed at Bochum. When on 7 June 1919 a new pilot started to stunt over the airfield, which was prohibited, Cremers took to the air to show the novice what 'real' aerobatics was like. Something went wrong, however, and poor Cremers crashed to his death.

CROMBEZ Henri Benjamin   Lieutenant   4,5,6,4,6

Born at Lombartzyde (West-Flanders) on 16 May 1893, Crombez never was a real fighter pilot in a fighter unit. He is mentioned here because he was one of the first pilots to operate as a fighter pilot before the first fighter unit was formed. 'Riri' Crombez was a pre-war pilot receiving his wings on 18 October 1910 (brevet nr.26). Then he left his Engineer Regiment for the 'Compagnie des Aviateurs' on 14 September 1913, being promoted to Caporal on 7 November 1913. On 5 August 1914, Sergent Crombez was the first Belgian pilot to have an aerial combat in his personal Deperdussin monoplane. Although all information about 1914 is lost, this was published in a newspaper. On 18 March 1915 Crombez was commissioned and he received his Nieuport N10 on 5 August 1915, being the first pilot to receive this scout. He baptised his aircraft Vampire and on 26 August the first offensive patrol was made and therefore he became, together with Adjt A.Behaeghe and S/Lt J.Olieslagers, one of the first three fighter pilots. In 1915 he flew 73 offensive patrols and was engaged in seven combats. The next year he was more and more engaged in reconnaissance and night-bombing missions and again he was the first to receive a new aircraft in the Belgian Army on 30 March 1916: the BE2c. From that moment on his career as a fighter pilot became history, although in early 1916 he had a Ponnier L1 scout at his disposal, again baptised Vampire. Promotion to Lieutenant and transfer to the 4me Escadrille occurred on 1 July 1917.

Crombez claimed his only victory on 14 October 1918 when he flew in his Spad XI (# Sp6) on a reconnaissance flight. In the proximity a French balloon was set on fire and Crombez didn't hesitate to attack the attacking German scout, which he shot down in flames. For this action, his 10th aerial combat during 100 OP's, he received a citation from the French Army and was, after the war, made a Chevalier de la Légion d'Honneur. From the Belgian Army he was made an Officier de l'Ordre de la Couronne, Chevalier de l'Ordre Leopold and decorated with the Croix de Guerre with Palme, Médaille de l'Yser, Médaille de la Victoire, Médaille Commémorative 1914-18, two citations, eight Chevrons de front and two Chevrons de blessure. From England he received the Military Cross gazetted on 22 March 1919 and Ethiopia made him Chevalier de l'Ordre de l'Etoile.

After the war he became a Lieutenant-auxiliaire with the Engineers on 31 March 1920, being discharged into the Reserves on 8 June 1921. He was promoted Capitaine-en-second on 26 March 1922 and was pensioned out on 1 December 1933, and promoted to Major-Honoraire on 21 April 1934. He died 27 January 1960.

	1918							
1*	14 Oct	D	Spad	6	—	—	DES(f)

* obs. Lt du Roy de Blicquy, possibly Ltn zS Max Stinsky (2 victories), MFJ IV, kia.

DALLEMAGNE François Marie Arthur Lambert   Sergent   11

Born at Liège on 25 February 1897, he volunteered in February 1915 to join the section of armoured cars. Here he stayed until transferred, on 2 August 1916, to the 13me Régt de Ligne. He managed a transfer to the Aviation Militaire on 30 January 1918, went to Juvisy to qualify in April and received his wings on 20 August. Dallemagne was posted to the 11me Escadrille de Chasse on 4 October and made his first offensive patrol on 5 October. The only aerial combat in which he was involved occurred on 15 October when he, together with his flight commander, 1er Sgt Maj R.Mulders and Sgt F.Waroux, attacked a group of Fokker scouts. On 1 November he overturned his Sopwith Camel, but without too much damage. He was in the air for only 24 hours and 10 minutes during 19 offensive patrols.

Francis Dallemagne was decorated with the Médaille Militaire 2nd class with Palme, Croix de Guerre with two Palmes, Croix du Feu, Médaille du Volontaire Combattant 1914-18, Médaille de la Victoire, Médaille Commémorative 1914-18, six Chevrons de front and one

Chevron de blessure.

After hostilities, Dallemagne went to France and helped his father sustaining an agricultural property. In 1924 he went back to Belgium and was in charge of a workshop, producing sporting guns and afterwards in a steam engine factory. He loved fishing, hunting, nature in all aspects and children ... for he was the father of 16 children! He died, terminally ill, at Liège, January 30, 1975.

de CHESTRET de HANEFFE (Baron) Louis Marie Fernand Ghislain
Sous-Lieutenant 4,5,10

Born at Donceel (province of Liège) on 30 March 1889, he was an Engineer when war came and volunteered on 4 August 1914. On 6 August 1915 he managed a transfer to the Aviation Militaire, becoming a Sergent the next day. He appeared in the Ordre Journalières de l'Aviation Militaire on 23 April 1916 and flew on his first reconnaissance mission five days later with the 4me Escadrille de Reconnaissance. On 28 May 1916 he was promoted to 1er Sergent During August he transferred to the newly formed 5me Escadrille de Chasse, being made a 1er Sergent Major on 6 August. Like his brother Pierre, he shot down an enemy aircraft on his first aerial combat. Louis de Chestret, however, had more luck for his victory was made official, whilst his brother's victory was not confirmed. Promotion to Adjudant occurred on 10 December 1916. Louis de Chestret was finally commissioned on 7 November 1917 as an Engineer-officer attached to the Aviation Militaire. When the Groupe de Chasse was formed, Louis de Chestret only flew 31 more offensive patrols in which only two combats occurred. Only once did he fly together with his brother (7 June 1918). His last official combat occurred on 10 June when he, together with Adjt R. de Leener, saw an enemy two-seater protected by four scouts. Whilst De Leener attacked one of the scouts, de Chestret took the opportunity to attack the two-seater, but to no avail. In the afternoon de Chestret was attacked by two Bristol fighters.

On 12 June Louis de Chestret took off for his 118th offensive patrol from which he did not return. He attacked, well behind the German lines, an enemy aircraft which he actually destroyed, but had to crash-land his Spad due to fuel shortage. Severely injured after his 13th combat, he was transported to Iseghem in a Military Hospital, being badly treated and then went to a Ghent Hospital. When he was sufficiently cured to be transferred to a prison camp, he did not wait for official approval and left on his own. He escaped on 28 July and walked the 100 km distance to the Dutch border. Here he stayed for a few days with an uncle and again left for the Belgian front in August. He did not reach the front until 17 November 1918.

For his actions at the front he was made a Chevalier de l'Ordre de la Couronne for flying over 300 hours above the front and was decorated with the Croix de Guerre with citation, Médaille de l'Yser, Médaille de la Victoire, Médaille Commémorative 1914-18, Médaille du Centenaire and eight Chevrons de front, one chevron de blessure. After being promoted to Lieutenant auxiliaire in the reserves on 26 June 1919 he was pensioned out on 1 August 1924. In 1929 he left for Morocco were he started a kapok factory. During his spare time he was a devoted fisherman for trout. Baron Louis de Chestret de Haneffe died at Rabat (Morocco) on 7 February 1978.

	1916							
1*	17 Nov	Fokker	Nieup	5	—	15.15	FTL
	1918							
_**	12 Jun	EA	Spad	10	—	11.30	DES

* whilst alone he attacked a formation of 4 scouts (Jasta 8 ?) and although hit in the fuel tank, he managed to make one scout force-land. ** de Chestret crash-landed near his victim and was taken prisoner.

de CHESTRET de HANEFFE (Baron) Pierre Louis Marie Ghislain
Sous-Lieutenant 5,1,9

Born at Donceel (province of Liège) on 14 October 1894, he volunteered for the 3rd Division on 4 August 1914 becoming a Sergent the same day. One year later he transferred to the Aviation Militaire, with a demotion of his rank to private. One day later he regained his stripes and was made a 1er Sergent on 28 May 1916. On 6 August 1916 he became a 1er Sergent Major. The first patrol of Pierre Pétar de Chestret was made on 30 March 1916 and four days later he crash-landed for the first time due to engine trouble, at Alveringhem. The first months of his flying career were spent at an artillery observation unit. The first test flights on a Nieuport scout were made in August 1916 and the first offensive patrol in a scout occurred on the 29th. In his first aerial combat he forced an enemy aircraft to land behind its lines, therefore the possible victory could not be confirmed, whilst his brother Louis de Chestret had more luck in his first aerial combat, for his victory was confirmed. Promotion to Adjudant occurred on 10 December 1916. On 9 June 1917, Pierre de Chestret claimed his only confirmed victory. During a protection flight he was attacked by two scouts: Pierre de Chestret was hit in the chest, but managed to continue the combat. Somehow he managed a loop and shot down his surprised attacker. De Chestret crash-landed after this combat and was claimed (believing the official letters) by a 27-victory ace. A few days after the combat, news spread that the red-painted Albatros or Halberstadt fighter was flown by the German ace Karl-Emil Schäfer, Jasta 28, who was killed over Bixschoote. This rumour of course was false, for Schäfer had been killed four days earlier by Lt H.Satchell/Lt T.Lewis, 20 Sqdn, RFC. For this victory Pétar was made a Chevalier de l'Ordre de Leopold II and decorated with the Croix de Guerre with citation. On 7 November he was commissioned. After recovery, the first offensive patrol with the newly formed Groupe de Chasse was flown on 6 June 1918, almost a year after the previous patrol! He was involved in a three vs three combat, together with Capt W.Gallez and Adjt P.Dubois on 11 August. One of the Fokkers was forced to land, but none of the Belgians received a confirmed victory. On 22 September 1918 he became a Flight Commander, taking the place of Lt W.Coppens of the White Flight. 18 aerial combats were fought during 117 OP's.

After the war he was made a Chevalier de l'Ordre de la Couronne and was decorated with the Médaille de l'Yser, five chevrons de front and one chevron de blessure. He was made a Lieutenant on 26 June 1919 and left for occupied Germany on 26 August. Here he married Mrs M.Laloux on 24 April 1922. Suffering from a disease contracted at the front from which he never recovered, he was discharged to the Reserve List of the 2me Régiment de l'Aviation Militaire on 10 August 1931. He stayed a born hunter (this time for deer) and started a factory which made materials for beer brewing. The factory, which he built up successfully, was sold to an American when de Chestret reached his 65th birthday in 1961. Baron Pierre de Chestret de Haneffe died 6 June 1975.

	1916		N16				
_	13 Nov	EA	#N1	5	Eesen	15.00	FTL
	1917						
_	24 May	C	Nieup	5	Clercken	19.00-20.20	FTL
1*	9 Jun	Alb D	Nieup	5	Bixschoote	12.45	DES
	1918		HD				
_**	11 Aug	Fokker	#12	9	Tervaete	10.00	FTL

* shared with S/Lt C.Ciselet (1) ** together with Capt W.Gallez and Adjt P.Dubois.

DECLERCQ René Auguste Marie Alphonse   1er Sergent Major   11

Born at Liège on 10 December 1896, Declercq managed to escape occupied Belgium and volunteered in London on 25 January 1915. He was posted to the 10me Régtd'Artillerie where he was promoted Brigadier in 1916. On 23 February 1917 he was posted to the 4me Régt d'Artillerie from where he was sent to Etampes as a student pilot on 27 December. He qualified as a pilot on 18 June and was sent to the Parc d'Aviation at Calais on the 27th. Declercq was posted to the 11me Escadrille de Chasse on 9 July and flew his first sortie on the same day. He had his first aerial combat on 3 August and on 16 August he attacked, together with Capt P.Hiernaux, Lt E.Wouters and Adjt J.Lamarche, a two-seater at 4,000 m over Houthulst Forest. After diving to 300 m the German observer ceased firing and the two-seater seemed to fall out of control. It is, however, not mentioned in Declercq's claim list, as details are missing. He was made a 1er Sergent on 25 August. On 30 August his aircraft turned over after landing at the airfield, but Declercq was unhurt. On another occasion Declercq did not return from an offensive patrol. This occurred on 28 September 1918, the first day of the Belgian Liberation Offensive during the attacks on Houthulst Forest and the famous Hindenburg line. Adjt Lamarche saw him at 08.15 east of Blankaert Chateau two or three km behind the German front lines. He must have been at some 400 m above the ground and there were no German scouts in the neighbourhood, so it appears he had engine trouble. He must have reached the Belgian lines, however, for the next day he flew his next two patrols. He made his only claim on 3 October when he, flying alone, attacked a two-seater over Staden. He followed his adversary to Lichtervelde where he attacked twice more flying at a height of only 50 m. When he turned to attack a fourth time, he saw the two-seater crash to the ground. Declercq was promoted to 1ère Sergent Major on 27 October. With the 11me Escadrille de Chasse Declercq flew 71 sorties and took part in 10 aerial combats.

He finally reached the rank of Adjudant on 29 December and was demobilized on 31 January 1919 and was awarded the Croix de Guerre, Médaille du Volontaire Combattant 1914-18 and obtained two Chevrons de front and one citation for his victory (although the citation mentioned the claim as being 2 October).

René Declercq was still alive in October 1984.

	1918							
1	3 Oct	C	—	11	Lichtervelde	08.10	DES	

de CROMBRUGGHE de LOORINGHE (Baron) Marcel Alphonse Eugène Josephe Ghislain Gerard Marie   Lieutenant   4,5,4,5,6,2,3,1,9

Born at Ixelles, Brussels on 23 January 1894, he volunteered on 31 July 1914 into the 22me Régiment de Ligne. On 3 August he transferred to the 2me Régiment de Guides where he was made a Maréchal-des-Logis the day after his arrival. On 5 September 1914 he was made Adjudant. He was finally commissioned as a Lieutenant-auxiliaire with the 4me Chasseurs à Cheval on 14 January 1915 and managed a transfer to the Aviation Militaire in June when he became an observer for Escadrille IV. On 8 October 1915 he was promoted to Sous-Lieutenant and the promotion to Lieutenant occurred on 26 March 1916.

De Crombrugghe was wounded on 11 November 1915, a bullet smashing his arm. His pilot, Lt J.Dony had to make a forced landing near to the railway-line Furnes-Dixmude, close to a first aid post. For this action de Crombrugghe received a citation. He stayed in hospital till 31 January 1916 and went to the 5me Escadrille, only to return to the 4me Escadrille on 16 March. The next transfer, again to the 5me, occurred on 18 May and on 28 June he went to the 6me Escadrille. His next transfer, to the 3me Escadrille, was made on 8 July 1917 from where he moved to the 1ère Escadrille de Chasse on 26 August. Here he became the observer to Cdt F.Jacquet, except for a period in August 1918 when he again was hospitalised in Cabour. After his first victory, de Crombrugghe received his second citation on 12 October 1918. On 27 October 1918, with his pilot Jacquet, he attacked a two-seater north of Lovendeghem at 0815. This aircraft dived into its lines in a strange way near Ghent. This was possibly a Marine Feldflieger Abteilung machine, which lost Leutnant Walter Fromme.

During the war he flew 102 offensive patrols of which 85 were flown with the Groupe de Chasse. Nineteen out of 23 aerial combats were fought with this pursuit group. De Crombrugghe received the following decorations: Chevalier de l'Ordre de la Couronne, Croix de Guerre, Médaille de l'Yser, Médaille de la Victoire, Médaille Commémorative 14-18 and eight Chevrons de front.

After the war he was discharged to the reserve-corps on 5 June 1920 and was pensioned out on 13 February 1925. He moved to Indonesia in 1920, came back to Belgium to marry Comtesse S.de Borchgrave d'Altena on 9 June 1921 and again departed for Indonesia. Two years later he moved to Java, after having some difficulties with his Dutch patron. He gave the name 'land Sawangan' to his plantation and led it through the crisis of the thirties. When Japan invaded the island in 1941, de Crombrugghe managed to escape with his wife and six children to Australia in a light aeroplane, where he co-operated in starting a brewery close to Perth, which he owned until 1946. That year he returned to Java, trying in vain to regain his property. After failing to do so, he departed for Belgium in 1948 but one year later he emigrated to Zimbabwe. Here he stayed until 1962. He returned to Brussels where he became terminally ill and died on 2 May 1978.

	1918						
_*	5 Jun	Fok DrI	Spad	9	Houthulst	06.42	OOC
1**	4 Oct	Rumpler C	Spad	9	Gits	—	DES
2***	6 Nov	C	Spad	9	e.Ghent	09.00	OOC

* Pilot Cdt F.Jacquet, witnessed by ground troops of the 2me Division d'Armée Belge. ** Pilot Cdt F.Jacquet. *** Pilot Cdt F.Jacquet. This was probably Gefr Jakob Dick/??, FAA 5, kia.

DELAUNOIT Arsène François Cyrille   Adjudant   3,11

Born at Geraardsbergen (East-Flanders) on 2 November 1893, he was studying Industrial Engineering, when drafted into duty on 4 July 1913. With his unit, the 9me Régt de Ligne, he went to war and in January 1916 he was made a Caporal. Delaunoit transferred to the Aviation Militaire and qualified at Hendon on 16 January 1916 (RAC nr.2284). He received his wings on 8 August and was posted to the 3me Escadrille d'Observation later in the year. With this unit he was promoted to Adjudant on 21 October 1917. He flew 19 OP's and protection flights in a Sopwith Pup and was engaged in two combats before being posted to the newly formed 11me Escadrille de Chasse in May. Delaunoit was one of those pilots who was wanted by Cdt F. Jacquet to form his Groupe de Chasse in March 1918. His first patrol on 17 May turned out to be his last, for two days later, on his motorbike, he was run over by a lorry driver fleeing from a bombardment. The lorry driver didn't even stop and left poor Delaunoit alone with a smashed leg. The war was over before Arsène Delaunoit could return to the front. Adjt A.Delaunoit was decorated with the Croix de Guerre, Médaille de l'Yser, Médaille de la Victoire, Médaille Commémorative 1914-18, five Chevrons de front and was twice mentioned in dispatches.

He retired on 20 September 1919 and was commissioned as a Sous-Lieutenant de Réserve on 14 August 1920. He became an Industrial & Commercial Engineer afterwards who was much involved with the Belgian Congo and died at Uccle, Brabant, on March 24, 1979, aged 85.

DE LEENER Robert   Sous-Lieutenant   1,5,10

'Bob' De Leener was born 3 June 1890 at Gommerages (province of Brabant) and was a draftee in 1911 with the 9me Régt de Lanciers. When war broke out, he was studying justice. From 29 August 1914 onwards he was a motorbike rider in the 3me Division d'Armée. One year later, 1 August 1915, he transferred to the Aviation Militaire where he became a Caporal on the 29th. Almost a year later, on 25 June 1916, becoming a Sergent only a few days earlier, he made his first test flight with his new unit, the 1ère Escadrille de Chasse. He flew his first war flight on 20 July. Promotion to 1er Sergent occurred on 6 August and promotion to 1er Sergent Major came on 29 October. He received a first citation on 13 August 1916. In his first year he flew 18 offensive patrols, but did not see any action in the form of aerial combats, nor pursuits. De Leener was made an Adjudant on 30 January 1917 and was finally commissioned on 7 November. On 15 November 1917, he received a second citation, together with the Croix de Guerre for his total of more than 150 hours over the front lines. In April 1918 he became a flight commander in the renumbered 10me Escadrille de Chasse. On 9 June 1918, flying with S/Lt P.de Chestret and Adjt M.Siraut, the Flight was attacked at 12.50 pm by two Bristol Fighters over Houthulst Forest. He gained his only official claim on 16 September attacking, for the very first time, a balloon. The 'drachen' hung over Zarren at 1,000 m and caught fire almost immediately. For this feat De Leener received a third citation on 30 September. On 23 October he did not return from an offensive patrol. The reason is not known, but on the 24th he was again over the front flying his next patrol. As a fighter pilot he flew on 260 sorties and fought 23 aerial combats during which one official and one probable victory were claimed.

He was made a Chevalier de l'Ordre de la Couronne and awarded with the Médaille de l'Yser, Médaille de la Victoire and Médaille Commémorative 1914-18. De Leener was demobilized on 29 September 1919, and was made a Sous-Lieutenant in the Corps of Engineers on 26 June 1919. Ten years later, 24 April 1929, he went to the Pilot School and was discharged into the Reserves, at his own request on 31 August 1931. He was pensioned out on 19 January 1940 and reached the rank of Capitaine de Réserve on 27 June 1946. He died 23 April 1962.

	1918						
_*	1 Jun	C	Spad	10	Houthulst	12.45	FTL
1	16 Sep	balloon	Spad	10	Zarren	14.30	DES

* together with S/Lt E.Desclée and Adjt M.Siraut.

de MAELCAMP d'OPSTAELE (Baron) Leon Charles Etienne   1er Sergent   1

Born at Brussels on 13 August 1896, he arrived at the front in July 1917, flying his first Offensive Patrol on the 21st. After ten sorties, however, de Maelcamp crashed to his death on 22 August with 1er Sergent Major Lucien Hallet in the latter's Farman 170 HP two-seater at Les Moëres aerodrome at 18.45, doing a training flight. De Maelcamp fought three combats, which were all fought in one sortie in Adjt Andre de Meulemeester's Yellow Flight .

De Maelcamp was posthumously made a Chevalier de l'Ordre de Leopold and awarded the Croix de Guerre.

DEMANET Arsène Jean Joseph   Capitaine-Commandant   1

Born 8 January 1884 at Liège, he joined the Army in May 1907 and was attached to the 4me Régt d'Artillerie. With this unit he was commissioned on 25 December 1910. He gained his wings before the war, on 30 July 1912, receiving brevet nr. 63. Married in September, he went to the Compagnie des Aviateurs on 15 October 1913. Demanet commanded Escadrille I, based at Liège during the first days of the war. After the withdrawal from Liège and Antwerp, the Escadrille had its base at La Panne, still under the command of Demanet, who arrived at the front with one of the first Nieuport N10's on 14 June 1915. Only one day later, however, he landed somewhat uncomfortably and wrote-off the new aircraft. Meanwhile Demanet was promoted to Capitaine on 28 February. In October 1915 Capt Demanet became one of the first six fighter pilots of the Belgian Army; his Nieuport scouts were decorated with a four-leafed clover on the cowling.

When in February 1916 the 1ère Escadrille de Chasse was formed, out of the former Escadrille I, Demanet stayed at his post as CO until he had a quarrel with S/Lt L.Robin in the summer of that year. The quarrel ended when Demanet struck Robin (who was known to be some kind of a rogue). This led to the removal of Demanet as acting CO and he was put on the inactive list for three months, from 5 December (Ordre Journalières de l'Armée (OJA) 8 December 1916), and then was transferred back to the 1er Régt d'Artillerie on 10 March 1917, the arm where he had started his military career. Whilst with the Aviation Militaire he flew 33 offensive patrols but saw no aerial combats.

During his time as Artillery officer he commanded Battery nr.48 until 10 November 1918, the day before the Armistice, when an explosion, probably of his own ammunition, put an end to his life at Landuit, near Eke (province of East-Flanders). Capitaine-Commandant A.Demanet was made a Chevalier de l'Ordre de Leopold II and was decorated with the Croix de Guerre, Médaille de l'Yser, four citations and was made a Chevalier de la Légion d'Honneur and received the French Croix de Guerre.

de MEULEMEESTER Andre Emile Alfons   Lieutenant   1,9

Born at Bruges 28 December 1894, he volunteered immediately to the Aviation Militaire Belge on 26 January 1915. On 8 April 1917 he was officially assigned to the 1ère Escadrille de Chasse although he already had been with it as early as October 1916 when he made his first war flight as a Sergent. 'Mystère' as he was nicknamed by his companions, appeared to be a good piano-player. He was severely wounded after his fifth claim on 21 August 1917, while shooting down a two-seater but was himself hit by the German gunner who put de Meulemeester in hospital for over a month. On 21 February 1918, de Meulemeester, together with Capt H.Symons of 65 Sqdn, RFC, shot down an Albatros DV over Dixmude for his seventh victory. Adjt G.Kervyn de Lettenhove, who assisted in the combat, was not credited. On 11 July Mystère was again wounded, this time engine trouble caused him to crash-land behind Belgian lines inflicting numerous contusions to his face and loosing some teeth. According to Willy Coppens, de Meulemeester was a great pilot, although very small and looking more like 'a sack of bones' than a man. He was indeed a very aggressive pilot who had, during the days of the Groupe de Chasse (March to November 1918) flown over 200 patrols in which he had more than 55 airfights. Four official victories were claimed, as well as five probables, and six fights in which his guns jammed (a disaster that occurred frequently in the Belgian Army). Most of his victims disintegrated in the air. De Meulemeester was commissioned on 21 May 1918. Twice he was attacked by English planes: the first time on 29 June 1918 when a DH4 attacked him three times and secondly on 7 July when his Yellow Flight (Adjt Georges Kervyn de Lettenhove and S/Lt 'Gusto' de Mevius) was attacked by one DH4 and a flight of Sopwith Dolphins. Gusto de Mevius was actually shot down and had to force-land after this attack!! As the most aggressive Belgian fighter pilot, Mystère was engaged in 185 aerial combats during 511 sorties. One of his Hanriots was #HD30.

He was made a Chevalier de l'Ordre Leopold, Chevalier de l'Ordre Leopold II with Palme and decorated with the Croix de Guerre with Palme, five citations from the Belgian and French Armies, and six Chevrons de front and one Chevron de blessure, together with the French Croix de Guerre with Palme and the Italian Medaglio d'Argento al Valore Militare.

De Meulemeester, disgusted at being made a Lieutenant de Réserve on 21 November 1918, left the Army on 17 July 1919 and never flew again. He went into the family Brewery business and died in Bruges on 7 March 1973.

	1917						
_	1 Feb	Rumpler C	Nieup	1	Lombartzyde	15.15	FTL
1*	30 Apr	C	Nieup	1	Leke	09.00-11.15	DES
_ **	2 May	C	Nieup	1	Schoore	07.10	FTL
2***	12 Jun	C	Nieup	1	Vladsloo	15.40	DES
_ §	15 Jun	D	Nieup	1	Keyem	11.15	DES(f)
3	10 Jul	C	Nieup	1	Ramscapelle	20.00	DES
4	20 Jul	C	Nieup	1	km-post 20-21 of the Yser river	06.20	DES
_ §§	23 Jul	D	Nieup	1	Kortewilde	15.50	OOC
_ §§§	5 Aug	D	Nieup	1	S.Dixmude	16.00-16.30	OOC
5	21 Aug	Alb C	Nieup	1	Yser front	—	DES
_ ¶	30 Sep	C	Nieup	1	Roulers	10.40	FTL
_ ¶¶	1 Oct	C	Nieup	1	Beerst	15.45	OOC
_ ¶¶¶	18 Oct	Albatros	Nieup	1	Tervaete	09.15	OOC
_	28 Oct	D	Nieup	1	s Keyem	15.45	OOC
6†	4 Nov	Alb DIII	Nieup	1	Kloosterhoek	07.45	DES
_	17 Nov	Albatros	HD	1	Leke	11.30-11.35	OOC
	1918						
_	16 Feb	C	HD	1	Pervyse	11.04	OOC
_††	21 Feb	C	HD	1	Clercken	08.50	OOC
7†††	21 Feb	Alb DV	HD	1	Dixmude	14.50	DES(f)
8‡	17 Mar	C	HD	9	Dixmude	11.00	DES
_‡‡	26 Mar	Pfalz DIII	HD	9	Dixmude	17.00	CAPT
_	11 Apr	C	HD	9	Schoore	18.15	OOC
9 ‡‡‡	3 May	C	HD	9	Schoorbakke	11.35	DES
_ §§§	9 May	C	HD	9	Fort Knocke	13.15	OOC
10✪	17 May	C	HD	9	Houthulst	10.30	DES
_❑	25 Aug	C	HD	9	Houthulst	09.30	OOC/FTL
_	2 Oct	Halb C	HD	9	Beveren/Lys	18.25	OOC
11	5 Oct	balloon	HD	9	Thourout	07.05	DES

* together with a British Sopwith. ** together with Adjt J.Goethals, Sgt F.de Woot de Trixhe and Sgt G.de Mevius. *** shared with Sgt G.Kervyn de Lettenhove. This was a FA3-aircraft. § together with S/Lt J. Olieslagers, who was credited for this victory

and Sgt C.Verbessem. §§ single-handed he attacked a formation of five scouts and claimed one out of control. §§§ together with S/Lt G.de Mevius. ¶ together with Adjt W.Coppens. Possibly a Kasta 18 aircraft which lost Gefr Friedrich Egner, kia. ¶¶ with S/Lt J.Olieslagers and Adjts W.Coppens & J.Goossens-Bara. ¶¶¶ shared with S/Lt M.Orban, 5me Escadrille, probably Ltn Xaver Dannhuber, Jasta 26, a ten-victory ace who would end the war with 11 victories, wia. † together with Sgt G.Kervyn de Lettenhove who did not receive an official victory. †† together with S/Lt G.de Mevius and Adjt G.Kervyn de Lettenhove. Possibly Vizewachtmeister Friedrich Hothorn of FA7, kia. ††† shared with Capt H.Symons, 65 Sqdn, RFC in Camel B5600 and Adjt G.Kervyn de Lettenhove, who was not credited. ‡ Ltn dR Friedrich Bücheler/??, FA13, kia. ‡‡ together with S/Lt G.de Mevius and Adjt G.Kervyn de Lettenhove (this was Flgmt Hans Groth in Pfalz DIII 5923/17, MFJ II, kia). ‡‡‡ shared with Adjt G.Kervyn de Lettenhove (4). ★ Uffz Andreas Ertl/Obltn d R Viktor Hepe, FA288b, kia..❑ together with S/Lt G.de Mevius and Adjt G.Kervyn de Lettenhove. Possibly Flugzg Matrose Josef Gernhardt of Seefrontstaffel II, kia.

de MEVIUS Gustave David Hubert Ghislain (Baron)   Sous-Lieutenant
5,4,1,9

'Papa Gusto' de Mevius was born 4 November 1882 at Ixelles, Brussels. Before the war he was an engineer who volunteered on 10 September 1914 and was made a Caporal on 12 October with the Section auto-mitrailleurs belonging to the 10me Régtd'Artillerie. He was made a Sergent on 23 March 1915 and transferred to the Aviation Militaire on 15 January 1916. More than a year later he was sent to the front on 2 February 1917 with the 5me Escadrille. Promotions to 1er Sergent and 1er Sergent Major occurred on 8 April 1917 and 17 June 1917 respectively. He transferred to the 4me Escadrille d'Observation on 24 July 1917. Here he became an Adjudant on 9 August. During his time as an observation pilot he had two combats. In the second, on 30 September, he was flying with observer Cdt R.d'Hendecourt when they were attacked by 9 scouts over Tervaete. One was last seen spinning out of control and the others abandoned the fight. This was possibly FlugObermaat Erich Golembiewski of Seeflug Stat. Flandern I who was killed in action on that day. He finally transferred to the 1ère Escadrille de Chasse on 7 October 1917. Here he mainly flew with Adjt A.de Meulemeester's Yellow Flight, together with Sgt G.Kervyn de Lettenhove. He was hospitalised at Cabour from 28 December 1917 to 3 January 1918. Adjt G.de Mevius received the Croix de Guerre on 16 April 1918 for flying over 150 hours over the front. On 22 April, Gusto de Mevius was shot down by a two-seater crew. Whilst the Yellow Flight attacked, the latter hit de Mevius' fuel tank. Three days later he claimed his only official victory whilst flying at 4,000 m. They spotted a formation of 25 scouts from which one was isolated and shot down. In May, de Mevius was commissioned and was made a Chevalier de l'Ordre de la Couronne, for his victory and for flying over 300 hours over the front. Papa (daddy) Gusto was again shot down on 7 July 1918, this time by British scouts! One another occasion, 14 October, S/Lt G.de Mevius must have believed he was on his last patrol; together with S/Lt de Meulemeester he attacked a two-seater protected by eleven scouts. At that moment de Meulemeester's guns jammed and he broke off the fight. De Mevius was left alone and there was nothing left than to fly his way out. Whilst trying to avoid the scouts, he managed to attack first one of the Fokkers which dived into the clouds, then he attacked the two-seater, but de Mevius found his guns jammed as well! He got away safely anyway. Gusto de Mevius flew 260 offensive patrols and fought 46 combats. Three times he had to abandon attacks due to gun failures.

He was decorated with the Médaille de l'Yser, Médaille de la Victoire, Médaille Commémorative 1914-18 and obtained eight Chevrons de front. S/Lt G.de Mevius was also decorated with the French Croix de Guerre on 12 November.

After hostilities he was discharged and transferred to the réserve list where he reached the rank of Capitaine on 24 June 1928. Meanwhile he married in August 1921 and had four children. He started to work as an Engineer at the Stella-Artois Brewery in Louvain and died on 24 January 1931 at Rhisnes, aged 48. His eldest son became the Administrator of this, the most famous Belgian brewery.

	1917						
_ §	2 May	C	Nieup	1	Schoore	07.10	FTL
_ §§	30 Sep	D	Strut	4	Tervaete	15.00-16.15	DES
	1918						
_ §§§	21 Feb	C	—	1	Clercken	08.50	OOC

_*	26 Mar	Pfalz DIII	HD	9	Dixmude	17.00		DES
1**	25 Apr	Pfalz DIII	HD	9	Boitshoucke	11.15		DES(f)
_***	9 May	C	HD	9	Fort de Knocke	13.15		FTL
_#	9 Jul	C	HD	9	Menin	10.45		OOC
_##	25 Aug	C	HD	9	Houthulst	09.30		OOC
_###	2 Oct	Halb C	HD	9	Beveren/Lys	18.25		FTL

§ together with Adjt J.Goethals, 1Sgt A.de Meulemeester and 1Sgt F.de Woot de Trixhe. §§ observer Cdt R.d'Hendecourt (the observer's fourth unofficial claim). Possibly Flug.Ob Erich Golembiewski of Seeflug Stat.Flandern I, kia. §§§ shared with Adjt A.de Meulemeester and Adjt G.Kervyn de Lettenhove. * together with Adjt A.de Meulemeester and Adjt G.Kervyn de Lettenhove (this was Flgmt Hans Groth in Pfalz DIII 5923/17, MFJ II, kia). ** shared with Adjt G.Kervyn de Lettenhove (this was Flgobmt Bruno Fietzmann, MFJ II, kia, shot down in Pfalz DIIIa 5942/17). *** together with Adjt A.de Meulemeester, the observer was obviously killed # together with Adjt G.Kervyn de Lettenhove. ## together with S/Lt A.de Meulemeester and Adjt G.Kervyn de Lettenhove. The two-seater seemed to force land at Staden, the observer apparently badly wounded or dead with his guns pointing straight into the air. Possibly Flugzg Matrose Josef Gernhardt of Seefrontstaffel II, kia. ### together with S/Lt A.de Meulemeester.

de MONTIGNY Charles Albert Marie Paul   Adjudant   5,10

Born 4 June 1892 at Antwerp, he volunteered in the first days of August 1914. He finally managed a transfer to the Aviation Militaire, qualifying as a pilot on 29 May 1917, receiving his wings 28 July 1917, at Etampes. On 5 August he was made a Caporal and was transferred to the 5me Escadrille de Chasse on 12 December 1917. Here he received his promotion to Sergent on the 23rd. On 8 March 1918 he came to the rescue of an English two-seater attacked by a German scout. The latter fled and 1Sgt de Montigny in turn was attacked by the Englishmen! Later that day he attacked the front-line trenches at Tervaete from 200 m altitude. Together with Lt J.Goethals and Adjt C.Wouters, he was engaged in a combat on 23 May fighting off seven scouts with orange tails. In April he was made a 1er Sergent Major and on 25 June reached the rank of Adjudant. De Montigny was shot down on 5 June 1918 by Ltn zur See Theo Osterkamp for an unconfirmed victory at 17.30 and force landed at La Panne. His Spad was destroyed but de Montigny remained unharmed. De Montigny shot down a runaway balloon on 18 July over the Blankeart Lake at 3,400 m. Unfortunately the nationality of the balloon was not recognised, so the victory was never official. Adjt de Montigny was again shot down on 15 October during his 215th OP and 29th combat. In a fight with 15 Fokkers, the patrol (Lts L.Robin, M.Orban, E.Wouters and Adjt G. Coppens d'Eeckenbrugge) was attacked by these scouts from above and de Montigny was immediately hit by one of them but continued the fight and shot down his adversary, broke of the fight and managed to land inside Belgian lines. The very shy de Montigny was severely injured in his legs and thigh-bone. An amputation was apparently needed, but de Montigny refused. He then became a victim of the influenza epidemic and died at the Calais Military Hospital on 30 October 1918. One of the nurses who attended his wounds was the wife of Jean Olieslagers.

Adjt C.de Montigny was made a Chevalier de l'Ordre de Leopold, Chevalier de l'Ordre de la Couronne and was decorated with the Croix de Guerre.

	1918							
1	30 May	balloon	Spad	10	Leffinghe	13.15		DES
_*	18 Jul	balloon	Spad	10	Blankaert Lake	10.30		DES
_**	14 Aug	D	Spad	10	—	11.15		OOC
_***	7 Oct	C	Spad	10	n Dixmude	06.05		DES
2#	15 Oct	D	Spad	10	Roulers	07.35		DES(f)

* this was a runaway balloon of unknown nationality. ** this scout attacked two English two-seaters, Adjt de Montigny came to the rescue and the scout appeared to be hit and fell out of control (possibly Flgmt Karl Goldenstedt, MFJ I, kia). *** only credited to Lt J.Goethals. (2) # possibly FlgObmt Schonebaum, MFJ V, wia.

de MUNCK Charles Alphonse   Sous-Lieutenant   1

Born at Brussels on 16 February 1894, he joined the transport service as a militarised civilian in August 1914. On 6 September he volunteered for the Army and was assigned to the Engineers. Here he was made a Caporal on 1 June 1915. Five days later he transferred to the Aviation

Militaire and Caporal de Munck arrived at the front on 25 March 1916. On that day he made a first reconnaissance flight on board 1Sgt J.Goethals' Nieuport N10. Two days later he tried such an aircraft himself for the first time. The first offensive patrol was flown on 1 April and on this flight he attacked his first enemy. The German, apparently a novice too, made for home as fast as he could. A few days later, de Munck was promoted to Sergent and on 28 May he was a 1er Sergent. In August came promotion to 1er Sergent Major and he made it to Adjudant on 6 December 1916. During his tour at the front he flew on 122 sorties and was engaged in ten aerial combats in various types of Nieuports which were all decorated with a clover on its cowling. One probable claim was made, and once his machine guns failed whilst attacking a DFW two-seater over Ypres. In February 1918, he was sent to Juvisy, France, as an instructor in the Pilot School. Here he was commissioned on 12 October and stayed at the School till the end of the War. De Munck left the army as a disabled ex-Serviceman on 29 September 1919.

For his feats de Munck was made a Chevalier de l'Ordre de la Couronne and was decorated with the Croix de Guerre, Médaille du Volontaire Combattant 1914-18, Médaille de la Victoire, Médaille Commémorative 1914-18 and seven Chevrons de front. Charles de Munck died at Schaarbeek, Brussels on 31 May 1952.

	1916		N12					
–	21 May	EA	#229	1	Beerst		pm	OOC

DE NEEF Abel Louis Camille Fernande   Lieutenant   1,9

Born at Louvain on 15 December 1884, he was working in a garage as a coach-builder in Paris when war came over Europe. He volunteered on 2 August 1914 and was a Caporal lorry driver who received his Sergent stripes on the day of his 20th birthday. He managed a transfer to the Aviation Militaire on 1 January 1915 and qualified on 17 April 1915, receiving the Aero Club de France brevet nr.1876. He received his wings on 1 May 1915, being made a 1er Sergent the day after. On 3 October he was made 1er Sergent Major. On 1 January 1916 De Neef joined the 1ère Escadrille, becoming an Adjudant on the same day. He finally reached the front in a brand new Nieuport N10 on 11 January, not flying his first combat flight until the 14th, due to bad weather. The first offensive patrol was made two days later. On 19 January he made his first pursuit at Ypres and on the 23rd he had his first aerial combat over Bergues (France). When the 1ère Escadrille de Chasse was formed, De Neef was, together with 1er Sergent Roobaert, the first to fly an offensive patrol for the new unit. He was injured after a crash-landing due to engine trouble on 30 July 1916 and his Nieuport was written off. De Neef was hospitalised for some time and did not make his next sortie until 25 September. On 7 February 1917 he was transferred to the Military Academy in Cazeau where he was commissioned on 15 December 1917. During his stay in Cazeau he managed to take some 'refresher courses' with his old unit, for he became a Flight Commander in the 1ère Escadrille in the summer of 1917. De Neef was engaged in 37 aerial combats during 209 OP's.

In 1918 he returned to the Pilot School at Juvisy where he saw out the war, and after the war he was demobilised on 29 September 1919. He was decorated with the Médaille Militaire 2me classe, Croix de Guerre, Médaille de la Victoire, Médaille Commémorative 1914-18 and six Chevrons de front. In 1939 he was made a Chevalier de l'Ordre de Leopold II.

After living and travelling to several countries, he finally died at Louveciennes, France, on 20 March 1970.

	1916							
–	1 Jul	EA	N10	1	Houthulst		10.00	FTL

(de) PETROWSKI Alexandre Sergeivitch   Sous-Lieutenant   1,5,10,7

Born at St-Petersburg, Russia on 21 December 1885, 'Sacha' went to Belgium before the war where he lived in Brussels. Probably it was here that the word 'de' was added to his name. He was the 11th pilot in Belgium to receive his pilot's certificate on 31 May 1910 and still resided in Brussels when war broke out. He immediately joined the Aviation Militaire Belge for he could not go to Russia and volunteered on 5 August 1914, becoming a Caporal the first day. On 6 September, flying with Sgt Benselin, he threw a few bombs and fléchettes at a bivouac near Lebbeke. On 1 October he was made 1er Sergent and on the 30th of that month was commissioned. In the meantime on 25 September, Petrowski, together with Sgt Benselin forced a Taube to land, on the St Agatha-Berchem airfield, near Brussels. The German pilot was dead. This was actually the very first aircraft shot down, for the pilot was hit by rifle fire from either Petrowski's or Benselin's carbine (only four shots were fired!). The Taube was originally sent into the air to stop Petrowski from bombing the airfield at St Agatha-Berchem. After the battle of the Yser in October 1914, Petrowski was transferred to the Pilot School in Etampes where he stayed until 15 September 1916. At this date he went back to the front and to the newly formed 5me Escadrille de Chasse and by the end of the month Petrowski had flown on a few offensive patrols. Meanwhile Petrowski was promoted a Lieutenant on 6 January 1916. During 1917 he managed to travel for three months to his native country where he stayed until 30 November.

When the Groupe de Chasse was formed in March 1918 Petrowski went to the newly formed 7me Escadrille d'Observation and, on his request, was discharged on 22 July 1918. With this last unit, however, he flew many protection flights in a Hanriot, one of which he crashed on 22 March. During the War he flew 72 OP's and participated in only three aerial combats. Petrowski was made a Chevalier de l'Ordre Leopold II on 31 May 1917 and decorated with the Croix de Guerre. After the war, he moved to Jersey, in the Channel Islands.

	1914						
_*	25 Sep	Taube	MF	1	St Agatha-Berchem	16.00-18.00	FTL

* observer Sgt. Benselin.

DE RUYTER Gaston François Felix Corneille   Sergent   11

Born at Huy (province of Liège) on 23 December 1895. One of the first Boy scouts, formed in Belgium by Comte de T'Serclaes and Dr.Depage, he was awarded a medal with a certification for his bravery during a fierce fire at Laroche on 26 August 1913. A good student, he graduated at the Athenée Royal in his home town and volunteered on 4 August 1914 with the 12me Régt de Ligne. Here he was involved in heavy fighting during the first weeks of the War. After the recapture of Ramscapelle, during the Battle of the Yser, he was posted to the 5me Régt de Ligne on 21 October, where he was promoted a Sergent in November. Promotion to Adjudant occurred on 28 February 1915. He was not only known to be a fearless soldier, but also as a poet. He was an actor as well and even wrote his own performance, called *On vole à Juvisy* (Flying at Juvisy), concerning the Pilot School at the latter place. De Ruyter was replaced as a soldier at his own request and transferred to the Aviation Militaire on 28 February 1918. He qualified at Juvisy, and was posted to the 11me Escadrille de Chasse on 2 October 1918 flying Sopwith Camels. Five days later, however, he crashed to his death, getting into a spin during a test flight. He only flew on one sortie on 5 October, from 06.45 till 08.20, with Adjt J.Lamarche and Sgt F.Dallemagne at 1,200 m altitude. Sgt G.De Ruyter was made a Chevalier de l'Ordre de Leopold II and decorated with the Croix de Guerre and Médaille de l'Yser.

DESCLÉE Edmond Marie René Henri Jude Gabriel   Lieutenant   6,5,10,7

Born 16 September 1891 at Tournai, the tall (1m 85) Desclée studied law, and when war came he volunteered on 3 August 1914. On 15 February 1915 he transferred to the 'Compagnie des Aviateurs' and became a Caporal the same day. On 1 April 1915 he moved to the Parc d'Aviation at Calais and finally arrived at the front on 22 June in a Maurice Farman 80 HP. Promotion to Sergent followed on 18 July. He was engaged in many night-bombing sorties which he flew well into 1916. On 1 August 1915 he was promoted to 1er Sergent and to Adjudant on 3 October.

On 1 July 1916 he flew his first offensive patrol and had his first fight on 20 July. The first special feat happened on 7 September 1916 when he, together with Adjt A.Orban, flew to

Antwerp and back. He actually received a citation for this on 11 September, and was commissioned on 2 October 1916. Desclée's Nieuport N23 had a message in its comet's sign warning each German he'd better run with the words *va ou je te pousse* (beat it or I'll make you). On 23 July 1917 he shot up a hostile aircraft on its airfield. On 14 May 1918, after throwing some leaflets over the German front-lines, he was engaged in a combat, together with S/Lt A.Orban and 1Sgt Maj C.de Montigny, against five Albatros scouts. Desclée's Spad was riddled with bullets but he managed to land safely. On another occasion he attacked a two-seater, together with S/Lt R.De Leener and Adjt M.Siraut. The two-seater went into a spin and dived in a very strange way towards its lines. Probably the pilot was hit and made a forced landing or even crashed. Due to the low clouds the result could not be seen and therefore no claim could be made. On yet another occasion (26 June 1918, the day he was promoted to Lieutenant) he attacked a runaway balloon over Dixmude at 4,500 m, without result. With the Groupe de Chasse Lt E.Desclée flew 78 sorties and took part in 9 combats. He transferred to the 7me Escadrille d'Observation on 20 September where he saw out the war after flying a total of 234 OP's in which 40 combats were fought. For his feats he was made a Chevalier de l'Ordre de la Couronne with Palme, Chevalier de l'Ordre Leopold II and was decorated with the Croix de Guerre with Palme, Médaille de la Victoire, Médaille Commémorative 1914-18 and obtained eight Chevrons de front. From France he received the Croix de Guerre on 11 November 1918 with a citation in the Ordre Journalière Aéronautique de l'Armée Française des Flandres.

He was demobilized on 31 March 1920, but died in a crash in an army aircraft on 13 June 1924 at Nivelles, only 33 years old.

	1918							
_*	1 Jun	C		Spad	10	Houthulst	12.45	FTL

* with S/Lt R.De Leener and Adjt M.Siraut.

de WOELMONT (Baron) Frederic Felix Henri Marie Ghislaine
Lieutenant 4,6,10

Born at Brussels on 24 February 1893, he joined up well before the outbreak of the war and was already commissioned when German troops first violated the Belgian border. Baron de Woelmont was serving as a Sous-Lieutenant with the 11me Régiment de Ligne and transferred to the 4me Régiment Chasseurs à Cheval in September 1914. He finally moved to the Aviation Militaire on 8 October 1915 as an observer and was cited for the first time eight days later for his bravery during some artillery-spotting sorties with his pilot, Adjt P.Braun. With the latter he became a fighter-duo in late December 1915 when Braun received a Nieuport 10 two-seater. He made 18 offensive patrols in 1915. Co-operation with Adjt Braun did not last for long and de Woelmont took his position as an artillery observer again. On 16 March 1916 he was shot down by enemy artillery fire near Nieuwcapelle with his pilot, Sgt E.Lambert. The next crash-landing occurred on 2 July on board of Capt J.Dony's aircraft, again shot down by gunfire. Lt de Woelmont stayed at his post until well into 1917 although he only flew 26 hours 25 minutes over the front during that year; in the first month of the year, he was recalled to Cazeaux for a refresher course on air firing. After one month he was sent back to the front, but whilst all the other observers and pilots went back to their units, de Woelmont stayed a few days in Paris. He was accused of desertion in face of the enemy and sent back to his old cavalry unit on 27 March. By the grace of King Albert, close friend to de Woelmont's parents, and by their persuasion, he was sent back to the Aviation Militaire on 15 June. Lt de Woelmont even received a new citation in November 1917 by the 1ère Armée Française. In 1918 de Woelmont qualified as a pilot in Juvisy on 27 August, and was sent to the 10me Escadrille de Chasse on 18 September. His first offensive patrol, on 25 September, came to a sudden end, for he suffered engine trouble. When Cdt J.Dony died on 2 October, de Woelmont was given command of this unit until 6 October when Lt L.Robin took over. With the 10me Escadrille, Lt F.de Woelmont flew 32h 40 minutes during 24 sorties out of a total of 59 OP's. Only once did his machine guns fire, at a two-seater, over Oostwinkel on 23 October at 09.50 am. Only four other combats were fought during the entire war. For his feats he was made a Commandeur de l'Ordre de la Couronne, Commandeur

de l'Ordre Leopold II, Officier de l'Ordre Leopold and he was decorated with the Croix
Militaire 1ère Classe, Croix de Guerre with Palme, Croix du Feu, Médaille de l'Yser, Médaille
de la Victoire, Médaille Commémorative 1914-18 and eight Chevrons de front. He also received
the Croix Commémorative de la Maison du Roi Albert and was a Commandeur of the Swedish
Order of the Swords.

After the war, de Woelmont stayed in the army, was promoted to Captain in 1920 and
transferred to his old unit (4me Régt Chasseurs à Cheval) on 1 April 1920. On 26 March 1921
he was promoted to Capitaine-Commandant and again transferred to the Aviation Militaire on
24 September, where he was made a CO of the Groupe de Chasse in 1927, based at Nivelles.
Two years later he became a Major and on 7 July 1932 he replaced Lt-Col Raoul de Cartier at
the Ministry of Military Affairs and reached the rank of Lieutenant-Colonel on 26 December
1933. The following month he became the Officier d'Ordonnance for King Leopold III of
Belgium and was made a Chef d'Etat Major de la Défense Aerienne du Territoire (DAT) in
1935. On the eve of World War II, in May 1940, Lt-Col F.de Woelmont commanded the three
Belgian Groupes de Chasse and moved with the remains of this Groupe to France on 14 May.
After the capitulation of the Belgian Army, de Woelmont went back to Belgium on 20 August
and again became the Officier d'Ordonnance for King Leopold on 10 September. He was finally
discharged at his own request on 14 July 1947, shocked by the way King Leopold was treated,
and died 21 September 1960 in Soiron at the family's chateau.

---

de WOOT de TRIXHE (Baron) Fernand   1er Sergent   1

Born at Presseux-Sprimont (Province of Liège) on 19 October 1896, he volunteered on 2 August
1914 for the duration when he joined the 6me Régt d'Artillerie. In September 1915 he managed
a transfer to the Aviation Militaire. He went to Hendon were he qualified as a pilot on 21
November 1915 (RAC nr.2076). In January 1917 de Woot was posted to the 1ère Escadrille de
Chasse where he made his first sortie on the 26th with Capt F.Jacquet. His first war flight
occurred on 29 January.

On 18 March, he had the honour of flying a protection patrol to King Albert when the
latter, flown by Capt F.Jacquet in a newly arrived and updated Henri Farman, went over the lines
at Dixmude. On 2 May he was one of the proud pilots to welcome the great French ace Charles
Nungesser at the aerodrome, but on the 31st of that month Sgt de Woot crashed to his death at
Les Moeres airfield. He had flown 59 patrols and was engaged in two aerial combats during four
months at the front. Baron F.de Woot de Trixhe was made a Chevalier de l'Ordre de Leopold II
and received the Croix de Guerre and Médaille de l'Yser.

	1917							
_*	2 May	C		Nieup	1	Schoore	07.10	FTL

* with Adjt J.Goethals, 1Sgt A.de Meulemeester and Sgt G.de Mevius.

DONY Jules Arthur Joseph   Capitaine-Commandant   6,5,10

Jules Dony was born 3 April 1890 at Ixelles, Brussels. He became a regular soldier on 17
December 1908 and was commissioned on 25 March 1911. Dony received his pilot's certificate
before the war, on 2 June 1913 (nr. 74) and was detached to the Compagnie des Aviateurs on 15
October of that year. He was made a Chevalier de l'Ordre de la Couronne on 20 September
1913.

During the first days of the war he was attached as an observer to the French Escadrille
MS26, but transferred to the Aviation Militaire Belge in October 1914. Here he was promoted
to Capitaine in March 1915. At first, he was an observation pilot, but in December 1915 Dony
started to fly offensive patrols. On 26 December 1915 he crash-landed due to engine trouble. His
Nieuport was demolished and Dony sustained several facial injuries. He was posted to the 5me
Escadrille on 1 February 1916 and when in August 1916 the 5me Escadrille de Chasse was
formed, Capt J.Dony took command of this unit. On 23 March 1918 he flew a ground strafing
mission with Adjts Coppens d'Eeckenbrugge and Wouters between Clercken and Woumen.

Dony reached the rank of Capitaine-Commandant three days later. On 15 September he was attacked by four Fokker scouts, but was rescued by English Sopwith Camels over Gheluvelt. Dony appeared to be a good CO, but did not get the chance to fly too much. He stayed at his post until 1 October 1918, the day he was killed in an accident, whilst taking off for his second OP of the day. Earlier he had emptied his machine guns at two enemy aircraft stationed at their airfield south of Roulers. With the Groupe de Chasse he flew on 48 out of a total of 144 OP's and fought seven out of 12 aerial combats.

Cdt J.Dony was made a Chevalier de l'Ordre de Leopold, was decorated with the Croix de Guerre and obtained seven Chevrons de front. From the Allies he received the Russian Ordre de St-Stanislaus 3me classe and was made a Chevalier de l'Ordre de la Légion d'Honneur with the French Croix de Guerre avec 2 Palmes.

DUBOIS Pierre Albert Marie   Sous-Lieutenant   1,9

Born at St-Gillis, Brussels, on 21 July 1894, he went to the army on 7 July 1913 and was with the 1er Régt Grenadiers at the outbreak of the war. On 26 May 1915 he transferred to the Engineers from where he went to the Aviation Militaire. On 1 May 1916 he was promoted a Caporal and Dubois received his wings on 22 November 1916 at Hendon. The next promotion (Sergent) occurred on 13 May 1917 and on 9 June he was sent to the 1ère Escadrille de Chasse. Promotion to 1er Sergent occurred on 22 July and to 1er Sergent Major on 24 September. On 25 November, he became an Adjudant.

When the Groupe de Chasse was formed, Adjt P.Dubois was the first to score for the new unit. He usually teamed up with Capt W.Gallez and Adjt W.Coppens and besides the Thistle, insignia for the 9me Escadrille de Chasse, his Hanriot carried two white lightning-flashes on a blue upper tail surface. Pierre Dubois was commissioned on 22 September 1918. With the 1ère and 9me Escadrille he flew 223 sorties and fought 27 aerial combats. On one of these, a three vs three fight on 11 August, one of the opposing Fokkers apparently made a crash-landing. Dubois was also the last fighter pilot to have an accident on 10 November, when he crashed while landing. The Hanriot was a write off, but Dubois was unharmed.

S/Lt P.Dubois was made a Chevalier de l'Ordre de la Couronne and was decorated with the Croix de Guerre and citation (for his victory), and received in 1919 six Chevrons de front. He also received a citation from the 6th French Army. After hostilities he was named a Sous-Lieutenant de Réserve on 22 March 1919; he married on 17 June 1921. He stayed in close contact with aircraft, however, for he became the Chef de Service at the SABCA airlines at Zaventem (which later changed its name to SABENA airlines). He stayed on the réserve list, was promoted to Capitaine on 25 December 1932, and was pensioned as a Major de Réserve Honoraire on 14 May 1947. He died at Zaventem on 12 May 1956, aged 61.

	1917						
_*	24 Sep	C	Nieup	1	Fme Bien Acquis	13.30	OOC
	1918						
1**	12 Mar	C	HD	9	St-Georges	09.10	DES(f)
_***	11 Aug	Fokker	HD	9	Tervaete	10.00	OOC

* together with 1Sgt G.Kervyn de Lettenhove he attacked two two-seaters which both fell apparently out of control. ** the observer was seen to jump out of the plane without parachute at 3,000 m. Capt W.Gallez and Adjt W.Coppens were involved in the fight, but not credited. *** together with Capt W.Gallez and Lt P.de Chestret de Haneffe. This was Ltn Martin Uebe FA26, kia.

FRANCHOMME Maurice Charles Louis Fernand   Lieutenant   1,5

Born on 27 December 1892 at Schaarbeek, Brussels 'Teddy' served in the army from 1 August 1912 and was recalled to duty on 30 July 1914. Here he served with the 31me Régt de Ligne. Teddy Franchomme managed a transfer to the Compagnie des Aviateurs, but was reassigned to the 1er Régt de Guides in December of the same year. From there he went to England, qualifying as a pilot at Hendon on 4 June 1915, receiving RAC certificate nr.1304. After receiving his wings, Franchomme was assigned to the Parc d'Aviation at Calais from where he was posted to the 1ère Escadrille de Chasse in June 1916. He flew his first sortie on 19 July and fought his first aerial combat on 6 September, three days after receiving a new Nieuport N11 (#N5004) which was baptised ZY, marked with a chequered blue-red & white band on the upper side of the fuselage, just aft of the cockpit. This was repeated on the wheel covers. Early 1917 he was promoted to Adjudant and on 26 June Franchomme left the front for the Pilot School at Etampes and afterwards at Juvisy. At the latter he was commissioned on 7 November, receiving a citation nine days later for his front-line work. Franchomme flew 111 OP's and was engaged in 17 combats, for which he was awarded with the Croix de Guerre with three Palmes, Médaille de l'Yser, Croix du Feu, Médaille de la Victoire, the Médaille Commémorative 1914-18 and Médaille de Liège.

After hostilities Teddy went to the 6me Escadrille d'Observation, stationed at Evere, Brussels in 1919, stayed in the army and was promoted a Capitaine into the réserves on 25 December 1929. He reached the rank of Capitaine-Commandant five years later and achieved a successful flight on 20 December 1934 to the Belgian Congo in a de Havilland Comet, teamed with Ken Waller, who was a pilot and instructor with the Cinque Ports Flying Club near Hythe, England. On 1 September 1939, Franchomme was again called to duty and became the Commanding Officer as a Major of the 1er Groupe, Régt Troupes Auxiliaires Aériennes (TA.Aé). Here he served during the 18-day campaign of May 1940, until he was made a PoW at Lotenhulle, East-Flanders, on the 29th and transferred to the Military Hospital at Ghent. He escaped from here on 6 June and returned to Brussels. Franchomme was again caught on 6 June 1942 and sent to Huy where he was imprisoned, only to be released two days later for having reached the age of 45. Franchomme returned to Brussels and went into the Resistance for the rest of the war, finally being recalled to duty on 22 September 1944 following the liberation. He was assigned to the Belgium Military Mission and attached to the 2nd Tactical Air Force, HQ, becoming a flying officer in the RAF (nr 199.490). For his feats during WWII he was made a Commandeur de l'Ordre de la Couronne, Commandeur de l'Ordre de Leopold II and decorated with the Croix de Guerre 1940 with Palme & lion vermeille, Médaille Civil 2me classe 1940-45, Médaille du Combattant Resistance, the French Croix de Guerre 1939-45 and the British War Medal 1939-45.

Franchomme was finally demobilized on 21 February 1946 and promoted to Lieutenant-Colonel in September 1947. He was also Chairman of the Belgian Aéro Club. Franchomme died at Bruxelles on 19 June 1976.

GALLEZ Walter Jean Marie   Capitaine-Commandant   4,6,1,9

Born at Schaarbeek, Brussels, on 31 May 1890, he entered the Military Academy on 17 December 1908 and was commissioned as early as 25 March 1911, whilst serving with the 6me Régt de Ligne. On 26 September 1911 he transferred to the Régt Grenadiers and one year later changed this unit for the Engineers. He became ill for three months, but when recovered, he asked for a convalescence period of four months. This meant leave without payment and loosing his seniority of rank. However, during this period he took the opportunity to learn to fly. He finally qualified as a pilot on 19 June 1914, receiving civilian brevet nr.103. On 6 July he was promoted to Lieutenant and went to the Military Pilot School at Brasschaat near Antwerp. Gallez was the first man in the air, together with his team-mate Lt Hagemans. Two days later, the same crew had to force-land due to engine trouble, at Waremme. This hamlet, however, was surrounded by German troops and both Gallez and Hagemans escaped in civilian clothes, leaving their Farman behind. A few days later, it was successfully brought back, thanks to Baron Pierre de Caters.

During the first two years of the war Gallez wasn't a fighter pilot, although he flew some offensive patrols in 1915. On 30 March 1916 Gallez was promoted to Capitaine. On 26 September he was seriously wounded in the thigh and went to hospital until 29 November. In January 1917 he joined the 6me Escadrille d'Observation and finally managed a transfer to the 5me Escadrille de Chasse on 1 July. Here he fought his first combat on 19 September. Whilst S/Lt M.Orban engaged three scouts at a very low altitude over Hazewind, Gallez came to the rescue and forced one to dive into its lines.

During Capt Dony's absence, Gallez was the acting commander of the unit and was such a good leader that he took command of the 1ère Escadrille de Chasse on 12 December 1917, a post he held till the end of the war. He claimed his only official victory on 25 April 1918, together with Adjt W.Coppens, when they attacked a group of 25 scouts over flooded Flanders at 5,000 m. Promotion to Capitaine-Commandant occurred on 26 September 1918. Because of his convalescence leave, back in 1913, Gallez was not promoted earlier. On the contrary, when he asked the Belgian Government to reinstate his seniority (approved of by Cdt F.Jacquet) he received a strange answer; eight days imprisonment, without salary, or visits. On 14 October Gallez was slightly wounded in combat, hit by anti-aircraft gunfire, during his protection flight for Lt W.Coppens and Sgt E.Hage who were both shot down by AA fire. His Hanriot carried a blue tail surface with a white swallow's tail painted on it.

Gallez was known to be righteous, modest and a born leader. He commanded but never ordered, a simple question was sufficient. He had flown 287 OP's and was engaged in 32 combats during his time at the front with his various units.

He was made a Chevalier de l'Ordre de Leopold II and decorated with the Croix de Guerre, Médaille de l'Yser, Médaille de la Victoire, Médaille Commémorative 1914-18, eight Chevrons de front and the following Allied decorations; the British Military Medal, the Russian Order of St-Anna, 3me classe and a French citation for his leadership of the most famous Belgian Fighter Squadron during the 1918 offensive in Flanders.

Late in the 1920's he was also made an Officier de l'Ordre de la Couronne. Gallez asked to be discharged to the réserve-list on 6 May 1921 and turned his back on the army, disgusted from what had happened to him and to some friends during the war. He emigrated to the Dutch East Indies and started to work in a rubber plantation. Here his management style soon showed for he became the owner of the plantation a few years later. He was finally pensioned out of the army on 12 March 1932 and died in January 1942.

	1918							
_*	12 Mar	C	HD	9	St-Georges	09.10	DES
1**	25 Apr	D	HD	9	St-Georges	12.20	DES
_***	11 Aug	Fokker	HD	9	Tervaete	09.05	OOC
_#	8 Oct	C	HD	9	Gits	12.00	FTL

* shared with Adjts W.Coppens and P.Dubois, the latter being credited. ** shared with Adjt W.Coppens, possibly a Jasta 36 pilot. *** together with S/Lt P.de Chestret de Haneffe and Adjt P.Dubois. This was Ltn Martin Uebe FA26, kia. # together with Lt J.Olieslagers, Adjt G.Kervyn de Meerendré, Sgt E.Hage and Sgt J.Lemaire.

GERARD Léon   Adjudant   1,9

Léon Gerard was born 23 June 1896 at Halle (province of Brabant) and presented himself at the Aviation Militaire Belge on 14 August 1914. He stayed at Calais from 11 October 1914 to 31 January 1916 from where he was posted to the 2me Escadrille the following day. On 5 March he was posted to the 4me Escadrille where he stayed till 29 October. Next day he was sent to France to qualify as a pilot. On 12 August 1917 Gerard was posted to the Parc d'Aviation at Calais, waiting for a move to a front-line unit. This occurred on 3 September when he was posted to the 1ère Escadrille de Chasse. He was wounded on active service on 15 January 1918 and hospitalised until 26 March and rejoined his, now renumbered, Escadrille les Chardons.

When, on 13 June 1918, the airbase of Les Moeres was bombed by German aircraft, everybody went outside to the burning aircraft to rescue what was possible. Willy Coppens heard from the room next to his a sorrowing cry from someone who was wounded. This appeared to be Gerard whose photograph of his last conquest (girlfriend), which was hanging over his bed, had fallen on his forehead.

Whilst with the 9me Escadrille he reached the rank of 1er Sergent Major on 21 July 1918. On one occasion, 15 August 1918, he flew an offensive patrol with flight commander Lt W.Coppens and 1Sgt Maj M.Jamar. At 4,500 m they spotted a Fokker pursuing a British aircraft. 1Sgt Maj M.Jamar dived, followed by Lt W.Coppens. Gerard however did not dive and Coppens hesitated, because he thought his flight was in turn about to be attacked by a stronger German force from above. Jamar, however, went on with his attack and shot the Fokker down east of Ypres. Gerard was not always one to hesitate for he was engaged in 16 aerial combats during 149 sorties. He also survived three crash-landings.

In September Gerard was posted to the Parc d'Aviation at Calais where he saw out the war. For his feats he was decorated with the Croix de Guerre, Médaille de la Victoire, Médaille Commémorative 1914-18 and obtained eight Chevrons de front and one citation.

GOETHALS Jacques   Sous-Lieutenant   2,1,5,10

Born at Courtrai (West-Flanders), 18 November 1889, he volunteered on 22 February 1915 for the Aviation Militaire. He received his civil brevet on 5 February 1915 at the Farman School in Etampes and the following March received his wings. Posted to the 2me Escadrille at the end of July, he flew a night-bombing mission on 1 August over Houthulst Forest. This bombardment was called the bombardment en masse for 13 aircraft were involved. Promotions followed; to Sergent on 8 August; 1er Sergent on 10 October, 1er Sergent Major on 24 March 1916 and Adjudant on 11 June. Meanwhile Goethals saw many aerial combats. The first three as an observation pilot back in 1915 and fourteen as a fighter pilot in 1916. Adjt Goethals was also one of the first Belgians to attack the German trenches in 1915. On 21 May 1916 he was wounded in action over Mariakerke and was out of action until 6 July. In January 1917 he was sent to Cazeaux, France, for a refresher course on air firing and on returning he was posted to the 5me Escadrille de Chasse on 11 July. Two months earlier Goethals had been commissioned. During 1917, his Nieuport N23, (# N998) carried a sparrow-hawk as a personal marking. It is possible that Goethals' first official victory was claimed on 3 July 1917. On this day Adjt E.Thieffry shot down two hostile aircraft within two minutes, the first Belgian to claim a double. Another victory was claimed, as well as an aircraft shot down by Belgian AA fire. There are, however, no surviving combat reports of this date, so this claim remains a bit of a mystery. Another possible victory was claimed on 27 September, the day he attacked an Albatros scout that had just shot down an Allied aircraft which crashed burning. This Albatros seemed to fall out of control into its lines. The only German pilot who downed an aircraft in this area, at the same time, was Ltn Xaver Dannhuber, Jasta 26, (a Bristol fighter, A7180, 48 Sqdn, RFC over Pervyse for his fifth victory of an eventual 11), but there are no records showing that Dannhuber was forced to land or even crashed.

Goethals was killed in action on 9 October 1918 whilst attacking a two-seater. He was surprised by Jasta 29 pilots and shot down in flames by Obltn Harold Auffarth for his 23rd victory over Hazewind at 13.40. A brave pilot, he flew 302 OP's and was engaged in 75 combats.

S/Lt Goethals was made a Chevalier de l'Ordre de la Couronne and decorated with the Croix de Guerre avec 2 Palmes, seven Chevrons de front and posthumously the Médaille de la Victoire and Médaille Commémorative 1914-18.

	1917		Nieup				
_*	2 May	C	N998	1	Schoore	07.10	FTL
_**	3 Jul	EA	N998	1	N.Dixmude	13.30	DES
_***	27 Jul	D	N998	5	Dixmude	20.15	OOC
_#	27 Sep	Albatros	N998	5	Tervaete	18.40	OOC
	1918						
_##	23 May	C	Spad	10	Houthulst	07.40	FTL
_	11 Jun	C	Spad	10	Houthulst	19.32	FTL
1###	7 Oct	C	Spad	10	N.Dixmude	06.05	DES
2§	9 Oct	C	Spad	10	Hazewind	13.40	DES

* shared with 1Sgt A.de Meulemeester and Sgts G.de Mevius and F.de Woot de Trixhe. ** was this the first official claim of Goethals ? *** possibly Ofstv Karl Gregor (2 vict.), Jasta 29, wia. # possibly the ace Ltn X.Dannhuber, Jasta 26. ## shared with Adjt E.Weekers. Possibly Flg Max Thomas/Ltn dR Rudolf Giesecke of Bomb.Geschw. 5, Staffel 6, kia. ### with Adjt C.de Montigny who was not credited § it is possible that this victory is the one mentioned on 7 October. He was cited on 18 October: 'fearless fighter pilot, has downed an enemy aircraft on 9 October 1918'.

GOOSSENS-BARA (Baron) Jules Alphonse Louis Marie Jean
Lieutenant   3,1,9,7

Born at Brussels on 29 January 1894, he volunteered on 3 August 1914. He was sent to the Grenadiers Régiment, but on the 8th he transferred to the 2me Régiment Carabiniers. Transfer to the Aviation Militaire occurred on 2 July 1915, becoming a Caporal on 29 August. The first war flight was flown in October 1916 and on the 16th of that month Sergent Goossens made his first crash-landing due to engine trouble. Five days later, the Voisin two-seater, manned by Goossens and observer Lt De Cubber, was attacked by three scouts who put 25 holes in the Voisin, leaving them to crash-land near Steenkerke. Both Goossens and De Cubber received a citation, for landing their machine behind the Belgian lines. Promotions to 1er Sergent and 1er Sergent Major occurred on 31 December 1916 and 8 April 1917 respectively. Goossens was made an Adjudant on 17 June 1917, whilst flying with the 1ère Escadrille de Chasse where he arrived shortly before his promotion. During this period Goossens had a personal marking which was practically the same as the later Polish national marking: a two-coloured square, divided in four squares, although the colours are not known. On 30 September, a most beautiful day, he started on an offensive patrol together with Lt P.Hanciau. They were caught in a big cloud and lost sight of one another. Goossens returned to the base expecting to see Hanciau there as well. Poor Hanciau, however, had been by then shot down. On 11 November 1917 S/Lt Goossens received the Distinguished Conduct Medal from Maj Shields, CO of 48 Sqdn, RFC. When the Groupe de Chasse was formed in March 1918, Goossens was one of those pilots who requested a transfer to another unit and went to the new 7me Escadrille d'Observation of CO Cdt Jules Jaumotte in May. With the Groupe de Chasse he only flew 11 sorties. He had one combat in which a German two-seater was shot down, but was not claimed by Goossens. On 21 April a Rumpler two-seater was shot down by a Belgian pilot behind the Belgian lines and set on fire by its crew. Goossens was the only Belgian pilot who had a combat with a Rumpler that day, but apparently did not see it fall out of control, for he did not make a claim. On 31 May, with his new unit, he was promoted to Lieutenant.   For his actions as a fighter pilot (157 OP's and 15 combats), he was decorated with the Croix de Guerre with citation. Other decorations were the two Palmes & Bronze Lyon to his Croix de Guerre, Croix du Feu, Médaille de la Victoire, Médaille Commémorative 1914-18 and six Chevrons de front.

After the war he was made a Lieutenant de Réserve on 29 December 1920. Jules Goossens-Bara died at Brussels, 9 April, 1972.

	1917							
_*	1 Oct	C	—	1	Beerst	15.45	OOC
	1918							
_	21 Apr	Rumpler C	HD	9	Lampernisse	09.30	CAPT

* shared with S/Lt J.Olieslagers, Adjt W.Coppens & Adjt A.de Meulemeester.

GORDINNE Charles Ferdinand Joseph Marie   Sous-Lieutenant   1,9,5

Born at Liège on 13 February 1894, he was a private with the 14me Régt de Ligne from September 1913. Here he stayed till 6 April 1916 when he obtained a transfer to the Aviation Militaire. He was made a Caporal on 8 June, six days after qualifying at Bournemouth (RAC nr.3023). He went to the Military Pilot School in France and received his wings on 6 April 1917. Charles Gordinne was posted to the 1ère Escadrille de Chasse in July 1917, together with his brother Robert, but both stayed only one year in the fighter unit. Charles arrived on 4 July as a Sergent and was promoted to 1er Sergent on 19 August and to 1er Sergent Major on 21 October. Promotion to Adjudant occurred on 23 December. Charles Gordinne was known to be a very nice man, always making fun and entertaining the squadron, but unfortunately he did not have the right aggressive attitude needed to be a fighter pilot. When in March 1918 the Groupe de Chasse was formed, he was posted to the 5me Escadrille d'Observation in June and flew on 112 offensive patrols and took part in 12 aerial combats. Two of these combats were fought during the same sortie with an interval of five minutes, but on both occasions, Gordinne had to break off the fight with his machine gun jammed. He was commissioned on 12 October whilst with his new unit. S/Lt C.Gordinne was decorated with the Croix de Guerre with citation, Médaille de l'Yser, Médaille de la Victoire, Médaille Commémorative 1914-18 and was made a Chevalier de l'Ordre de la Couronne in 1928.

He was demobilised in September 1919, made a Sous-Lieutenant de Réserve on 26 April

1920 and a Lieutenant de Réserve on 12 December 1920. He retired at his own request on 5 June 1939 and died in the early 1960's.

GORDINNE Robert Joseph Marie   Adjudant   1,9,5

Born at Liège on 10 February 1895, he was a student at the outbreak of the war. He was assigned to the Transport Corps of the 3me Division d'Armée on 2 August 1914. Here he stayed until 5 April 1916 when he, together with his brother Charles, transferred to the Aviation Militaire. Whilst Charles went to Bournemouth, England, Robert qualified as a pilot in Etampes, France. He arrived at the front on 6 July 1917 as a Caporal and was promoted to Sergent on 15 July, 1er Sergent on 24 September and to 1er Sergent Major on 25 November. Promotion to Adjudant occurred in January 1918. Like his brother, Robert Gordinne was a companionable fellow who was always into a joke, but, again like his brother, he lacked the aggressive mind of a fighter pilot. It is understood, however, that the Gordinne brothers were very good pilots. Therefore he was posted to another unit on 2 June 1918. As a fighter pilot he only flew 66 sorties and hardly saw any aerial actions during which he fought only two combats. For his feats he was decorated with the Croix de Guerre, Médaille de la Victoire, Médaille Commémorative 1914-18 and obtained seven Chevrons de front.

After the war he was reduced to the rank of Sergent at his own request on 23 March 1919, but worked his way up until he was commissioned on 22 June 1920.

S/Lt R.Gordinne was killed in a flying accident on 22 February 1921 over Krefeld, occupied Germany.

GUILLON Leon Jean Adolphe   Sergent   11

Born at Brussels on 5 October 1895 he volunteered at Nieuport in September 1914 after crossing the German front-lines. He was a wireless operator attached to the Belgian Headquarters and moved to the Aviation Militaire in January 1918, where he qualified as a pilot in March at Juvisy and was made a Caporal on 12 May and a Sergent on 25 August, five days after receiving his wings. Leon Guillon arrived at the front too late to become an ace. He had, however, the qualities to become one. He flew his first combat flight on 13 September 1918 and the first victory could have been claimed on 3 October when he attacked and surprised a two-seater, but at the fatal moment Guillon's guns jammed. On 15 October Sgt L.Guillon attacked a Fokker scout with a yellow horizontal line on the fuselage at 2,500 m. After firing 50 rounds at a short distance, the German's head fell forward and he flew in a straight line pointing downwards. Guillon pursued the German for a time, apparently hit and not making any attempt to defend himself. At about 50 m from the ground, Guillon was himself attacked by two adversaries and could not see the result of his own combat. The second claim was a victory over a 'drachen'; his second attempt on such a target. Guillon flew only 41 sorties and did not fly in November. He was only engaged in 11 combats and all were fought in October.

He was made a Chevalier de l'Ordre de la Couronne and decorated with the Croix de Guerre with Palmes, Médaille de l'Yser, Médaille du Volontaire Combattant 1914-18, Médaille de la Victoire Belge & Interalliée and also received the French Croix de Guerre. After the war Guillon was promoted to Adjudant on 2 March 1919, but died as a Great War invalid in July 1927.

	1918						
	15 Oct	Fokker	HD	11	Sleijhage	07.40	DES
2*	26 Oct	balloon	HD	11	Asseneede	15.00	DES

* Gefr Johann Ampenberger of Bayerische Ballonzug 202, kia or Vfw Gustav Fuchs of Bz 148.

HAGE Etienne Eduard Antoine Marie Joseph   Sergent   9

Born at Courtrai on 7 June 1896, he volunteered during the first days of the war and was attached as an observer to the Artillery. Here he stayed until he obtained a transfer to the

Aviation Militaire in the first months of 1917. He was sent to the Pilot School at Etampes, qualified on 26 February 1918, received his wings on 19 April, and was finally posted to the 9me Escadrille de Chasse in September 1918. Hage became second only to Lt W. Coppens in downing observation balloons, a very dangerous task. He flew his first offensive patrol on 16 September as a wingman to S/Lt P.de Chestret and with Adjt P.Dubois and 1Sgt G.Kervyn de Meerendré. Six days later he joined the flight of Lt W.Coppens. With the latter he downed two aircraft on 2 and 3 October, but these fell too far behind the lines. There was also a lack of communication between Headquarters and front-line troops at that moment, so the victories would never be claimed. On 14 October both men took off at 05.40 for what was to become their last patrol. The 'drachen' over Praat Bosch, Dixmude was to be destroyed, which Lt Coppens did at 06.00. Five minutes later Coppens downed the balloon over Thourout, but was severely wounded by AA fire (see his biography for further details). Sgt Hage went on and a few minutes later he set the balloon over Leffinghe on fire. Here Hage received a direct hit from another AA unit and was severely injured in the arm. With great difficulties he put his Hanriot on the ground close to the Military Hospital at Hoogstade. For his actions Sgt E.Hage was made a Commandeur de l'Ordre de Leopold II with Palmes and was decorated with the Croix de Guerre with Palmes, Médaille du Volontaire Combattant 1914-18, Croix du Feu, the French Croix de Guerre with Palmes and Médaille Militaire, and the unusual Commandeur de l'Ordre du Sacre Coeur de Jerusalem. He had flown 31 OP's during which six combats were fought. A look at his claim list shows that every opponent he attacked fell victim!

After the armistice, Hage stayed in the army and reached the rank of Lieutenant. During this period he married Mrs Goetsbloets and went into car racing. Here he turned out to be a great driver. In 1923 he achieved a speed record driving a Bugatti; in 1924 2nd place in the Monte Carlo rally behind Jacques Ledure; in 1925 1st in the 24 hours race at Francorchamps; in 1926 3rd in the Monte Carlo rally; 1927 1st in the Belgium-Nice rally and in 1928 again 1st in the 24 hours race at Francorchamps. In 1933 he stopped his racing and military career and was placed onto the réserve list. He undertook notary studies, and he became a lawyer in 1935 working at the notary's office of his father in law. Lieutenant de Réserve E.Hage was again called to active duty in 1939 and was a Liaison Officer of the Aviation Militaire in World War II. He was not taken prisoner of war because of his profession. Hage then started a wireless-net signalling information to London. After World War II, Hage was decorated with the Médaille du Volontaire Combattant 1940-45 and was pensioned out in 1954 as a Major Honoraire. He gave his notary's office to his eldest son in 1962 and retired until his sudden death at Hasselt on 18 February 1988, the last Belgian fighter pilot of the Great War to die, at the age of 91.

	1918						
1	29 Sep	balloon	HD	9	Armentières	07.00	DES
2*	2 Oct	balloon	HD	9	Quesnoy	07.25	DES
_**	2 Oct	C	HD	9	Handzaeme	—	OOC
_**	3 Oct	C	HD	9	Menin	07.10	DES
_***	8 Oct	C	HD	9	Gits	12.00	FTL
3†	14 Oct	balloon	HD	9	Leffinghe	06.15	DES

* Luftschiffen Walter Liebich, Bz 124, kia. ** with Lt W.Coppens. *** with Capt W.Gallez, Lt J.Olieslagers, Adjt G.Kervyn de Meerendré and Sgt J.Lemaire. † Bz 153.

HANCIAU Paul Charles Gustave   Lieutenant   1

Born at Ixelles, Brussels, on 26 January 1885 he gained his wings before the war on 23 February 1911, receiving civilian brevet nr.34. When on 6 August 1914 an aircraft was donated to the Aviation Militaire by the Societé des Aviateurs Belges, P.Hanciau volunteered as its pilot. He did not fly this aircraft very long, for on 14 August he had to crash-land his aircraft at Wilrijk, Antwerp. He was assigned full time to the Aviation Militaire on 6 May 1915 and in November he started to fly his first offensive patrols. On 31 January 1916 he transferred to the 1ère Escadrille de Chasse and had his first aerial combat on 5 February with his observer Lt Romeo Verhaegen. He flew on 64 offensive patrols that year and forced three hostile aircraft to return to their lines. During the war, he was known to be a pilot who hardly suffered any damage to his planes which were all baptised 'Soit!' (let it be).

After 156 OP's and six aerial combats, Hanciau was killed in action on 30 September 1917. He started with Adjt J.Goossens-Bara for the afternoon sortie. Slightly apart from one another, Hanciau was surprised by ten Albatros scouts and hit in the carotid artery. He had the strength to turn away and head for the Belgian lines, where he started to land at 14.45 near Alveringhem, close to some Belgian troops at rest. A few metres from the ground, however, the Nieuport N23 suddenly dived to the earth with its pilot dead. Hanciau was made a Chevalier de l'Ordre de Leopold, received the Croix de Guerre and obtained four Chevrons de front.

HEYVAERT Willy Leon Marie Hilaire   Adjudant   4,3,11

Born at Gentbrugge, near Ghent (East-Flanders) on 25 February 1896, he volunteered during the first days of the war. He left his unit for the Pilot School at Etampes in December 1916. Here he was promoted to Caporal on 15 April 1917, and received his wings on 12 May. He was posted to the 4me Escadrille de Reconnaissance on 21 July and was promoted to Sergent a few days later. In September he became a 1er Sergent and in November he was a 1er Sergent Major. He was cited for his recce-work together with his observer, Lt L.Robin on 2 December 1917. In May 1918 Capt F.Jacquet persuaded Adjt W.Heyvaert to join the newly formed 11me Escadrille de Chasse and his first offensive patrol was flown on the 20th. Heyvaert was forced to land after his third aerial combat on 28 June, crash-landing his Sopwith Camel at the Furnes-Ypres road and being slightly injured. On 1 July he received a brand new Camel, but crash-landed again, this time due to engine trouble, on 19 July. Heyvaert was wounded again and this time did not see further action. With the 11me Escadrille de Chasse, Heyvaert had flown 48 sorties and was engaged in four fights. Some 20 more OP's were flown with the recce units he had been assigned to, during which time he took part in four more combats. Adjt W.Heyvaert was decorated with the Croix de Guerre, Médaille de l'Yser and six Chevrons de front.

After the war he was discharged, was put onto the réserve list and attained the rank of Capitaine on 26 March 1940. Widower Willy Heyvaert died on 7 June 1944 at Pontet (Vaucluse), France.

HIERNAUX Paul Gustave Joseph   Capitaine-Commandant   1,9,11

Born at Brussels on 4 January 1888, he volunteered in October 1904 and was assigned to the 4me Régiment de Ligne. Here he was commissioned on 24 November 1911. Two days later he went to the Belgian Congo were he saw service until December 1912. He qualified as a pilot on 19 June 1914, receiving brevet nr. 98. On 29 July he transferred to the Aviation Militaire and was assigned to Escadrille I. He flew on many sorties over the Liège battlefield and was promoted to Lieutenant in November 1914. During 1915, Hiernaux (not taller than 1m 67) mainly flew as a reconnaissance pilot for the 3me Division d'Armée and flew only eleven offensive patrols during that year in which he saw four aerial combats. The first of these was the first dogfight in which Belgian aircraft were involved. On 26 February 1915, Lt F.Jacquet as an observer to three Farman aircraft fought off ten German Albatros and Aviatik two-seaters over the Belgian airfield at La Panne. Hiernaux was promoted to Capitaine on 21 July 1916, the day after he had flown over the front with a Russian Liaison Officer on board his Nieuport. He started his career as a fighter pilot in September 1916 and the first OP occurred on the 28th. Capt P.Hiernaux was second-in-command of the 1ère Escadrille de Chasse.

When the Groupe de Chasse was formed in March 1918, and a third Escadrille de Chasse came into existence, Capt 'Monsieur Paul' (as he was commonly called) Hiernaux was given command of this unit. With this escadrille he flew 82 sorties and took part in 19 aerial combats. He reached the rank of Capitaine-Commandant on 26 September 1918. During the war a total of 192 OP's were flown and Monsieur Paul was engaged in 25 aerial combats. Hiernaux was shot down on 15 October 1918. At 07.30 he was attacked by two Fokkers from Marinefeldjasta I, who left their formation to attack him. Oberleutnant zur See Gotthard Sachsenberg, CO of that unit, fired a few rounds at Hiernaux's Sopwith Camel which was hit in the fuel tank. Hiernaux crash-landed near Hooglede, but was unharmed. His Camel was written off, but

Sachsenberg was not credited with this victory for his victim fell well behind enemy lines. Monsieur Paul was made a Chevalier de l'Ordre de la Couronne, Chevalier de l'Ordre de Leopold II and decorated with the Croix de Guerre avec Palme, Médaille de l'Yser, Croix du Feu, Médaille de la Victoire, Médaille Commémorative 1914-18 and obtained eight Chevrons de front. He also received the French Croix de Guerre and Etoile de Service, the Italian Silver Medal of Merit, and the Ordre de l'Etoile from Ethiopia. In the years between the wars he received further decorations: Commandeur de l'Ordre de Leopold, Commandeur de l'Ordre de la Couronne, Commandeur de l'Ordre de Leopold II and Croix Militaire 2me Classe. Hiernaux was someone who never expressed his feelings and was hardly seen laughing or crying; he was stubborn, but always ready to volunteer for a task.

Hiernaux stayed in the army after hostilities and became the Commanding Officer of the IIIrd Group of the Aviation Militaire on 27 May 1922, was promoted to Major in December 1928 and reached the rank of Lieutenant-Colonel on 26 March 1937. On 26 September 1938 he was promoted to General-Major and became Commanding Officer of the Aviation Militaire. At this post he went to war for the second time but was taken prisoner on 28 May 1940 at Westende. He was sent to Germany and was repatriated on 19 May 1945. He retired on 23 June 1947 and died at Ixelles, aged 82, on 8 January 1970.

JACQUET Fernand Maximilien Leon   Capitaine-Commandant
1, GROUPE DE CHASSE

Born 2 November 1888 at Petit-Chapelle in the province of Namur, he joined the army as a cadet in October 1907. He was commissioned on 25 June 1910 and one day later was assigned to the 4me Régt de Ligne. He qualified as a pilot (brevet nr. 68) on 25 February 1913 and at the outbreak of the war was with the Escadrille Demanet (I) at Liège. On 17 April 1915 Jacquet was the first Belgian who officially shot down a German plane together with his observer, Lt H. Vindevoghel. Jacquet was not only a pursuit pilot, but also an observation pilot and always asked for 'les missions speciales'. He was promoted to Capitaine in November 1915. After Capitaine-Commandant Demanet's removal as CO of the 1ère Escadrille de Chasse in December 1916, Jacquet took command of this unit. Jacquet became Belgium's first ace on 1 February 1917, although it was his 13th claim. On 18 March 1917 he was the first pilot to be honoured, in flying King Albert over the front lines. During this period, however, having no observer because of Lt L.Robin's transfer, Jacquet flew a few OP's in a single-seater, but soon abandoned these flights. Jacquet wore spectacles and was not sure of himself whilst flying alone. Therefore he worked out tactics for his gunner, which proved quite successful. Jacquet mainly flew to the sea, which was so near, gaining height and then flew back to the Belgian lines from over enemy territory, hoping to find and surprise a lone enemy aircraft. On 27 October 1918, with his usual observer Lieutenant Marcel de Crombrugghe de Looringhe, he attacked a two-seater north of Lovendeghem at 0815. This aircraft dived into its lines in a strange way near Ghent. This was possibly a Marine Feldflieger Abteilung machine, which lost Leutnant Walter Fromme. He was engaged in some 126 aerial combats in various Farman types, Sopwith 1½ Strutter and Spad XI on 344 sorties. He himself wanted a Brisfit but this was refused for the BF2b was not a standard aircraft in the Belgian Army. He was promoted to Capitaine-Commandant in December 1917. When the Groupe de Chasse was formed in March 1918, Jacquet took command of this Groupe at the insistence of King Albert.

Jacquet was decorated an Officier de l'Ordre de la Couronne, Chevalier de l'Ordre Leopold I, Croix de Guerre with six citations, Croix Civil 3rd class, Médaille de la Victoire, Médaille Commémorative 1914-18, eight Chevrons de front, Chevalier de la Légion d'Honneur, French Croix de Guerre, the Russian St-Anna Order and he also was the only Belgian pilot to receive the British Distinguished Flying Cross.

In 1920 he left the army and started a Pilot School at Gosselies near Charleroi in 1921 and was pensioned out of the army on 14 July 1930. During World War II he was an active member of the Resistance, until made a prisoner in 1942 at Huy in the Ardennes. Fernand Jacquet died 12 October 1947 in Beaumont.

	1915						
1*	17 Apr	Alb C	MF	1	Roulers	15.20-16.55	DES(f)
_**	20 Jun	EA	MF	1	—	—	OOC
_**	26 Jul	Aviatik C	MF	1	Westende	18.20	FTL
	1916						
2***	20 May	Hydr C	MF	1	Nieuport	20.30	DES
_***	26 May	Aviatik C	MF	1	Thourout	18.20	OOC
_***	27 May	Aviatik C	MF	1	Couckelaere	19.25	FTL
_***	22 Jun	LVG C	MF	1	Staden	08.30	DES
3***	23 Jun	Fokker	MF	1	Couckelaere	08.00	DES
_***	30 Jun	Aviatik C	MF	1	Handzaeme	19.00	FTL
_***	8 Jul	LVG C	MF	1	Middelkerke	16.50	OOC
_#	30 Jul	LVG C	MF	1	Houthulst Forest	12.00	DES
4 ##	30 Jul	LVG C	MF	1	Houthulst	16.30	DES
	1917						
5***	1 Feb	Rumpler C	MF	1	Lombartzyde	15.15	DES
	1918						
_###	5 Jun	Fok DrI	Spad	GdC	Houthulst	06.42	OOC
6###	4 Oct	Rumpler C	Spad	GdC	Gits	08.00	FTL
7❏	6 Nov	C	Spad	GdC	e. Ghent	09.00	FTL

* obs Lt H.Vindevoghel. ** obs Lt L.Colignon. *** obs Lt L.Robin. # obs Lt L.Robin, together with Sgt Barthes/mec Baudoin of the French Esc.MF36. ## possibly a Marine Feldflieger Abteilung II aircraft. They lost Ltn dR Albert Siebert on this day. After this victory Jacquet circled around to shoot at the cars and men surrounding the downed aircraft. ### obs Lt M.de Crombrugghe de Looringhe. ❏ obs Lt M.de Crombrugghe de Looringhe. This was probably Gefr Jakob Dick/??, FAA 5, kia.

JAMAR Maurice Alphonse Felix Walter   Adjudant   9

Born at Liège on 21 June 1896, he studied for a technical profession in his hometown. He volunteered on 13 January 1915 and went to the Aviation Militaire on 30 August 1917, qualifying at Etampes on 25 September. With military brevet nr. 1578, obtained on 6 December 1917, Jamar was promoted to Sergent on 24 February 1918 and was posted to the 9me Escadrille de Chasse on 3 April 1918. He claimed two victories of which only one was made official. The confirmed victory was over an observation balloon, claimed flying Lt Coppens' Hanriot # HD45. Two observers baled out successfully. On 30 July, at 08.00 Jamar was attacked by five English scouts over Bixschoote. The second claim was made on 15 August. He took off with Flight Commander Lt W.Coppens and wingman 1Sgt Maj L.Gerard. East of Ypres they spotted a German Fokker pursuing an English two-seater. Jamar dived, followed by Coppens. The latter hesitated because Gerard did not follow. Maurice Jamar took no notice of this and attacked the Fokker who fell in flames. This claim, however, was given to a pilot of the British 204 Sqdn. General Headquarters, charged with the confirmation of Belgian Aviation Militaire's claims, ruled this victory was made over the English front and therefore could not be given to a Belgian pilot! Jamar reached the rank of Adjudant on 29 September 1918. On 3 October Adjudant 'le Cawé' Jamar was shot down, probably by AA fire, whilst attacking an observation balloon over Rumbeke and taken prisoner. It is, however, possible that Jamar was the 37th victim of Leutnant Josef Jacobs, who claimed two Camels over Rumbeke. With the Groupe de Chasse he had flown 103 sorties and was engaged in 15 combats.

For his feats he was made a Chevalier de l'Ordre de la Couronne, Chevalier de l'Ordre de Leopold II and decorated with the Croix de Guerre, Médaille de la Victoire, Médaille Commémorative 1914-18, seven Chevrons de front and was cited three times.

Jamar stayed in the army and was commissioned on 22 June 1920. He retired as a Lieutenant in 1928 and was made a Capitaine Honoraire on 26 June 1931. Jamar was killed in an aircraft, when he crashed at Oran, Algeria on 28 January 1937, only 40 years old.

Maurice Jamar had a brother, Gustave, who was an outstanding pilot with the observation squadrons during the war. Once hostilities ended Gustave became famous as a lawyer and was well known for his pioneering work in Belgian Congo.

	1918						
1*	10 Jul	balloon	HD	9	Leffinghe	09.10	DES
_**	15 Aug	Fok DVII	HD	9	Ypres	08.25	DES(f)

* victory claimed in Lt W.Coppens' HD45. Possibly Bz 83, who lost Luftschiffer August Rakonski, kia. ** victory credited to a 204 Sqdn, RAF, pilot, possibly Flugobermatrose Friedrich Gröchke, Seefront Staffel II, wia.

KERVYN de LETTENHOVE (Baron) Georges Maria Ghislain Gerard Bruno
Sous-Lieutenant   1,9

Born at Wakken (West-Flanders) on 11 February 1897, Baron Kervyn volunteered on 25 November 1915 with the 1er Régt de Guides. It was not really what he wanted and inspired by his brother Charles, who was a pilot at the 4me Escadrille d'Observation, he managed a transfer to the Aviation Militaire on 13 December. He went to Hendon, receiving his civilian brevet on 27 April 1916. The military brevet was obtained on 11 October. After being promoted to Sergent he reached the front on 27 May 1917, and came under the protecting wings of Adjt A.de Meulemeester. He rapidly scored two victories, but then his claims stalled. On 21 October 1917 he was made an Adjudant. Why he is not credited with a certain (shared) victory on 4 November is strange. Flying with Adjt A.de Meulemeester at 3,000 m, they observed five Albatros scouts out-manoeuvring four British aircraft. One German pilot found himself a bit apart from the rest and was promptly attacked by de Meulemeester. After a short burst the latter attacked another Albatros, leaving the first one to Kervyn. The plane lost height rapidly to 800 m where it suddenly fell like a stone into the floods of the Yser river, all this time being attacked by Kervyn. During that month, Kervyn undertook 21 OP's during which 21 combats were fought. Ten of them occurred during two sorties on November 13th and one of these attacks was fought single-handed against six Albatros scouts from Jasta 18 from which Ltn. H.Auffarth had just shot down a French Sopwith 1½ Strutter for his sixth victory. On 25 April 1918 the Yellow Flight of Adjt A.de Meulemeester attacked a formation of 25 scouts. Adjts G.Kervyn and G.de Mevius isolated a Pfalz scout and shot it down in flames. A few days later the same manoeuvre was repeated and Kervyn scored his fourth confirmed victory, this time with Adjt de Meulemeester, while 'Papa Gusto' de Mevius was on the look-out for other planes. On 1 August, out on a lone patrol at 4,900 m, he was attacked at 09.35 over Boesinghe by two 204 Sqdn Camels out of a formation of 15. He was followed until only 50 m over Elverdinghe. On 11 September Kervyn de Lettenhove was commissioned.

From June 1917 to November 1918 he flew 402 sorties and was engaged in 138 combats. His guns jammed four times whilst attacking an adversary.

He was made a Commandeur de l'Ordre de la Couronne, Commandeur de l'Ordre de Leopold II, Officier de l'Ordre de Leopold and received the Croix de Guerre with Palme, Croix du Feu, Médaille du Volontaire Combattant 1914-18, Médaille de la Victoire, Médaille Commémorative 1914-18 and Médaille Commémorative du Centenaire. He also obtained five Chevrons de front.

After the war he stayed in the army and in September 1925 went to the Ministère de la Défense Nationale, where he worked with the Département Aéronautique. In May 1926 Kervyn was commissioned as Chef de Bureau at the same Ministry and three years later, on 26 March 1929, reached the rank of Capitaine. He left the Ministry to go into the army again and became a CO of an Escadrille de Reconnaissance in December 1931. Two years later he was the CO of a Groupe de Chasse. After advanced pilot training, he was promoted to Capitaine-Commandant in 1935 and again left the army for the Ministère de la Défense Nationale, Service de l'Aéronautique. From October 1936 Kervyn was hospitalised for some 100 days, only to return to duty in January 1940. During World War II he was a liaison officer to General Gort of the BEF, and was made a PoW after the Belgian capitulation on 28 May 1940. He was repatriated on 1 July 1945, recalled to duty and reached the rank of Lieutenant-Colonel on 6 June 1946, after being made a Commandeur de l'Ordre de Leopold and decorated with the Croix Militaire de 1ère Classe and the Médaille Commémorative 1940-45. He became Adjoint de l'Inspecteur General de l'Aviation later in the year, becoming Inspecteur General himself in February 1947. Three months later, Kervyn was promoted the Aide de Camp to the Prince Regent, Charles,

Top left: Romantic view of the first Belgian (unofficial) victory by Lt Alexandr 'Sacha' Petrowski and Sgt Maurice Benselin in September 1914. *(Author's collection)*

Top right: Maurice Farman MF60 in which Cdt Fernand Jacquet gained five confirmed victories. *(CDH)*

Above: S/Lt Alberique Rolin (left) and Adjt John de Roest d'Alkemade, 4me Escadrille d'Observation, who flew over occupied Antwerp, Malines, Vilvoorde & Ghent on 7 September 1916.

(ASA/E.Rerren)

Left: Nieuport Bébé N11 with S/Lt Henri Crombez standing in front. *(CDH)*

Top left: Ponnier L1 scout with a personal marking on the cowling (S/Lt Abel De Neef?).

(CDH)

Top right: The first Spad SVII purchased by the Aviation Militaire Belge and given to S/Lt Edmond Thieffry. *(CDH)*

Middle left: Hut at Coxyde Military airfield in 1916, used by the 1ère Escadrille de Chasse.

(G.Lecomte)

Middle right: Crash-landed Nieuport, with the personal markings of both S/Lt E.Thieffry (wheel coverings) and S/Lt E.Desclée (*va ou je te pousse*) in the Comet's tail.

(Baron Siraut)

Bottom: Two Nieuport N16s, the first (#N3) was that flown by S/Lt Edmond Thieffry, flanked by #N1, flown by Adjt Pierre de Chestret de Haneffe. *(CDH)*

Top left: Mixed bag of aircraft at Les Moeres in the summer of 1917. *(ASA/E.Rerren)*

Top right: S/Lt José Orta (left) and Lt Louis de Burlet, 3me Escadrille d'Observation. The first observation crew credited with a victory. *(CDH)*

Middle: The Hanriot HD1 # HD8, flown by Lt Jean Olieslagers after his crash-landing on 4 November 1917 at Les Moeres. *(M.Olieslagers)*

Bottom: Fighter Pilots in 1917 (L to R):
S/Lt M.de Crombrugghe de Looringhe (2),
S/Lt G.de Mevius (1), S/Lt P.Braun (2),
S/Lt J Goossens-Bara, S/Lt A.De Neef,
Adjt L.Gerard, S/Lt P.Dubois (1),
S/Lt A.de Meulemeester (11), S/Lt C.Gordinne,
Lt J.Olieslagers (6), S/Lt E.Thieffry (10),
S/Lt A.Mouton, Cdt J.Dony, Lt W.Coppens (37)
& Cdt P.Hiernaux.
(Baron E.de Crombrugghe de Looringhe)

Top left: Aerial view of Les Moeres airfield in 1918. *(ASA/E.Rerren)*

Top right: Les Moeres airfield on 12 April 1918 at 5,400 m. *(ASA/E.Rerren)*

Middle left: The remnants of the DFW two-seater shot down on 8 May 1918 by Adjt Maurice Siraut, 10me Escadrille. Siraut is standing on the right, listening to a ground witness. *(Baron Siraut)*

Middle right: HM King Albert in the back seat of Lt Crombez' Spad XI. *(ASA/E.Rerren)*

Bottom: The 9me Escadrille de Chasse, 28 July 1918 (L to R): Adjt G.Kervyn de Meerendre, Lt J.Olieslagers (6), Adjt L.Gerard & Adjt M.Jamar (1) (Green-White Flight); Capt W.Gallez (1), Lt W.Coppens (37), S/Lt Pierre de Chestret de Haneffe (1) & S/Lt P.Dubois (1) (White Flight); S/Lt G.Kervyn de Lettenhove (4), S/Lt A.de Meulemeester (11) & S/Lt G.de Mevius (1) (Yellow Flight).

Top left: King Albert on the beach at La Panne, where the Royal Villa was situated.

(ASA/E.Rerren)

Top right: 1Sgt Victor Benoidt, 9me Escadrille, in a Nieuport at the Pilot School.

(G.Lecomte)

Middle left: Queen Elisabeth is helped in the back seat of Lt Crombez' Spad XI by Cdt Richard (CO 4me Escadrille).

(ASA/E.Rerren)

Above left: King Albert was on the alert for hostile aircraft and even carried a machine gun on board his Spad XI (pilot Lt Crombez).

(ASA/E.Rerren)

Above right: Lt Aimé Behaeghe, 1ère Escadrille, died at Dumbo, the Belgian Congo in December 1916. He was a fighter pilot before the formation of the first fighter squadron.

(nos Héros, morts pour la patrie)

Top: S/Lt Charles (L) and 1Sgt Robert Ciselet at Les Moeres airfield. Robert was shot down by Ltn E.Böhme, Staffelführer of Jasta Boelcke, on 20 November 1917. *(G.Lecomte)*

Above left: S/Lt Pierre *Bambino* Braun, 5me Escadrille, killed in an accident in December 1917, after gaining his second victory. *(Koninklijk Legermuseum, Brussel)*

Above right: S/Lt Roger Castiau, a fighter pilot in 1915, before the formation of the first Escadrille de Chasse. *(ASA/E.Rerren)*

Right: S/Lt Charles *Sidi* Ciselet, 5me Escadrille, 1 victory, seated on his Spad SVII #Sp2. Note yellow strip bordered with red bars. *(CDH)*

Top left: Lt Willy Coppens, 9me Escadrille, 37 victories, standing in front of his HD1 #HD 17.

(Koninklijk Legermuseum, Brussel)

Top right: 19 May 1918, five minutes after Adjt Willy Coppens' fifth victory. Standing at #HD24 are (L to R) Adjt P.Dubois (1), Cdt F.Jacquet (7), Adjt G.Kervyn de Lettenhove (4), 1 Sgt Maj G.Kervyn de Meerendre, Lt M.de Crombrugghe de Looringhe (2), Adjt A.de Meulemeester (11)

and Lt J.Olieslagers (6).   *(Mrs M.Olieslagers)*

Bottom left: Adjt Edmond Weekers, S/Lt Jacques Goethals, Lt Willy Coppens and S/Lt Andre de Meulemeester off duty.   *(G.Lecomte)*

Bottom right: Adjt Gabriel Coppens d'Eeckenbrugge, 10me Escadrille listed first concerning engine-troubles.

(Koninklijk Legermuseum, Brussel)

Top left: Adjts Leon Cremers, Robert Mulders & Jean van der Voordt, 11me Escadrille, standing in front of a Camel.

(Author's collection)

Top right:Capt Leon Colignon (left), killed in September 1918 flying a Sopwith Camel and Adjt Arséne Delaunoit who only flew one sortie as a fighter pilot in May 1918. *(ASA/E.Rerren)*

Above left: Sgt Francis Dallemagne, 11me Escadrille, who scored more after the war than during the conflict! *(P.Dallemagne)*

Above right: Adjt Leon Cremers, 11me Escadrille, who was killed in 1919 whilst flying aerobatics. *(G.Lecomte)*

Right: Lt Henri *Riri* Crombez, one victory, one of the first fighter pilots in 1915. *(ASA/E.Rerren)*

Top left: S/Lt Louis de Chestret de Haneffe, 10me Escadrille, 1 victory. He crashed close to his second victim but managed to escape from imprisonment.   *(Koninklijk Legermuseum, Brussel)*

Top right: S/Lt Pierre *Pétar* de Chestret de Haneffe, 9me Escadrille, 1 victory, standing in front of his Hanriot #HD12.

(Koninklijk Legermuseum, Brussel)

Bottom left: 1Sgt Mr René Declercq, 11me

Escadrille, one victory, seated in a Camel in the summer of 1918.   *(G.Lecomte)*

Bottom right: 4me Escadrille d'Observation in 1916 (L to R): ?, Adjt A. Glibert (KIA), S/Lt Vertongen, S/Lt Sterpin, S/Lt Ch.Coomans (KIA), S/Lt A.Petrowski, S/Lt E. Desclée, Adjt M.Siraut (1), Adjt Ch.Ciselet (1), S/Lt J.de Meeus (1) (KIA), Lt M.de Crombrugghe de Looringhe (2) and Adjt R.Rondeau.

(Baron E.de Crombrugghe de Looringhe)

Top left: S/Lt Robert *Bob* De Leener, 5me Escadrille, one victory, in front of his Spad SVII.

(G.Lecomte)

Top right: S/Lts *Bob* de Leener, *Teddy* Franchomme, Edmond Desclée and Max Orban (in the cockpit), all 5me Escadrille de Chasse.

(ASA/E.Rerren)

Above left: Yellow Flight (L to R): S/Lts *Gusto* de Mevius (1), Andre de Meulemeester (11) & Georges Kervyn de Lettenhove (4).

(La Guerre Aériennes Illustrée)

Above right: Cdt Arséne Demanet, CO 1ère Escadrille who was removed to his former arm (Artillery) in 1917, where he was killed on 10 November 1918.

(ASA/E.Rerren)

Right: S/Lt Andre de Meulemeester, 9me Escadrille, 11 victories, in front of his Hanriot, ready for take-off.

(Koninklijk Legermuseum, Brussel)

Top left: S/Lt Andre *Mystère* de Meulemeester, 9me Escadrille, in a less formal pose.

(Author's collection)

Top right: S/Lt *Gusto* de Mevius, 9me Escadrille, one victory, standing in front of his Hanriot.

(Koninklijk Legermuseum, Brussel)

Above left: S/Lt *Papa Gusto* de Mevius, 9me Escadrille.   *(G.Lecomte)*

Above centre: Adjt Charles de Montigny, 10me Escadrille, two victories, who was mortally wounded on 15 October 1918 and died on the 30th.

(Koninklijk Legermuseum, Brussel)

Above right: S/Lt Charles de Munck, 1ère Escadrille, in front of his Nieuport Bébé #N229.

(ASA/E.Rerren)

Top left: S/Lt Abel De Neef, 1ère Escadrille, standing in front of his Nieuport N12.

(*ASA/E.Rerren*)

Top right: Sgt Gaston De Ruyter, 11me Escadrille, who only flew one war flight before crashing to his death. (*G.Lecomte*)

Above left: S/Lt Edmond Desclée, 10me Escadrille, who claimed one unconfirmed victory during 40 combats. (*G.Lecomte*)

Right: 1Sgt Fernand de Woot de Trixhe, 1ère Escadrille who crashed to his death in May 1917. Note RFC wings.

(*Koninklijk Legermuseum, Brussel*)

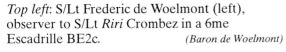

Top left: S/Lt Frederic de Woelmont (left), observer to S/Lt *Riri* Crombez in a 6me Escadrille BE2c. *(Baron de Woelmont)*

Top right: Cdt Jules Dony, CO 10me Escadrille, who was killed in an accident in October 1918. *(G.Lecomte)*

Bottom left: S/Lt Pierre Dubois, 9me Escadrille

de Chasse. He claimed the first official victory of the Groupe de Chasse in March 1918. *(Koninklijk Legermuseum, Brussel)*

Bottom right: Lt Maurice *Teddy* Franchomme, 1ère Escadrille in front of one of his Nieuports. He later became an instructor at the Pilot School. *(ASA/E.Rerren)*

Top left: Lt Marcel de Crombrugghe de Looringhe (left), two victories and Capt Walter Gallez, one victory before both went to the 9me Escadrille de Chasse. *(E.de Crombrugghe de Looringhe)*

Top right: Adjt Leon Gerard, 9me Escadrille, who was 'wounded' during a bomb raid in June 1918. *(ASA/E.Rerren)*

Above: S/Lt Jules Goossens-Bara, DCM, 9me Escadrille in his Nieuport. Note his personal insignia (with unknown colour scheme). *(ASA/E.Rerren)*

Right: S/Lt Jacques Goethals, 10me Escadrille, two victories. He was downed by Obltn H.Auffarth in October 1918. Note his gun installation. *(ASA/E.Rerren)*

Top left: S/Lt Charles Gordinne, 9me Escadrille, standing behind Lt J.Olieslagers' Sopwith Camel #Sk7. *(Koninklijk Legermuseum,Brussel)*

Top right: Adjt Robert Gordinne's Sopwith Camel, 1ère Escadrille, after the crash.

(ASA/E.Rerren)

Above left: S/Lt Charles Gordinne, known as a companionable fellow. *(G.Lecomte)*

Above: Sgt Leon Guillon, 11me Escadrille, top scoring pilot for his unit with two victories, standing in front of his Hanriot.

(ASA/E.Rerren)

Left: Adjt E.Weekers (left) joking to Adjt Robert Gordinne after the latter's crash at Les Moeres airfield. *(G.Lecomte)*

Top left: Sgt Etienne Hage, 9me Escadrille, who shot down three 'drachens', here at the Zurich Meeting in 1920, flying a Morane.

(ASA/E.Rerren)

Top right: S/Lt Paul Hanciau, 1ère Escadrille, killed in action on 30 September 1917, but apparently not claimed. *(CDH)*

Above left: Adjt Willy Heyvaert, 11me Escadrille, who was badly injured in a crash on 19 July 1918.

(Koninklijk Legermuseum, Brussel)

Above right: Cdt Paul Hiernaux, CO 11me Escadrille, who later rose to the rank of General-Major and commanded the Aviation Militaire in the1940 Campaign.

(G.Lecomte)

Right: Cdt Fernand Jacquet, CO 1ère Escadrille and Groupe de Chasse, seven victories. One of the few air aces who wore spectacles.

(CDH)

Top left: Cdt Fernand Jacquet (7), left and Louis Robin (4) during the days of their successes in 1916.

(G.Lecomte)

Top right: Adjt Maurice *le Cawe* Jamar, 9me Escadrille, who scored his only victory in Lt Coppens' Hanriot.

(G.Lecomte)

Bottom left: S/Lt Georges Kervyn de Lettenhove, 9me Escadrille, four victories, who later rose to the rank of General-Major and commanded the Belgian Air Force after 1945.

(Koninklijk Legermuseum, Brussel)

Bottom right: S/Lt Georges Kervyn de Lettenhove, 1ère Escadrille, in the summer of 1917, after scoring his second victory.

(G.Lecomte)

Top left: Adjt Georges *Edmond* Kervyn de Meerendre, 9me Escadrille, who crash-landed on his first patrol on 7 April 1918.

(G Lecomte)

Top right: S/Lt Robert Lagrange, 1ère Escadrille, who crashed to his death in the first Nieuport scout delivered to the AMB in July 1915.

(G.Lecomte)

Above: Adjt Ernest Nenesse Lambert and friend, 10me Escadrille, in a Nieuport N12.

(ASA/E.Rerren)

Right: Adjt Jacques *James* Lamarche, 11me Escadrille, here in a 3me Escadrille RE8.

(ASA/E.Rerren)

Top left: S/Lt Jacques Ledure, 10me Escadrille, who gained his two victories in ten days in his first month as a fighter pilot. *(G.Lecomte)*

Top right: Sgt Jules *Pout* Lemaire, 9me Escadrille, who could easily have been nicknamed Tom Thumb. *(G.Lecomte)*

Above left: Adjt Edmond Leonard, 10me Escadrille, who was a fighter pilot for only two weeks before he was accidentally wounded. *(G.Lecomte)*

Middle right: Sgt Leon Lhermitte, 10me Escadrille, who was shot down in flames on his first sortie on 22 October 1918. He immediately took to the air for his next OP! *(ASA/E.Rerren)*

Above right: Sgt Max Martin, 11me Escadrille. He was shot down in flames by Ltn Franz Piechulek, Jasta 56 on 4 October 1918. *(G. Lecomte)*

Top left: S/Lt Georges Medaets, 10me Escadrille, two victories over drachens in 1918. *(G.Lecomte)*

Top centre: S/Lt Maurice Medaets, 10me Escadrille, who scored his two victories during the Third Battle of Ypres in 1917. *(CDH)*

Top right: S/Lt Alfred Mouton, 9me Escadrille, who went to the Pilot School in 1918.

(Koninklijk Legermuseum, Brussel)

Above left: Adjt Robert Mulders, 11me Escadrille. He was the youngest fighter pilot in the Aviation Militaire Belge. *(G.Lecomte)*

Above right: Lt Jean Olieslagers, 9me Escadrille, six victories. He was the first Belgian fighter pilot to claim a victory in 1915.

(M.Olieslagers)

Top left: Lt Jean Olieslagers enjoying his meal.
(G.Lecomte)

Top right: Green/White Flight (L to R): Adjt Georges Kervyn de Meerendre, Lt Jean Olieslagers (6) & Adjt Maurice Jamar (1).
(G.Lècomte)

Above left: S/Lt Adrien *Max* Orban, 10me Escadrille, the eldest Belgian fighter pilot.
(Koninklijk Legermuseum, Brussel)

Middle right: Adjt Gilbert Ory, 9me Escadrille, who claimed two victories, both credited to Lt Jean Olieslagers, in May 1918.
(ASA/E.Rerren)

Above right: Russian S/Lt Alexandre Sasja Petrowski, 1ère Escadrille, who was discharged in July 1918, at his own request.
(CDH)

Top left: Lt Louis Robin, 10me Escadrille, four victories as an observer to Cdt Jacquet in 1916-17. He later became the CO of 10me Escadrille.
(G.Lecomte)

Top right: Adjt Robert Rondeau, 11me Escadrille, who scored two victories late in the war.
(G.Lecomte)

Middle left: Adjt Egide Roobaert, 1ère Escadrille, who died accidentally when he was obliged to land at sea.
(ASA/E.Rerren)

Bottom left: S/Lt Edmond Thieffry, 5me Escadrille, 10 victories. Photograph taken on 21 March 1917, six days after his first victory.
(ASA/E.Rerren)

Bottom right: S/Lt Jules Tyck, 1ère Escadrille, volunteer who asked to be withdrawn from the Army in 1916.
(ASA/E.Rerren)

Top left: S/Lt Jean *Albert* Van Cotthem, 1ère Escadrille de Chasse, one victory whilst an instructor at the Aerobatics School at Calais in 1918. *(ASA/E.Rerren)*

Top right: Adjt Jean *Charmant* van der Voordt, 11me Escadrille who scored his only victory in a Sopwith Camel. Note the overpainted British cockade. *(Koninklijk Legermuseum, Brussel)*

Middle left: Adjt Jean *Charmant* van der Voordt sitting on the wreckage of his crashed Nieuport
(Author's collection)

Above right: Instructors and student pilots in France: Standing: *Teddy* Franchomme (L) and 1Sgt Maj Armand Verhoustraten, who was killed by ground fire. Seated: Honore Deplus (Instructor), 1Sgt Leon de Maelcamp d'Opstaele, killed in an accident & 1Sgt Robert Ciselet (killed in action).
(G.Lecomte)

Left: 1Sgt Maj Carlos Verbessem, 1ère Escadrille, seated on his Nieuport, bearing the green triangle. He was killed in action in December, 1917.

(ASA/E.Rerren)

Top left: 1Sgt Maj Joseph Vuylsteke, one victory, who was substitute to the renowned Lt Willy Coppens. *(G.Lecomte)*

Top right: Three student pilots in October 1917: L to R: Adjts Gabriel Coppens d'Eeckenbrugge, Charles de Montigny and Charles Wouters. *(G.Lecomte)*

Above left: Adjt Edmond Weekers, 10me Escadrille, who scored three victories, although none was credited. *(ASA/E.Rerren)*

Above right: Cdt Jules Jaumotte (left) and Lt Emile Wouters, successful observation team in 1915-16. Wouters became a fighter pilot in 1918 with the 11me Escadrille. *(ASA/E.Rerren)*

Left: 1Sgt Maj Fernand Waroux, 11me Escadrille de Chasse, who flew 42 Offensive Patrols during the last eight weeks of the war.

(Author's collection)

after the latter became the head of State (Regent) in the absence of King Leopold III. In December 1948, Kervyn de Lettenhove was promoted to General, went into the réserves in 1950 and was pensioned.

Baron Kervyn de Lettenhove died at Ixelles, Brussels, on 17 November 1979.

	1917							
1*	12 Jun	C	Nieup	1	Vladsloo	15.40	DES
_**	14 Jun	D	Nieup	1	Schoore	18.00	DES(f)
_*	5 Aug	D	Nieup	1	Tervaete	16.00-16.30	OOC
2***	21 Aug	EA	Nieup	1	—	—	DES
_#	24 Sep	C	Nieup	1	Fme Bien Acquis	13..30	OOC
_*	4 Nov	Alb DIII	—	1	Kloosterhoek	07.45	DES(f)
	1918							
_##	21 Feb	C	HD	1	Clercken	08.50	OOC
_###	21 Feb	Albatros	HD	1	E.Dixmude	15.00	DES
_§	26 Mar	Pfalz DIII	HD	9	Dixmude	17.00	DES
3§§	25 Apr	Pfalz DIII	HD	9	Boitshoucke	11.15	DES(f)
4*	3 May	C	HD	9	Schoorbakke	11.35	DES
_❏	9 Jul	C	HD44	9	Menin	10.45	OOC
_❏❏	25 Aug	C	HD44	9	Houthulst	09.30	OOC

* shared with Adjt A.de Meulemeester. The first aircraft was a FA3-aircraft.** shared with S/Lt J.Olieslagers who was credited and 1Sgt A.de Meulemeester, possibly Vzflgm Bottler, MFJ I, wia. *** possibly Ltn dR Alfred Träger (3 victories), Jasta 8, wia # together with Adjt J.Goossens-Bara, he attacked two two-seaters which both fell out of control. ## shared with Adjts A.de Meulemeester and G.de Mevius, not credited. ### shared with Adjt A.de Meulemeester and Capt H.Symons, 65 Sqdn, RFC in Camel B5600. Both pilots were credited. § shared with Adjts A.de Meulemeester and G.de Mevius: this was Flgmt Hans Groth of MFJ II, kia in Pfalz DIII 5923/17. §§ shared with S/Lt G.de Mevius, this was FlgObmt Bruno Fietzmann, MFJ II, kia in Pfalz DIIIa 5942/17. ❏ shared with S/Lt G.de Mevius. ❏❏ shared with S/Lt G.de Mevius and S/Lt A.de Meulemeester. Possibly Flugzg Matrose Josef Gernhardt of Seefrontstaffel II, kia.

KERVYN de MEERENDRÉ (Baron) Georges Joseph Marie Ghislain
Adjudant   9

Edmond Kervyn de M, as he was called in the Ordres Journalières, was born at Drongen (East-Flanders) on 27 September 1895. He volunteered on 23 March 1915 at the Grand Parc d'Automobile before being sent to the Aviation Militaire. This occurred on 30 July 1917 and Kervyn received his civil brevet on 25 September 1917 at Etampes. After gaining his wings on 5 December (nr.1561), he was made a Sergent in February and was sent to the Parc d'Aviation at Calais in March 1918 before being sent to the front on 7 April 1918. Here he was assigned to the 9me Escadrille de Chasse. On his first patrol, the day of his arrival, he crash-landed his Hanriot due to engine trouble near Oost-Dunkerke. He was slightly injured but went on his next patrol April 12th. He fought his first aerial combat on 6 May as a wingman to Lt J.Olieslagers and with Sgt M.Jamar. It was in a three vs three fight at 6.40 am north of Dixmude. Kervyn de M was promoted to Adjudant on 29 September and was engaged in yet another 'dogfight' during which six Belgians fought against six German Albatros on 13 June. This Kervyn was also attacked by (five) British scouts. This occurred on 30 July on an offensive patrol with the same flight as the one mentioned above, over Bixschoote at 20.00.

Violin-player Georges Kervyn de M flew 131 sorties and took part in 14 combats. One probable victory was shared between five Hanriots on 8 October. Whilst attacking a two-seater, the observer collapsed in his cockpit, the guns pointing straight into the air and the pilot made a forced landing near Gits. Kervyn de M was decorated with the Croix de Guerre with Palme, Médaille du Volontaire Combattant 1914-18, Médaille de la Victoire, Médaille Commémorative 1914-18, obtained four Chevrons de fronts and was awarded the Greek Croix de Guerre 3rd class. In September 1919, he went on leave, was promoted a Sous-Lieutenant de Réserve in 1921 and a Lieutenant de Réserve on 26 June 1923. Kervyn moved to Switzerland, but died on Christmas Eve 1923 at Davos for some unknown reason, aged only 27.

	1918							
_*	8 Oct	C	HD	9	Gits	12.00	FTL

* with Capt W.Gallez, Lt J.Olieslagers, Sgt E.Hage, Sgt J.Lemaire.

LAGRANGE Robert   Sous-Lieutenant   1

Born at Ixelles, Brussels, on 18 March 1891 Lagrange was a model student at the Polytechnical School at Brussels. After his studies, he went to Brooklands, England to obtain his brevet as a pilot on 3 June 1914 (Belgian Civil Brevet nr. 96). He went to war as a volunteer with the Aviation Militaire and turned out to be a very active and brave pilot. Early in 1915 he crashed his Farman and was seriously injured. Hardly recovered, he returned to the front, received a Nieuport N10 two-seater in April and flew a mere 16 offensive patrols during which he was involved in three combats. Some 9 more war flights were flown in May. On the 17th between 04.15 and 05.15, he pursued a Zeppelin near Bruges, without success. When the first Nieuport scout arrived, he was the third man to fly it on 21 May. He asked and got permission to be one of the early fighter pilots. Therefore Lagrange went to Villacoublay (Versailles) to receive his scout, but crashed to his death whilst taking off on 1 July 1915. He was heading to the front with this new machine.

Lagrange was cited twice and was made a Chevalier de l'Ordre de Leopold and was decorated with the Croix de Guerre.

LAMARCHE Jacques Marie Albert Gustave   Adjudant   3,11

Born at Liège on 26 May 1896, 'James' volunteered on 1 August 1914 with the 3me Division d'Armée. He actually stole a German ambulance to break through their lines, to join the Belgian Army. He left his unit on 3 October 1915 for the 2me Régt Lancers where he was promoted to Brigadier (Caporal) on 15 January 1916. He transferred to the Aviation Militaire on 30 October, received his Civil brevet on November 2nd, and qualified as a pilot at Etampes on 10 May 1917 reaching the rank of 1er Sergent on 21 October. He was severely wounded after a forced landing on 17 November 1917. With the 3me Escadrille he attained the rank of Adjudant on 24 February 1918. The following May he was persuaded by Capt F.Jacquet to join the Groupe de Chasse. Lamarche joined the new 11me Escadrille and was seen almost daily over the front. He fought 19 aerial combats during 139 sorties. Four of these combats were fought in one sortie, 27 October. Two probable victories were claimed. Five more OP's were flown as a recce-pilot during which one more combat was fought. Adjt J.Lamarche was made a Commandeur de l'Ordre de Leopold II, Officier de l'Ordre de Leopold, Officier de l'Ordre de la Couronne and decorated with the Croix de Guerre, Médaille de l'Yser, Croix du Feu, Médaille du Volontaire Combattant 1914-18, Médaille de la Victoire, Médaille Commémorative 1914-18 and the Silver Medal of Merit of Serbia.

He was demobilised on 10 July 1919 and commissioned as a Lieutenant de Réserve on 14 August 1920. Two months later he joined the regular army again until 24 September 1923, when he was put into the Réserve list. Here he attained the rank of Capitaine-Commandant. Meanwhile, in civilian life, he was a Company Manager, who had not only studied at Liège but also in a Private College at Folkestone, Kent. He also did a great deal of car racing and in 1927 he finished fourth in the Monte Carlo Rally. The same year he won the Klausenrennen in Austria. The most heroic deed of his racing career surely was a Trans-African rally in 1928. The rally in a Belgian FN car ran from Algiers (Algeria) all the way to Cape Town (South Africa).

Lamarche was called to duty during the 18-day campaign of the Belgian Army during World War II as a Commanding Officer of one of the Groupes de Chasse (5 & 6/III/2). Thanks to his skill and experience gained during the previous war, his groupe was the only one who gained a few aerial victories. Lamarche in fact was also one of the very few WWI fighters who flew during the 1940 campaign (24 patrols in 19hrs and 35min). For his feats during WWII, Capt Lamarche was decorated with the French Croix de Guerre 1939-45 avec Etoile d'Argent and was cited. After WWII Lamarche reached the rank of Lieutenant-Colonel on 26 September 1946 and on 1 July 1953 he retired. He died at Brussels, the result of cardiac failure, on 13 December 1971, aged 75.

	1918						
_	11 Aug	D	HD	11	Staden	09.05	OOC
_*	14 Oct	Fokker	Camel	11	Houthulst	13.50	OOC

* this was one of a formation of 7 Fokkers. 'First it fell like a leaf, then like a stone' according to Lamarche. Obltn Fritz von Roth, Jasta 16, was wounded in combat on this day, but is seems unlikely this was Lamarche's work.

LAMBERT Ernest   Adjudant   ?,5,10,?

Caporal 'Nenesse' Lambert was first mentioned in the Aviation Militaire's diaries on 21 February 1916 when he flew his first test flight with his front-line unit. He was an artillery-spotter and was first wounded in action, when he was hit by artillery fire on 18 March. His Farman became unsteerable and Sgt Lambert crash-landed at Nieuwcapelle, with his observer, Lt F.de Woelmont. He had been promoted to Sergent earlier that month. In May he was promoted 1er Sergent and made his first offensive patrol on 10 May on board 1Sgt Maj C.Ciselet's Nieuport N10. He returned to his previous observation unit and had a bad landing, turning upside down, one week later. His observer on this occasion was Lt Constant Coomans. He again started to test scout aircraft in August and September and finally made his first offensive patrol in a single-seater on 28 September. Next month, another sortie was made and in November yet another followed. He crash-landed again on 27 November which caused him some injuries and left his aircraft destroyed. During 1916 he only flew on four sorties. After the formation of the Groupe de Chasse, he did not stay long with his unit and left early June. 49 OP's were flown and Lambert was engaged in five aerial combats. Little else is known of his activities.

LEDURE Jacques Eduard   Sous-Lieutenant   2,10

Born at Saint-Gillis, Brussels on 26 March 1893, he studied commercial science in Antwerp until his liability to service in September 1913. He was still serving with the 9me Régiment de Ligne when war broke out and he stayed with this unit till 21 January 1916. On that day he went to England and qualified as a pilot, receiving RAC brevet nr. 2521 at Hendon on 1 March. The following August, the 23rd, he gained his wings at Etampes, France. On 5 April 1917 he joined the 2me Escadrille d'Observation as a Caporal. Ledure was cited by General Nollet, Commanding Officer of the 36me Division d'Armée Française, on 11 July 1917 for his bravery. He reached the rank of Adjudant on 21 October 1917, still with this unit and received the Croix de Guerre and another citation. From March 1918 on he started to fly more and more protection flights in one of the unit's single-seaters, gaining some fame and was, like some ten other pilots, persuaded by Capt F.Jacquet to join the Groupe de Chasse. Before being posted to the 10me Escadrille in August, on 6 June, Ledure destroyed the Belgian runaway balloon nr.2 which fell near Bollezeele. Sgt Depret and Cpl Ullens de Schooten jumped at 1,300 m well before Ledure hit the balloon. Only two binoculars were lost (to nearby British soldiers). His first patrol with his new unit occurred on 6 August and on his second sortie, he had his first aerial combat as a fighter pilot when he, together with S/Lt Orban and Adjt Wouters, attacked an enemy two-seater. The next combat was good for his first claim. On his first attack on an observation balloon, Ledure sent it down in flames, diving from 2,300 m on his target over Staden. From then on Ledure started to do some more balloon strafing and claimed a second balloon still in his first month as a fighter pilot. On this occasion, Ledure himself was hit by a nearby AA unit and crash-landed his Spad, but was unharmed. There was another remarkable patrol on 4 October. Starting out on a lone sortie at 07.30 flying at 1,400 m, at 07.50 he attacked a two-seater at 900 m over Zarren; at 08.12 Ledure attacked the balloon over Courtrai and three minutes later he attacked a similar target over Iseghem. There he was intercepted by five Fokker scouts and he had to run for home. As the Fokkers abandoned the pursuit, Ledure turned back and again attacked the balloon over Iseghem at 08.20. This time his guns failed! Ledure landed safely at Les Moeres at 09.00.

On 60 offensive patrols with the 10me Escadrille de Chasse, he was engaged in 16 aerial fights of which eight were attacks on balloons. On two of these attacks his guns jammed. 23 more OP's were flown with the 2me Escadrille and seven more combats were fought.

S/Lt J.Ledure was made an Officier de l'Ordre de Leopold avec glaives, Officier de l'Ordre de la Couronne, Officier de l'Ordre de Leopold II and was decorated with the Croix du Feu, Médaille de la Victoire, Médaille Commémorative 1914-18, seven Chevrons de front, French

Croix de Guerre, Italian Medal of Merit and Italian Croix de Guerre.

He stayed in the army after hostilities and became a test pilot in the Technical Service and was in charge of the engine repair department. Between April and July 1922 he was sent to England on attachment to 4 Sqdn, RAF at Farnborough. For many years he had been a member of the Director's board of the Aéro Club Royal de Belgique and a member of the Sporting Committee of the Royal Automobile Club de Belgique. For this latter reason he did a great deal of car racing between 1923 and 1931 and won the Monte Carlo Rally in 1924. In this race, Etienne Hage was second. In civilian life he was an agent for the Castrol Oil Company in Belgium and from 1927 to 1930 attached to the Shell Company in Belgium, attending to the technical side of the lubrication oil department. Meanwhile he was also an agent for various aero engine makers (French & English) and was Director of the American Aircraft Company in Antwerp. Ledure was again called to duty on 24 August 1939 and acted as CO to 6 Squadron, 2nd Régt, Belgian Air Service, equipped with the Fairey Fox. Afterwards he was transferred to the Centre General de Renseignements de l'Aviation in which capacity he stayed at Bruges till 26 May 1940 to establish contact, in vain, with the English Service.

He then moved to France to the Etablissements d'Aéronautique Belge to take care of the technical side of assembling the Brewster fighters that were to be delivered to Belgium. On 27 June he left Bordeaux for Gloucester from where he tried to join the RAF in July through Lt-Col L.F.E. Wouters, Military & Air Attaché in London and former fighter pilot himself. The latter sent a letter to Wing Commander Porri, Foreign Liaison Officer, who was not keen to have a Captain who had reached the age of 45 in his fighter squadrons. Therefore Capt Ledure went to America where he joined the United States Air Force and there reached the rank of Major. After World War II he returned to Belgium, was promoted a Capitaine-Commandant de Réserve, retired in 1947, but died on 16 May 1948, the result of a car accident whilst racing at Chimay.

	1918						
_*	6 Jun	balloon	Camel	2	Bollezeele	—	DES
1	21 Aug	balloon	Spad	10	Staden	14.10	DES
2	31 Aug	balloon	Camel	10	S.Clercken	13.20	DES

* Belgian balloon nr.2 which was burnt at 5,200 m.

LEMAIRE Jules Lambert Adolphe Emile Hector Henri   Sergent   6,9

Born at Dinant (Province of Namur) on 7 February 1895, 'Pout' Lemaire volunteered on 7 August 1914 at the 5me Corps des Volontaires until 15 October. On 27 October, during the Battle of the Yser, he was posted to the 1er Régt Carabiniers. Here he was wounded on 3 November. A piece of his left ear was torn off and after first aid by a French doctor, serving with the Fusiliers Marins at Dixmude, Lemaire was evacuated to Ecailles, Calais. After recovering Lemaire transferred on 1 April 1915 to the Parc d'Aviation at Beaumarais from where he was sent to the front as a motor-bike rider to the 4me Escadrille on 22 October. The next move occurred on 1 April 1916 when his new unit became the 6me Escadrille. The following move was made on 14 May to the 2me Escadrille. Lemaire, who was rather small, stayed here until 28 December 1917, when he was permitted to go to Juvisy as a student pilot. He qualified as a pilot on 30 January 1918 and received his wings on 20 August. He was posted to 6me Escadrille on 9 September, but instead joined the 9me Escadrille de Chasse on the 15th. He flew his first patrol on 21 September as a wingman to S/Lt P.de Chestret and with Sgt E.Hage. He was in the air for only 56 hours on 35 sorties. Lemaire was engaged in three combats and on one of these a two-seater was attacked between 5,000 m and 700 m. The attack stalled and the two-seater force landed near Gits with a dead observer onboard.

Lemaire was demobilised on 31 January 1919 and decorated with the Croix de Guerre with Palme, Médaille du Volontaire Combattant 1914-18, Médaille de l'Yser, Médaille de la Victoire, Médaille Commémorative 1914-18 and obtained six Chevrons de front.

He died at Montauban, France on 18 April 1945.

	1918						
_*	8 Oct	C	HD	9	Gits	12.00	FTL

* with Cdt W.Gallez, Lt J.Olieslagers, Adjt G.Kervyn de Meerendré and Sgt E.Hage.

LEONARD Edmond Jules   Adjudant   2,10

Born at Pepinster (Province of Liège) on 10 August 1885, Leonard was a volunteer from the first day of the war with the 'Grand Parc d'Automobile'. He transferred to the Aviation Militaire on 1 March 1917 where he qualified as a pilot on 24 April 1917 at Etampes and received his wings on 26 June. He went to the 2me Escadrille d'Observation on 26 October. Two days later he was promoted a Sergent, a 1er Sergent on 20 January 1918, 1er Sergent Major on 24 February and finally reached the rank of Adjudant on 21 April, still with the 2me Escadrille. Leonard was posted to 10me Escadrille on 1 August and flew a first offensive patrol on the 9th with Adjts E.Weekers and C.de Montigny. After seven sorties he flew his last OP on August 21st. He was engaged with two two-seaters on 13 August north of Ypres at 08.05 for his first and only combat, during a total of 26 OP's. Leonard appeared to be very seriously injured on the left hand and wrist on the 27th and was hospitalised at the Vinckem Military Hospital. Transferred to Mortain, he was on convalescence leave until 21 January 1919.

After hostilities Leonard was demobilised on 24 April 1919. For his feats, Leonard was decorated with the Croix de Guerre 1914-18, Médaille de la Victoire, Médaille Commémorative 1914-18 and obtained eight Chevrons de front. Leonard died on 20 June 1961, aged 75.

LHERMITTE Leon Gaston Joseph   Sergent   10

Born at Hotton (Province of Luxembourg) on 10 December 1894. Pre-war he had served with the 13me Régt de Ligne during 1912-1913 and was again called to duty on 1 August 1914 with the same unit. After severe fighting during the Battle of the Yser in October 1914 he was transferred to the Compagnie des Cyclistes, 4me Division d'Armée on 15 April 1915 where he was made a Sergent on 16 April 1916. During his stay in the trenches, Lhermitte never hesitated to do his duty and twice rescued a severely wounded comrade lying in no man's land. He stayed in the trenches until 30 January 1918 when he was sent to Juvisy. Here Sgt Lhermitte qualified as a pilot. He was posted to the 10me Escadrille de Chasse on 11 October, and flew on his first patrol on the 22nd. He took off at 08.00 in company with Lts L.Robin, F.de Woelmont, M.Orban, B.De Leener and Adjts M.Siraut and G.Coppens d'Eeckenbrugge. They were engaged by several Fokkers and Lhermitte was shot down in flames during his first combat at 08.50 over Handsbeek. He escaped unharmed and after his return to the airfield, only a few moments later, he immediately took to the air for his second OP! Afterwards Lhermitte went on to fly some eight more patrols. On one of these, 3 November, he fired some rounds at a two-seater. This was his only feat on nine patrols, flying only 12 hours and 10 minutes over the front.

Lhermitte was made a Chevalier de l'Ordre Leopold II with Palme and decorated with the Croix Militaire 2me classe, Croix de Guerre and the rare Etoile d'Or de Kara Georges from Serbia for his cold-bloodedness during his famous first combat.

After hostilities he rose to the rank of Adjudant and became an instructor, but died in an aircrash at the military airbase of Schaffen (Brabant), 2 March, 1920.

MARTIN Max Joseph Valere Ghislain   Sergent   11

Born at Bonneville (Namur) on 1 June 1895, he volunteered on 6 August 1914 and was a soldier with the 10me Régiment de Ligne. He stayed with this régiment until he transferred to the Aviation Militaire in January 1918, qualifying on 29 January and receiving his wings on 31 July at Juvisy. Sgt Martin joined the 11me Escadrille de Chasse in September, flew for the first time on 13 September and made his first offensive patrol on the 14th. He turned out to be a brave and good pilot and made 18 sorties. He was unfortunately killed in his fourth combat over Beveren/Roulers on 4 October at 07.15. Cdt P.Hiernaux led a flight with Adjt R.Rondeau and 1Sgt Maj J.van der Voordt and Martin. They took off at 06.30 and Hiernaux saw and engaged a flight of Fokkers belonging to Jasta 56 from which Martin failed to return. He fell victim to Ltn Franz Piechulek for his 14th and final victory in a black-white, black-yellow striped Fokker DVII.

Sgt Martin was posthumously made a Chevalier de l'Ordre de Leopold II, awarded the Croix de Guerre and cited once.

	1918							
_*	23 Sep	C		HD	11	Middelkerke	07.05	FTL

* with Adjt R.Rondeau and Sgt J.van der Voordt.

MEDAETS Georges Octave Ulrich   Sous-Lieutenant   5,10,2

Born at Schaarbeek, Brussels on 27 February 1896, Medaets went to England where he learned to fly at Hendon, receiving his brevet RAC nr.1874 on 12 October 1915. From there he volunteered for the Aviation Militaire on 7 January 1916, being promoted to Caporal two days later and receiving his wings on 2 August. He followed his brother, Maurice, to a front-line unit and joined the 5me Escadrille de Chasse in 1917 and reached the rank of Adjudant on 21 October of that year. After his brother had joined the 2me Escadrille d'Observation, Georges followed his example in July 1918 after scoring two victories over observation balloons, for which he was made a Chevalier de l'Ordre de la Couronne and received the Croix de Guerre. As a fighter pilot, he flew on 155 sorties and took part in 21 combats. His first victory was shared with Adjt E.Weekers, who was not credited although both attacked the same 'drachen'; Medaets fired first and when Weekers dived and started to fire, the balloon caught fire. Nevertheless, the Aviation Militaire concluded that Medaets was the one who had set the drachen on fire.

Whilst with his new unit, he was commissioned to Sous-Lieutenant on 11 September 1918. Medaets was decorated with the Croix du Feu, Médaille du Volontaire Combattant 1914-18, Médaille de la Victoire, Médaille Commémorative 1914-18 and obtained two Chevrons de front. He was also rewarded with the French Croix de Guerre avec Etoile Bronze.

After hostilities he went into the réserve and in the late thirties he commanded an observation unit (7/III/3Aé) and reached the rank of Capitaine. He was also involved in many flights to the Belgian Congo. The first occurred on 9 March 1926 with Lt J.Verhaegen and Adjt J.Coppens. The aéroplane used was a Breguet XIX, called Reine Elisabeth. This team was the first to make a to-and-fro flight and they did it in 100 hours effective time in the air. For this feat Medaets was made an Officier de l'Ordre de Leopold. In November 1927 he again left for a flight to the Belgian Congo with Lt Verhaegen. This time all went wrong; the aircraft fell at the Langres heights and Medaets was severely injured. Later decorations were Officier de l'Ordre de la Couronne and Officier de l'Ordre Leopold II.

When World War II swept over Europe, Medaets managed to get to England and volunteered as a pilot into the RAF. He was refused, however, due to some medical problems and Medaets therefore went to Brazil on 23 July 1940. After WW II he retired from the Belgian Army on 11 March 1947, whilst formally being suspected of desertion due to his emigration. He died at Sao Paolo, Brazil on 8 December, 1976.

	1917							
_*	27 Jul	EA		Nieup	5	S.Clercken	14.55-15.40	DES
	1918							
1**	30 May	balloon		Spad	10	—	15.30	DES
2	23 Jul	balloon		Spad	10	Zarren	05.15	DES

* with S/Lt P.Braun, possibly a Jasta 29 who had one pilot seriously wounded. ** with Adjt E.Weekers, who was not credited for this victory.

MEDAETS Maurice Paul August Jean-Baptiste   Sous-Lieutenant   5,10,2

Older brother to Georges, he was born on 11 April 1893 at Schaarbeek near Brussels, where he studied until he was liable to take up Military Service in August 1913. He joined the 1er Régt

Carabiniers and one month later was posted to the 9me Régt de Ligne. With this unit he went to war and was promoted to Sergent on 1 August 1915. He left the 9me Régt de Ligne for the Aviation Militaire on 25 September and qualified as a pilot in May 1916. Next month he was sent to the Parc d'Aviation at Calais where he obtained a seven days holiday to Switzerland! He was finally sent to the front on 1 February 1917 where he joined the 5me Escadrille de Chasse (this was really what he wanted). During the days of the Third Ypres offensive, Medaets claimed two enemy aircraft for which he was made a Chevalier de l'Ordre de la Couronne and received the Croix de Guerre. He was cited twice by the Belgian Army and once by the 36me Division d'Armée Française and also received the French Croix de Guerre. Meanwhile he had reached the rank of Adjudant on 19 August. At the end of the year, on 8 November, Medaets was engaged by a two-seater and was forced to land. His opponent was an aircraft probably belonging to Schutzstaffel 8. On 17 January 1918 Medaets was admitted to the Adinkerke Military Hospital where he stayed until 8 March. He joined the renumbered 'Comet' Escadrille and was commissioned on 13 May. His last aerial combat occurred on 26 June when he fired 400 rounds at a runaway balloon over Dixmude. As a fighter pilot, Maurice Medaets was engaged in 25 aerial combats during 125 sorties. On 1 August he left the 10me Escadrille for the 2me Escadrille de Reconnaissance where he was severely injured by ground fire on 21 October, whilst flying at 100 m on a reconnaissance sortie. For this he was made a Chevalier de l'Ordre de Leopold II. In a sorry state he was transferred to the Cabour Military Hospital on the 27th. Here he quickly recovered and on 8 November went to Paris for a convalescence period of twenty days. He again joined the 2me Escadrille, after the Armistice, this time based at Evere, Brussels.

For his feats during the Great War he was further made an Officier de l'Ordre de la Couronne, decorated with the Croix du Feu, Médaille de la Victoire, Médaille Commémorative 1914-18, and obtained seven Chevrons de front and one Chevron de blessure.

On 26 April 1920 he was promoted to Lieutenant de Réserve, after being placed on the réserve list on 10 April 1919. In March 1930, he reached the rank of Capitaine de Réserve and was at that time a CO of the 5th Squadron, 3rd Groupe, 3rd Régiment (5/III/3Aé) of the Aviation Militaire Belge and later that year he became the manager of the Societé Brocevin Bruxelles at Costermansville, Belgian Congo. Finally pensioned off on 11 February 1938, he left for Sao Paolo, Brazil, from where he wrote a letter to the Belgian Government to obtain a contribution as a war veteran in 1962.

	1917							
1*	21 Jul	C		Nieup	5	Pilckem	16.10	DES
2**	11 Sep	C		Spad	5	Grognies	12.16	DES

* possibly an aircraft belonging to Seeflug Stat.Flandern I, which lost Flugmeister Ludwig Meyer, kia. ** Gefr Paul Wörner/Ltn dR Kurt Dobberstein, FAA 233, kia.

MOUTON Alfred Jules Marie   Sous-Lieutenant   1,9,3

Born at Liège on 27 December 1887, Alfred Mouton was one of three brothers who enlisted in the Aviation Militaire. All of the brothers qualified as pilots in three different places. Alfred a 1m80 tall lawyer, volunteered on 4 August in the Colonne Estafettes & Reconnaissance, 3me Division d'Armée. From here he transferred to the 9me Régt d'Artillerie in June 1915 and went to England in January 1916 to gain his wings. He qualified at Hendon on 28 March 1917 and was assigned to the 1ère Escadrille de Chasse on 8 June where he reached the rank of Adjudant on 25 November. He only stayed for a year as a fighter pilot and moved to the 3me Escadrille d'Observation on 2 June 1918, flying on his last sortie as a fighter pilot on 26 May from 11.30 to 13.00, together with the Gordinne brothers, who were both to be discharged from the 9me Escadrille to the 5me Escadrille d'Observation. Mouton was a good pilot but not an aggressive one; six aerial combats were fought during 112 sorties. After a brief stay with the 3me Escadrille, he was sent as an instructor to the Pilot School in Juvisy on 14 September where he saw out the war, being promoted a Sous-Lieutenant on 22 September.

Mouton was decorated with the Croix de Guerre and obtained six Chevrons de front. He died at Liège on 9 December 1953.

MULDERS Robert Marie Ghislain Charles Emile   Adjudant   11

Born at Bruxelles on 25 July 1898, Mulders was the youngest fighter pilot engaged in the Belgian Army. He volunteered directly into the Aviation Militaire on 18 October 1915 reaching the rank of Caporal in September 1916. At his own request he was reduced to soldier and went to Etampes to the Pilot School. After qualifying as a pilot on 25 September 1917 (nr.1550) and receiving his wings on 6 December, he joined the newly formed 11me Escadrille de Chasse as a Sergent in May 1918 flying Sopwith Camels. He flew 112 sorties and took part in 13 aerial combats, including on 15 October an attack, as a flight commander and with wingmen Sgts Waroux and Dallemagne, on a strong formation of Marinefeld-Jasta IV or V which was in combat with a 10me Escadrille Flight (where Adjt C.de Montigny was mortally wounded). Mulders reached the rank of Adjudant on 27 October 1918 and for his feats was awarded the Croix de Guerre for over 150 hours over enemy lines, Médaille de la Victoire, Médaille Commémorative 1914-18 and French Croix de Guerre with Palme. He also obtained five Chevrons de fronts.

After hostilities he went into the Réserve reaching the rank of Capitaine on 22 March 1932. Meanwhile Mulders had started his own aviation-engine company, building Hispano-engines under license. Robert Mulders died at the age of 84 on 18 February 1983.

OLIESLAGERS Jean   Lieutenant   5,2,1,9

The 'Antwerp Devil' was born 14 May 1883 at Antwerp. Fascinated by speed he exchanged his pedal-bike for a motorcycle. In 1902 he became World Champion and became the first man on earth to reach over 100 km/h on a motorbike. In 1909 he bought a Blériot monoplane and in October of that year he received brevet nr.5. Seven world records stood against his name between 1910-1913. In 1910 he won the Meeting d'Aviation de Rheims and in June 1914 he was the equal of the Frenchman Roland Garros in an aérobatics-contest. When the German Army invaded Belgium he received a letter from the German Government asking him to give them a hand in observation. He refused, of course and presented himself together with his two brothers Max, a pilot and Jules, a mechanic who could also fly, and their three self-built Blériots, to serve in the Belgian Army. He soon became a Sergent and before the year ended he was already commissioned. On 6 August, Belgian Headquarters decided that Belgian aircraft should carry Belgian cockades. Olieslagers, after hearing this, painted his roundels himself, but with the outside colour black instead of red! Olieslagers was injured for the first time, on 5 January 1915, in the chest, left arm and leg after a crash-landing. He also became the first fighter pilot to claim a victory on 12 September 1915 and could have had many more victories to his name, but Olieslagers never took claiming seriously and hardly claimed anything. At the time of his first victory, his N10 was the only camouflaged Nieuport in the Aviation Militaire and bore the name *le Démon* (devil). Olieslagers also had many combats far behind the German lines. On 30 March 1916 he shot down an enemy aircraft over Praat Bosch, seeing it fall behind the wood. This one he claimed and the Guards of the 3rd Division confirmed the combat in which an aircraft fell out of control, but there wasn't an officer to confirm it, so the claim was never made official. 193 offensive patrols were flown in 1916 during which 52 aerial combats were counted. Nine unconfirmed victories were achieved. Olieslagers, who seemed to suffer from myopia, once lost consciousness and crashed his Hanriot at Les Moeres airfield on 4 November, 1917. Transferred to the Military Hospital at Beveren, he stayed unconscious for a few days, but recovered sufficiently to fly again in January 1918.

Olieslagers was an excellent pilot who took nearly all of the new pilots of his Escadrille under his wing and he hardly ever went on leave. He was in personal contact with Mr Lewis, the machine-gun inventor and therefore undertook many trips to London, but apart from this he always stayed at his airfield, working on his machine, in the hangars or in his 'garden'. With the 9me Escadrille de Chasse alone, he flew 141 sorties and was engaged in 15 aerial combats during which two aircraft were officially claimed. His brother Jules seemed to be a very good mechanic, for Olieslagers hardly suffered any engine trouble, although he did have engine trouble on 9 November 1918 when he had to land in a field close to Eecloo, East-Flanders. This turned out to be his 518th and last patrol during which 97 combats were fought.

Lt J.Olieslagers was made a Chevalier de l'Ordre Leopold and decorated with the Croix de Guerre with Palme, Croix de l'Yser, Croix du Feu, Médaille du Volontaire Combattant 1914-18, Médaille Commémorative 1914-18 and eight Chevrons de front. He was also made a Chevalier de la Légion d'Honneur and further received the French Croix de Guerre, Russian St-Stanislaus Order and Serbian Golden Medal. The Hanriot HD1 shown at the Brussels Air Museum is painted after Olieslagers' Hanriot during the war. After the war he went back to his hometown after being demobilised on 29 September 1919 and opened a garage. On 1 April 1921 he was pensioned out as a Lieutenant de Réserve. In 1923 Olieslagers was the man behind the opening of the Antwerp Airport in Deurne. At its entrance there now stands a statue to the honour of the Antwerp Devil. He died in March 1942 from cancer. His coffin was decorated with the Belgian flag and the National Hymn was played, although both were forbidden by the German occupation forces.

	1915						
1	12 Sep	Aviatik C	N10	2	Oudstuyvekenskerke	10.11	FTL
_	22 Sep	C	N10	5	Avecapelle	—	OOC
_*	30 Nov	C	N10	5	Furnes	11.15	OOC
	1916						
_	14 Mar	EA	N10	1	Dixmude	15.30	OOC
_	30 Mar	EA	N10	1	Praat Bosch	09.30	OOC
2‡	17 Jun	Fok DII	N11	1	Pypegaele	15.15	DES
_	25 Jun	LVG C	N11	1	Nieuwcapelle	17.15	OOC
_	25 Jun	Fokker	N11	1	Dixmude	17.20	OOC
_	28 Jul	LVG C	N11	1	Handzaeme	15.45	FTL
_	30 Jul	LVG C	N11	1	Houthulst Forest	am	FTL
_	31 Jul	LVG C	N11	1	Houthulst Forest	—	OOC
_	3 Aug	EA	N11	1	Ghistelles	10.00	FTL
_	28 Sep	Alb C	N11	1	Ghistelles	19.00	FTL
	1917						
_**	7 Feb	LVG C	Nieup	1	Clercken	12.00-13.05	FTL
_***	8 Feb	LVG C	Nieup	1	St-Jacques-Capelle	10.05-12.10	OOC
3¶¶	14 Jun	C	Nieup	1	Schoore	18.00	DES
4#	15 Jun	Fok DII	Nieup	1	Keyem	11.15	DES (f)
_##	4 Sep	Alb C	HD#8	1	Woumen	07.00-08.05	OOC
_###	1 Oct	C	HD#8	1	Beerst	15.45	OOC
	1918						
_¶	3 May	D	HD	9	Eesen	09.40	OOC
5 §	3 May	Fok DVII	HD	9	Westende	17.50	DES
6 §§	19 May	Alb DV	HD	9	Woumen	17.40	DES(f)
_§§§	8 Oct	C	HD	9	Gits	12.00	FTL

* together with S/Lt J.Tyck, Adjt C.Kervyn de Lettenhove/S/Lt R.d'Hendecourt. ‡ Ltn dR Heinz Warneken du Wurtemberg, born at Leipzig 22/2/1896, kia. ** Ltn Erich Ziemke (FA 19) died of wounds the next day at Handzaeme airfield. *** single-handed he attacked a formation of 3, one apparently was hit and force-landed behind his lines. ¶¶ possibly Vzflgmstr Bottler, MFJ I, wia. # Vfw Richard Schipfer, the leader of a patrol of three scouts belonging to Kampfgeschwader 4, kia. 1SgtMaj A.de Meulemeester and Sgt C.Verbessem were involved in the combat as well, but were not credited. ## his first flight in a HD1. The observer was hit, but the Hanriot as well; Olieslagers made a force landing. This was probably a Schutzstaffel 29 aircraft .### with Adjts W.Coppens, A.de Meulemeester and J.Goossens-Bara. ¶ possibly Obltn Friedrich Pohrt of Marine Landflieger Abteilung, kia. § this was Ltn de Réserve Walter Lippold of Marine Feldflieger Abteilung. §§ Vzfw Andreas Triebswetter, Jasta 16, (4 vict) who just downed the Belgian balloon over Loo, and also claimed by two British pilots (Lt W.E. Gray and Capt J.W. Pinder, 213 Sqdn, RAF). In fact Jan Olieslagers attacked first according to his combat report. Adjt G.Ory too was involved in this fight, but he was not credited §§§ together with Capt W. Gallez, Adjt G.Kervyn de Meerendré, Sgt E.Hage and Sgt J.Lemaire.

ORBAN Adrien Eugene Joseph Max   Sous-Lieutenant   4,1,5,10

Born at Herve (Province of Liège) on 22 July 1881, Max Orban was the oldest fighter pilot in the Aviation Militaire Belge. Before the war he already had a career as a lawyer. He had been a rower and in 1905, being part of an eight-men strong Ghent team, he won the Grand Challenge Cup at Henley on Thames. This team became the first to achieve a non-British victory in the prestigious race. As a skiffer he attended many races abroad, such as Athens, Constantinople, Prague, Bucharest, Lucerne and Monaco.

He volunteered on 3 August 1914 with the Aviation Militaire, although he was awarded the French Croix de Guerre avec Etoile d'Argent and cited for the rescue of a French 75. gun at the Yser river. This sounds odd being a member of the AMB, but this deed he performed during a period at the front while learning observation. The first test-flight Max Orban flew was on 10 October 1915, followed by a patrol six days later with his observer, Lt L.Orban, his brother. On 21 November he was one of the first pilots to test a BE2c, which was purchased by the Belgian Government and sent to the newly formed 6me Escadrille d'Observation in February 1916. Orban was awarded the Croix de Guerre on 12 March 1916 for the following feat. An Allied aircraft was downed by AA fire into the flooded area of no-man's land, so with two pals he managed to salvage the machine gun and engine under heavy German artillery fire. Promotion to 1er Sergent Major occurred on 24 March and in June Orban joined the 1ère Escadrille de Chasse, flying his first offensive patrol on the 30th. One month later he had his first aerial combat when he was attacked by a Fokker DII. Adjt A.De Neef, in the neighbourhood, came to his rescue. Orban was promoted to Adjudant on 6 August and one month later, 7 September, together with Adjt E.Desclée, they flew over Antwerp and Ghent in their Nieuport 10 scouts, protecting the Farman 120 HP of 1SgtMaj J.de Roest d'Alkemade/S/Lt A.Rolin. For this feat all four were cited in the order of the day. On 19 May 1917 he was finally assigned to the Aviation Militaire, posted to the 5me Escadrille and commissioned. With this Escadrille, he flew on Nieuport scouts and his personal Nieuport (# N5024) is now shown in the Brussels Air Museum. Orban claimed an Albatros on 18 October 1917 whilst patrolling over the lines with Adjt A.de Meulemeester. They were engaged by two Albatros scouts, and both men attacked the same scout, which dived away in a very strange way, apparently hit. This probably was Ltn Xaver Dannhuber of Jasta 26 (10 victories), who was wounded in the upper arm on this day during a combat. On a lone sortie on 2 July 1918 at 11.30 am he spotted a Gotha or Friedrichshafen bomber at 6,000 m. This aircraft was not fired at by any guns, so Orban decided to attack it. When reaching an altitude of 5,600 m he was disturbed by a Belgian Hanriot. He could not recognise the pilot, nor did he ever find out who it could have been, probably a recce-pilot, but nevertheless, Orban had to abandon his attack. S/Lt A.Orban flew a total of 251 OP's and was engaged in 47 aerial combats. He was made a Chevalier de l'Ordre de la Couronne and decorated with the Médaille de l'Yser, Croix du Feu, Médaille de la Victoire, Médaille Commémorative 1914-18 and obtained eight Chevrons de front. After the war he became a Lieutenant on 18 June 1919 and a Lieutenant de Réserve on 29 September. Max Orban then established himself in Antwerp where he took up his career as a lawyer.

When war swept again over Europe in 1940, Lieutenant de Réserve Orban was once more called to duty on 10 May. He was, however, arrested in his military clothes, at his home on that day by the Belgian Security Service. He joined his squadron, still under arrest, five days later, which was stationed in France. After the personal intervention of Lt-Col F.de Woelmont he was freed on 8 August. His arrest had been based on a mistake, but it was never cleared afterwards. After the Belgian capitulation Max Orban went back to Belgium on 20 August and again practised as a lawyer in Antwerp. He was not left alone during the years of the German occupation, for he was put into prison twice by the Geheime Feld Polizei, first in the autumn of 1940 and again in the autumn of 1943. He stayed sane by trout-fishing, travelling and playing chess. Orban died at Antwerp, on 23 May 1969 at the age of 88, the result of cardiac failure.

	1917		Spad				
_*	18 Oct	Alb D	#Sp5	5	Tervaete	09.15	OOC

* shared with Adjt. A.de Meulemeester, 1ère Esc. Probably Ltn X.Dannhuber, Jasta 26, wia.

ORY Gilbert Emmanuel Joseph   Adjudant   1,9,6

Born at Glons (Province of Liège) on 18 April 1891, he was a farmer who was drafted in 1910, serving with the 11me Régt de Ligne. Recalled to duty in the first days of the war, he was assigned to the Transport Corps detached to the 3me Division d'Armée. With this Corps he stayed until 27 February 1917. That day the 1m 81 tall Ory obtained his transfer to the Aviation Militaire. He received his civil brevet on 24 April and qualified in the army on 26 June, both while at Etampes, followed by the usual promotion to Caporal. On 17 October he joined the 1ère Escadrille de Chasse where he reached the rank of Adjudant on 24 March 1918.

On 3 May he was engaged in two aerial combats and on the second, his combat report was as follows: 'We (Ory, Lt J.Olieslagers and Adjt L.Gerard) were flying at 4,500 m over Nieuport coming from Dixmude. At 5.40 pm I noticed a scout over Westende heading for the sea. I immediately attacked and fired a few rounds, but my machine-gun jammed. I abandoned the attack and turned towards our lines, followed by the same scout. Once the jam cleared, I turned back to renew my attack. The German turned back as well, having certainly noticed another Belgian aircraft (Lt Olieslagers) heading in his direction and placing himself between the German and myself. At that time I was slightly higher than both and started to fire again. The German went into a spin and I circled round to watch the result. Meanwhile Lt Olieslagers followed the German.' From this combat report and that of his flight companions, Olieslagers and Gerard, Capt W.Gallez and Capt F.Jacquet concluded that the victory should be credited to Lt J.Olieslagers.

On his sortie of 19 May his combat report reads as follows: 'On my OP over Beerst at 3,000 m I noticed two parachutes close to the observation balloon over Loo which was set on fire. Then I saw a hostile scout heading for its lines. Without hesitation I attacked the aircraft over Woumen, together with two British Sopwith Camels (Capt J.W. Pinder and Lt W.E. Gray, 213 Sqdn, RAF) and one Hanriot (Lt J.Olieslagers). Again flying higher than any of the attackers I fired a few rounds and the German started to burn and crashed. This occurred at 5.40 pm.' From this combat report and that of Lt Olieslagers, Capt Jacquet and Capt Gallez concluded that both Belgians were to be credited with this victory. Olieslagers was credited, as well as the two British pilots. Ory wasn't for some unknown reason.

Adjt G.Ory had flown 131 sorties and took part in 19 combats. He flew his last offensive patrol on 6 September and nine days later moved to the 6me Escadrille d'Observation where he took to the air for the first time on the 18th. On 3 October, in the middle of the liberation offensive, he supplied the ground troops with food from a height of 300 m, thrown to the troops by his observer, Lt. Gilles. With the same observer he undertook some ground strafing on 2 November east of Lovendeghem.

Adjt G.Ory was awarded the Croix de Guerre, Médaille de l'Yser, Médaille de la Victoire, Médaille Commémorative 1914-18 and eight Chevrons de front. On 10 February 1919 he received the Serbian Golden Medal for Valour. He was commissioned on 1 May 1919 and placed onto the Réserve list on 29 June 1921. Gilbert Ory died at Brussels on 22 August 1984, aged 91.

	1918							
_*	3 May	Fokker	HD	9	Westende	17.50	DES(f)	
_**	19 May	Alb DV	HD	9	Woumen	17.40	DES(f)	

* this was Ltn Walter Lippold of Marine Landflieger Abteilung, kia. ** this was Vzfw Andreas Triebswetter, Jasta 16, (4 vict), kia.

ROBIN Louis Marie Omer August   Lieutenant   1,2,4,3,7,10

Born at Ixelles, Brussels on 1 June 1893, he went to the Military Academy in 1911 and was commissioned in December 1913 with the 5me Régiment de Lanciers. At the cavalry school in Ypres he was under the command of Jacquet's brother who informed Fernand Jacquet of the qualities of Robin, who was known to be some kind of a rogue. He went to war with his Régiment and took part in the battles of Antwerp and the Yser river. On 20 February 1915 he joined the Aviation Militaire, where he made his first offensive patrol as an observer to Sgt Willy de Roy on 14 March 1915. His first aerial combat occurred on 31 March with Lt F.Jacquet, when they attacked an Aviatik two-seater. On 29 September 1915 he flew over Brussels throwing some bombs on the Zeppelin hangars. His pilot on this occasion was S/Lt R.Castiau. On the night of 26/27 September he went on five different bomb sorties with the same pilot. On 15 October

1915, again with S/Lt Castiau, he overflew Ghent and Antwerp throwing some newspapers and a Belgian flag with the words 'zy zullen hem niet temmen' (the refrain of the Flemish hymn). In 1916 he became the main observer for Capt Jacquet and flew on 113 sorties, participated in 70 fights during which three official claims were made. Because of the problem between Robin and his CO, Cdt A.Demanet, the friendship between Jacquet and Robin broke down and he was transferred on 1 July 1917 to the 4me Esc, August to 3me Esc, 16 September back to 4me Esc. In 1917 Robin started a flying course and qualified as a pilot in Etampes. Posted to the 7me Escadrille d'Observation Photographique, Robin started to fly protection flights in a Hanriot scout and was seen in the air on OP's, even more often than real Belgian fighter pilots! He finally joined the 10me Escadrille de Chasse in October 1918 and was made its Commanding Officer on the 6th. With this unit he only flew 18 sorties, but was engaged in 11 combats. In one of these fights he forced a two-seater to land in Holland. During his wartime career as an observer and recce-pilot he flew 326 OP's and was involved in 117 combats.

Lt L.Robin was made an Officier de l'Ordre de la Couronne, Chevalier de l'Ordre de Leopold, the Fourragère aux couleurs de l'Ordre de Leopold and decorated with the Croix de Guerre with 8 Palmes and 4 lions, Médaille de l'Yser, Croix du Feu, Médaille de la Victoire, Médaille Commémorative 1914-18 and received 14 citations and eight Chevrons de front. By the Allied countries he was made a Chevalier de la Légion d'Honneur and decorated with the French Croix de Guerre with 2 Palmes and the Russian Ordre de Saint-Stanislaus 3me classe.

In 1920 he was the manager of the Belgian team for aerial combats, which won a gold medal at the Olympic Games in Antwerp, Belgium. Of course this was no Olympic sport, but just a demonstration. In 1921 he helped his former pilot, Fernand Jacquet to start the latter's Pilot School at Gosselies, near Charleroi, where he trained 56 pilots for the army. Robin was also the first Belgian to descend from an aircraft with a parachute. In October 1922 he again joined the Cavalry where he took command of the 2me Régiment de Lanciers. As a Lancer, he was an instructor at the Cavalry School, teaching topography. As a horseback rider he won the Inter-Allied Cross Country at the Ostende Hippodrome in August 1926. He was promoted to Major in May 1930.

When in 1940 Belgium was violated by Germany for the second time, Cdt L.Robin commanded the 7me Escadron d'autos blindés (armoured cars), belonging to the 2me Régt de Lanciers. After the capitulation on 28 May 1940, he asked his commanding officer, Lt-Col d'Orjo de Marchovelette, if he could get to the British Isles to join the RAF. This was refused by his CO and Robin was therefore taken prisoner. He was taken to Germany, first to Soest, then Tibor and finally Prenzlau in OFLAG IIa from where he was repatriated on 3 June 1945.

Robin retired on 1 June 1946 and was promoted a Colonel. When Jacquet died on 12 October 1947, Robin was one of the deeply affected speakers at his funeral. Louis Robin himself died at Etterbeek, August 9, 1976, aged 82.

	1916						
1*	20 May	seaplane	MF	1	Nieuport	20.30	DES
_*	26 May	Aviatik C	MF	1	Thourout	18.30	OOC
_*	27 May	Aviatik C	MF	1	Couckelaere	19.20	FTL
_*	22 Jun	LVG C	MF	1	Staden/Cortemarck	08.30	DES
2*	23 Jun	Fok DII	MF	1	Couckelaere	am	DES
_*	30 Jun	Aviatik C	MF	1	Handzaeme	21.00	FTL
_*	8 Jul	LVG C	MF	1	Middelkerke	16.50	OOC
_**	30 Jul	LVG C	MF	1	Houthulst Forest	12.00	DES
3***	30 Jul	LVG C	MF	1	Houthulst	16.30	DES
	1917						
4*	1 Feb	Rumpler C	MF	1	Lombartzyde	15.15	DES
_#	2 Jul	C	Strut	3	Ypres	13.40	OOC
	1918						
_##	3 Nov	C	Spad	10	Selzaete	12.00	FTL

* pilot Capt F.Jacquet. ** pilot Capt F.Jacquet, shared with Sgt Barthes/mec Baudoin of the French Esc.MF36. *** pilot Capt F.Jacquet. Possibly a Marine Feldflieger Abteilung II aircraft. They lost Ltn dR Albert Siebert on this day. After this victory Jacquet circled around to shoot at the cars and men surrounding the downed aircraft. # pilot S/Lt J.de Roest d'Alkemade. ## this aircraft landed in Holland.

RONDEAU Robert Gustave Florent   Adjudant   6,3,4,11

Born at Antwerp on 27 July 1894, he fulfilled his draft in the Aviation Militaire from 14 May 1914 as a soldier. He was assigned to 2me Escadrille in January 1915 where he stayed till April 1916. On the 16th, he moved as a lorry driver to 6me Escadrille where his brother Raymond was a distinguished pilot. Inspired by the feats of the latter, he obtained his transfer to the Pilot School on 1 September and qualified on 20 April 1917 at Etampes. On 1 July 1917 he was assigned to the General Staff from where he was sent to the observation units. Here he was promoted to Adjudant on 27 January 1918. Robert Rondeau turned out to be a brave pilot and Capt. F.Jacquet persuaded him to join the 11me Escadrille de Chasse on 12 May 1918. The first offensive patrol was flown on the 20th. Because of his experience, he was promptly made a flight commander. Most of his sorties were made with wingmen Adjt L.Cremers and Sgt J.van der Voordt, or Adjts W.Heyvaert and R.Mulders. On his second aerial combat, on 13 June, he joined five Hanriots of 9me Escadrille involved in a dogfight with six Albatros scouts. On 25 August he crash-landed his Camel which was a write-off, although Rondeau remained unhurt. On 2 September he managed to do the same thing all over, being uninjured again. Adjt Rondeau flew 154 sorties and fought 27 aerial fights in which he claimed three victories and twice he had to break off the fight due to machine-gun failure. For his two credited victories Rondeau was made a Chevalier de l'Ordre de la Couronne and decorated with the Croix de Guerre with Palme, Médaille de l'Yser, Médaille de la Victoire, Médaille Commémorative 1914-18, seven Chevrons de front, was cited three times with the Belgian army, received the French Croix de Guerre and was cited with this army once.

    In January 1919 Rondeau was commissioned and demobilised on 29 September 1919. He was promoted to Lieutenant de Réserve in June 1922 and retired in August 1931. Meanwhile he had married Mrs Renéaux from Paris, France in 1925. He died in July 1957.

	1918		HD1				
_*	23 Sep	C	73	11	Middelkerke	07.05	FTL
1	27 Sep	balloon	73	11	Clercken	11.30	DES
2**	9 Oct	Halb C	73	11	Cortemarck	15.20	DES
_***	19 Oct	EA	—	11	—	—	DES

* with Sgts M.Martin and J.van der Voordt. ** possibly Vfw Bruno Grütze/?? of Bomb.Geschw. VI, Staffel 7, kia. *** this is possibly the 9 October claim, but on November 14 he was cited by the French Army for his second victory dated *19*/10/1918.

ROOBAERT Egide Max Corneille   Adjudant   5,1

Born at St-Jans Molenbeek, Brussels, on 8 August 1894 he volunteered in the early days of the war and asked for a transfer to the Aviation Militaire. He joined Commandant Moulin's 5me Escadrille on 16 September 1915. Soon afterwards he joined the 1ère Escadrille and made his first offensive patrol one year before his death. He had his first aerial combat on Christmas Day 1915 stopping a German aircraft crossing Belgian lines. Next January he was promoted to 1er Sergent and when he made two offensive patrols on 24 February, he was the very first fighter pilot to fly an offensive patrol for an Escadrille de Chasse, which had just been formed. It could have been different, for seven days earlier he crash-landed due to bad weather, but Roobaert escaped unharmed. On 29 February he flew a protection flight over a German runaway observation balloon which landed close to the shore at St-Idesbald (two observers were rescued: one was taken on board a trawler, the other one swam to the beach). On 19 May, together with Capt F.Jacquet, he attacked such a balloon with Congreve rockets and nine days later he came to the rescue of the same Capt Jacquet who was engaged in a fight with his observer Lt L.Robin fighting off three enemies. Lt Robin did not fire because his guns jammed and when Roobaert attacked the nearest aircraft he found his guns jamming as well! In June he was promoted to Adjudant, flew a new single-seater, the Ponnier L1, an ill-conceived aeroplane with poor flying capabilities, and with Jacquet/Robin claimed an unconfirmed victory. On 6 September, on a lone sortie, Adjt E.Roobaert flew over the German airbase at Handzaeme, where he stunted for nearly an hour, all the time being shelled. During the same month he took off several times for balloon-strafing, but in vain. All his aircraft carried the name Fox-Trot.

Adjt E.Roobaert was killed during a test flight on 19 December 1916 when the engine of his Nieuport failed, Roobaert fell into the sea 1 mile off Zuydcoote-Bray Dunes. He was posthumously awarded the Chevalier de l'Ordre de la Couronne and Croix de Guerre. Roobaert flew 110 sorties and participated in 9 aerial combats.

	1916							
_*	22 Jun	LVG C	N12	1	Staden	08.30	OOC

* with Capt F.Jacquet/Lt L.Robin.

SIRAUT (Baron) Maurice Emile Albert Marie   Adjudant   5,10

Born at Ghlin, near Mons, on 4 December 1894, the 1m 70 tall Siraut volunteered on 18 August 1914 at the Transport Corps of the 5me Division d'Armée. He obtained a transfer to the Aviation Militaire on 31 October 1914 and went to Etampes where he stayed until 28 January 1917. On that day he joined the 5me Escadrille, flying Nieuport scouts, becoming a 1er Sergent on April 8. He was wounded in combat on 30 April in a fight against four scouts, being claimed by Ltn z S Theo Osterkamp, MFJ I for his first victory of an eventual 32. On 10 May he was again wounded, this time by shrapnel fire. Siraut reached the rank of Adjudant on 19 August 1917. When he attacked a two-seater on 12 April 1918, the latter had to abandon the fight and dived out of control, leaving a dark smoke trail. The fight, however, occurred behind the German lines and could not be confirmed by ground troops. Four days later he was cited for flying over 150 hours above the enemy lines with great skill. Siraut was luckier in his next combat. He attacked a DFW two-seater at 5,000 m and shot it down in flames. Siraut was also one of those Belgian pilots who were attacked by British aircraft. On 9 June during a sortie with S/Lt L.de Chestret and Adjt R.De Leener, they were attacked by two Bristol fighters over Houthulst Forest. On a sortie three days later with Adjt E.Weekers, both men were attacked by five Albatros scouts. The Belgian airmen were not at all impressed and although outnumbered turned and attacked an Albatros themselves; this action took the Germans by surprise and they left the scene. Adjt Siraut saw his last combat on 3 November when he attacked a two-seater which dived into the clouds. 27 aerial combats were fought during 244 sorties. Siraut was made a Chevalier de l'Ordre de Leopold I with Palme, Chevalier de l'Ordre de la Couronne and decorated with the Croix de Guerre with 4 Palmes, Médaille de l'Yser, Médaille de la Victoire, Médaille Commémorative 1914-18, six Chevrons de front and one Chevron de blessure. He also was awarded the French Croix de Guerre avec Etoile de bronze.

He was commissioned after the war, on 6 January 1919 and went on the Réserve list as a Lieutenant in September 1921. On the eve of the Second World War, Siraut was again called to duty on 26 August 1939 and taken prisoner at Lombardzijde on 28 May 1940, but released on 11 October 1941. After the war he retired on 31 December 1946. Widower Baron Maurice Siraut died at Leuze, Province of Hainnaut, on 25 January 1951.

	1918							
_	12 Apr	C	Spad	10	Merckem	09.25	OOC
1*	8 May	DFW C	Spad	10	Linde	09.20	DES (f)
_**	1 Jun	C	Spad	10	Houthulst	12.45	FTL

* Uffz Paul Fritz/Ltn Ulrich Haupt, FAA 240, kia. ** with S/Lt E.Desclée and S/Lt R.De Leener.

THIEFFRY Edmond   Sous-Lieutenant   4,5

Born 28 September 1892 at Etterbeek near Brussels, he became a lawyer a few days before the outbreak of the war and became a PoW early on. He managed to escape on a motorbike through Holland and got back to the Yser front. He received his military brevet in Etampes on 21 September 1915. A fearless pilot, he crashed nearly every plane he flew and therefore the Commander persuaded him to transfer to a single-seater unit. This unit (the 5me Escadrille de Chasse) saw him arrive on 11 December 1916. On 24 January 1917 he overflew Brussels throwing some leaflets for his fiancée and over his old school. His Nieuport was baptised, like Sous-Lieutenant Hanciau's Nieuport 'Soit !', the wheel covers, however, were decorated with

Thieffry's personal markings: white wheel covers with a red band. This was repeated on the top of the fuselage, just aft of the cockpit. It is, however, possible that the Nieuport used by Thieffry was Hanciau's former aircraft because the word 'Soit !' showed less clearly.

On the 3rd of July he became the first Belgian to score a double; two Albatros scouts belonging to the Marinefeld-Jagstaffel 1 within two minutes. For this action he was commissioned on 24 July while being made a Chevalier de l'Ordre Leopold and decorated with the Croix de Guerre. On an evening sortie on 31 August, he was engaged with two scouts at 19.10 west of Dixmude. One of the scouts, flown by Ltn Karl Hammes, Jasta 35b, outmanoeuvred and hit Thieffry's Spad and the latter was forced to land close to the Belgian front-line. This was Hammes' first of an eventual four victories. Thieffry's Spad #Sp1 was destroyed, but Thieffry came out of it unscatched.

Thieffry became the only ace of the 5me Escadrille de Chasse which wore the Comet as its sign. After 160 OP's and 53 combats, Thieffry was again shot down on 23 February 1918 whilst attacking a two-seater. Thieffry waited too long to open fire and the German got in a burst at the Belgian Spad which was seen to spin down over Woumen behind the German lines. His Spad was credited to Gefreiter Lunecke/Leutnant Sanbold of FA227. After several weeks it became clear that Thieffry was still alive and being treated in a Ghent Hospital, then in Stettin and Karlsruhe. There he escaped on 13 April 1918 but was recaptured in the Black Forest ten days later, being interned at Bad Aibling. From there he was brought to Ingolstadt at Fort Orft, Fort X and Fort 8 where he stayed till 27 November. He then left on his own and went to Switzerland and France arriving back in Brussels on 6 December 1918. On 18 December he took up civilian life again and became a lawyer and a politician in his hometown. He was still in love with flying and on 12 February 1925 he started with pilot Leopold Roger and mechanic Jef De Bruycker for the first flight to the Belgian Congo on board the Handley-Page W8F Princesse Marie José, a Sabena aircraft. 51 days later he arrived at Leopoldville. He undertook more flights which were not all a real success. Therefore he took the boat to the Congo for some liaison flights in that country. On one such flight he died on 11 April 1929. The plane was caught in a tropical storm and flung to the ground. Pilot Gaston Julien and Edmond Thieffry were both killed and mechanic, Eugene Gastuche, was the only survivor. The crash occurred 150 km from Albertville. For his work in the Congo he was made an Officier de l'Ordre Leopold I. Thieffry's wife was left with five young children.

	1917							
1	15 Mar	C	Nieup	5	—	17.00-18.00	DES	
2	23 Mar	C	Nieup	5	Ghistelles	15.35-17.30	DES	
_	24 Apr	C	Nieup	5	Nieuport	07.00-08.05	OOC	
_	26 Apr	Alb DIII	Nieup	5	Houthulst Forest	16.35-17.50	OOC	
3	12 May	C	Nieup	5	Houthulst Forest	07.00	DES	
4*	14 Jun	Alb DIII	Nieup	5	Westende	20.30	DES	
5**	3 Jul	Alb DIII	Nieup	5	n Dixmude	13.30	DES	
6**	3 Jul	Alb DIII	Nieup	5	n Dixmude	13.32	DES	
_***	10 Jul	Gotha	Nieup	5	Houthulst Forest	19.55	OOC	
7	16 Aug	Alb C	Spad	5	Gheluvelt	09.15	DES	
_	18 Aug	C	Spad	5	Westende	10.50	DES	
8#	22 Aug	D	Spad	5	Beerst	10.15	DES	
9##	26 Aug	EA	Spad	5	Slype	19.40	DES	
10###	16 Oct	D	Spad	5	Merckem	11.40	DES	
_	9 Nov	C	Spad	5	Oostkerke	09.30	OOC	

* possibly Vzflgmstr Kurt Lichterz, MFJ I, kia. Thieffry crash-landed himself after this victory at Steenkerke. ** One of these was Ltn z S Kurt Cruger, MFJI, kia. *** possibly Ltn dR Max Roselmüller of Kampfgeschwader III, Staffel 16, OHL, kia. # this was Flgmt Luitjen Luitjens, MFJI, kia. ## Uffz Carl Conradt, Jasta 17, kia. ### single-handed he attacked a formation of six scouts and claimed one of them. Possibly Uffz Hermann Huth, Jasta 36, kia.

TYCK Jules Ghislain Jacques   Sous-Lieutenant   3,1

Born at Antwerp on 26 April 1889 he engaged as a volunteer on 1 August 1914 with the Escadrille of Blériot monoplanes, consisting of civilian-pilots. Jules Tyck was one of those pre-war pilots who received his brevet (nr.8) on 7 May 1910. With this Escadrille of monoplanes, Tyck, a close friend to Lieutenant J.Olieslagers, distinguished himself repeatedly in his personal aircraft. On 20 August, however, his Blériot monoplane was totally worn out and he had to abandon it to fly two-seaters. On 25 September he was forced to land at Kontich, near Antwerp and crashed his aircraft. Jules Tyck was commissioned on 6 May 1915 after being the first pilot to fly protection flights from February 1915 onwards. He crashed two more aircraft during 1915 (31 July and 6 September). When the Grand Quartier-Général (GQG) decided to give the Aviation Militaire a few pilots who were to fly only protection/offensive patrols, Jules Tyck was one of those six airmen chosen, thus becoming one of the first specified fighter pilots in the Aviation Militaire Belge. On 14 February 1916 he was transferred to the 1ère Escadrille de Chasse and became the very first fighter pilot of this Escadrille to chase a German aircraft. Two days later he was the first man of the unit to have an aerial combat, but was forced to abandon the attack when his gun jammed. On 20 April 1916, however, he asked to be withdrawn from the army and this took place on 30 April. It turned out that Tyck was so exhausted he could not cope with the strain. Sous-Lieutenant Tyck had flown 106 sorties and participated in 14 aerial combats during which one probable victory was claimed.

For his short stay at the front he was made a Chevalier de l'Ordre de Leopold II and was decorated with the Croix de Guerre. He also obtained two Chevrons de front. Tyck moved to France, where he became ill and subsequently died at Hompnes on 21 October 1924, only 35 years old.

	1915							
_*	30 Nov	EA	N10	3	Furnes	11.15	OOC

* with S/Lt J.Olieslagers and Adjt C.Kervyn de Lettenhove/S/Lt R.d'Hendecourt. The aircraft was able to reach its own lines.

VAN COTTHEM Jean Albert   Sous-Lieutenant   1,Parc d'Aviation,9

Born at Okegem (West-Flanders) on 31 December 1890, Albert, as he was known, joined the army as a recruit with the Carabiniers Régiment from June 1910 till March 1912. In December 1913, after a reorganisation, he was attached to the 1er Battalion Carabiniers-cyclistes. With this unit he went to war, being mobilised on 28 July 1914, and was promoted a Caporal in September. On 4 June 1915 his request to join the Aviation Militaire was granted and after qualifying, Van Cotthem joined the 1ère Escadrille de Chasse in March 1916. Here he made his first flight on the 23rd, and on 31 March flew his first offensive patrol with veteran 1er Sergent J.Goethals. Before the year came to an end Van Cotthem had reached the rank of Adjudant. On 23 March 1917 he was involved in a fight with four scouts over enemy territory. His Nieuport was hit in the fuel tank, but Van Cotthem managed to reach Belgian lines where he crash-landed. He was the victim of Hptm Gustav Stenzel, Staffelführer of Jasta 8, for the latter's third victory. Van Cotthem was wounded on this occasion and awarded the Croix de Guerre. After he was injured a second time in December, he became a test pilot at the Parc d'Aviation at Calais where he was commissioned on 27 January 1918. He did not like this job and sometimes he was seen as far as the Belgian front-lines, 'testing' his aircraft. On one such occasion, on 18 March, he again flew to the front-lines when he spotted a Rumpler two-seater. With his machine guns loaded, he went straight for the enemy and forced him to land behind Belgian lines, where the two airmen were captured after they had destroyed their aircraft. After several attempts he was posted back to the front on 15 September, where he joined the 9me Escadrille de Chasse. His first patrol occurred on 28 September, during the liberation offensive of the Belgian Army, but did not fly in October, nor November for some unknown reason. During the war Van Cotthem had flown 80 offensive patrols during which he was engaged in nine combats.

S/Lt A.Van Cotthem was made a Chevalier de l'Ordre de la Couronne with Palme and received a Palme to his Croix de Guerre gained in 1917, Médaille de l'Yser, Médaille de la Victoire, Médaille Commémorative 1914-18, obtained eight Chevrons de front and was cited twice.

After the war Van Cotthem went onto the Réserve list in June 1921 and became a major flyer of private aircraft. He also became an instructor at Jacquet's Pilot School at Gosselies. An

International distance record stood against his name as well for several years. He retired from the Réserve list on 31 December 1944 as a Capitaine de Réserve and was promoted a Major Honoraire in March 1949. He died on 20 September 1962.

	1918						
1	18 Mar	Rumpler C	—	Parc d'Aviat.		—	— CAPT

van der VOORDT Jean Jules Georges Marie   Adjudant   11

Born at Antwerp on 15 December 1895, 'Charmant' van der Voordt presented himself as a lorry driver on 25 September 1914 and, after the fall of Antwerp, he escaped on 5 or 6 October to England. Here he volunteered on 15 February 1915 and was attached as a lorry driver at the Military Hospital l'Océan at La Panne on the same date. On 14 August 1917 van der Voordt was sent to Etampes as a student pilot and qualified as a pilot on 28 September. On 16 April 1918 he was sent to Calais where the Ecole d'Acrobatie was stationed and he was finally posted to the 11me Escadrille de Chasse on 5 May. At the Ecole d'Aviation, however, van der Voordt received his first citation: whilst flying a Maurice Farman two-seater at 4,000 m on 12 April 1918, the old two-seater suddenly fell into a spin with its inexperienced pilot and without an instructor! Charmant, however, stayed cool and got out of the spin, to land safely at the airfield. He flew on his first combat flight well behind his own lines on 17 May 1918 with two other novice pilots, Sgts R.Mulders and L.Cremers. His first offensive patrol occurred three days later as a wingman to Adjt R.Rondeau. One day later he flew on a lone sortie. Van der Voordt was engaged in his first aerial combat on 7 June when he was attacked by a Fokker scout. This German was not at all impressed by the fact that he was greatly outnumbered, for he attacked single-handed a patrol of six scouts. On the 24th of June, van der Voordt received a new Sopwith Camel with which he saw out the war. On 25 August he was promoted a 1er Sergent Major and on the 22nd he threw some 9,000 leaflets over Staden.

After claiming a possible victory in September, he was credited with shooting down a Fokker DVII in mid-October. The fact that it occurred in a dogfight between five Belgian Spads and three Belgian Sopwith Camels on one side and 12 to 15 Fokkers on the other side, and that after the loss of that particular Fokker, the others abandoned the fight, could mean that this probably was the Fokker flown by Ltn z S Reinhold Poss, an 11-victory ace and Staffelführer of Marine-Feldjasta IV, who was taken prisoner after being shot down by a Sopwith Camel. Adjt C.de Montigny of 10me Escadrille also claimed a Fokker after he was mortally wounded. By the end of the month van der Voordt was promoted to Adjudant. 17 aerial combats were fought in October out of the 24 he had in 115 offensive patrols, during 179 hrs 30 min of operational flying.

Van der Voordt was decorated with the Croix de Guerre avec 2 Palmes, Médaille de l'Yser, Médaille du Volontaire Combattant 1914-18 and French Croix de Guerre. He also obtained three citations and seven Chevrons de front. He was demobilised on 19 August 1919 became an exchange broker after the war and was one of the founder members of the Antwerp Aviation Club of which he became the Chairman. Over the years, he always told everyone that neither he nor any of his companions were the biggest heroes of the war, but rather the Officers, NCO's and soldiers living and fighting in the trenches! They endured a four-year hardship never experienced before in the history of mankind and he, as a pilot, only faced danger when flying. Jean van der Voordt died at his home at Hove near Antwerp on 5 August 1977, aged 81.

	1918							
_*	23 Sep	C	Camel	11	Middelkerke	07.05	FTL
1**	15 Oct	Fok DVII	Camel	11	N.Roulers	07.20	DES

* with Adjt R.Rondeau and Sgt M.Martin. ** this was possibly Ltn z S R.Poss (11 vict), Staffelführer of MFJ IV and taken PoW. His citation mentioned 'devoted fighter pilot who downed a hostile aircraft on 15 October 1918.'

VERBESSEM Carlos Albert   1er Sergent Major   1

Born at Ghent on 5 October 1891, he was an infantry recruit from the first day of the war, serving with the 2me Régiment de Ligne. He stayed with this regiment until 15 May 1915, when he received his transfer to the Compagnie des Projecteurs (searchlights) of the 4me Division d'Armée. Here he stayed until December 1915. On 24 April 1916 he managed a transfer to the Aviation Militaire as a student pilot at Etampes after he had qualified at Hendon on 16 April 1916. After receiving his wings on 6 April 1917 he was posted to the 1ère Escadrille de Chasse on June 7th, where he became a wingman to S/Lt Jan Olieslagers. On his first offensive patrol, he witnessed Olieslagers' 4th confirmed victory when the latter shot down a Fokker in flames. Verbessem turned out to be a very good pilot, but on 19 December 1917 was mortally wounded by a piece of shrapnel. He managed, however, to land his Nieuport, which carried a green triangle, at Wulveringhem without crashing it. Before this happened, Verbessem attacked a two-seater over Kortewilde at 13.00, but broke off the fight; perhaps it was then that he was hit. Verbessem flew 100 sorties and fought 23 combats.

1er Sergent Major C.Verbessem was posthumously made a Chevalier de l'Ordre de Leopold II and received the Croix de Guerre with Palme, Médaille de l'Yser and Croix du Feu.

	1917						
_*	15 Jun	D	Nieup	1	Keyem	11.15	DES(f)

* shared with S/Lt J.Olieslagers and 1SgtMaj A.de Meulemeester, the former being credited. Vfw Richard Schipfer, Kaghol 4, kia.

VERHOUSTRAETEN Armand Emmanuel Marie   1er Sergent Major   1

Born at Antwerp on 19 December 1890, he volunteered during the first days of hostilities and was attached to the Aviation Militaire, serving as a recruit with the 3me Escadrille. He was sent to the Pilot School at Hendon on 1 June 1916 where he qualified on 31 August 1916. After receiving his wings on 6 April 1917, he was posted to the 1ère Escadrille de Chasse on 1 August. Five months later, however, 1Sgt Maj Verhoustraeten was killed by machine-gun fire from the German trenches.

On 7 December, a very cold and misty day without air-activity, the front-line troops signalled a two-seater which was strafing front-line trenches. Two men were called for an intervention against the hostile aircraft. Adjt P.Dubois and Verhoustraeten were the first two volunteers who took off at 14.10. When both men arrived, it appeared that their prey had already gone. When Verhoustraeten turned to the German front-lines, he flew too close to the ground and was hit by ground fire. His Nieuport N23 crashed in flooded no-man's land, close to Dixmude.

1er Sergent Major A.Verhoustraeten had flown 60 sorties and fought 16 combats and was made a Chevalier de l'Ordre de Leopold and decorated with the Croix de Guerre.

VUYLSTEKE Joseph Marie Victor   1er Sergent Major   4,9-11

This subaltern was born at Menin, 7 October 1895. He joined the 2me Régiment de Volontaires at Bruges on 2 August 1914 and after training he was sent to the 3me Régt de Ligne on 23 October to take part in the last week of the Battle of the Yser. After a few transfers to other units, he was sent to the Aviation Militaire on 21 January 1918. After gaining his flying brevet at Juvisy, France, on 27 March 1918, he received his wings on 13 August. 'Steke', as he was known, was first posted to the 4me Escadrille on 8 September and was engaged in the combat in which the crew Adjt Gisseleire/S/Lt Roland were killed on 3 October. He was posted to the Groupe de Chasse on 16 October, as a substitute for the loss of Lt Willy Coppens two days before, where Vuylsteke flew his first offensive patrol on the 22nd. Steke only flew 15 sorties, but was engaged in another five aerial combats, four of them attacks on observation balloons. One was destroyed for which he received the Croix de Guerre with Palme, and on another occasion his machine guns jammed. When he carried out his last attack, on the balloon north-east of Ghent, he was intercepted by four Fokker scouts. His Hanriot, #HD68, was named Butterfly, and bore 11me Escadrille's paper bird insignia, although all his patrols were flown in company with 9me Escadrille. Vuylsteke was awarded another Palme and Lions to his Croix de Guerre, Médaille de l'Yser, Médaille du Volontaire Combattant 1914-18, Médaille de la Victoire, Médaille

Commémorative 1914-18, eight Chevrons de front and the British Distinguished Flying Medal. In the years between the wars Vuylsteke was also made a Grand Officier de l'Ordre de Leopold II, Chevalier de l'Ordre de Leopold with Palme, Chevalier de l'Ordre de la Couronne and received the Croix du Feu.

Vuylsteke stayed in the army, reached the rank of Major and was serving at the Bureau du Service de l'Aéronautique at the Ministry of Defence at the time World War II began. After the capitulation of the Army, he joined three different Resistance-groups and on 3 September 1944 he led a group of tanks in hot pursuit as the enemy retreated towards Germany. For his feats during WWII he was made an Officier de la Légion d'Honneur and was decorated with the Croix de Guerre Française with Palme and became a Honorary Member of the Order of the British Empire with the following citation: *This officer rendered distinguished service with clandestine organisations during the enemy occupation of Belgium. After the liberation of the country, he directed the Belgian Army Information Service in close liaison with the Allied Authorities, thus contributing largely to the safeguarding, and security of the armies and their lines of communication.* He was also awarded the Yugoslavian Order of St-Sava on 23 January 1946. After WWII he again volunteered on 21 January 1945 and rose to the rank of Lieutenant-Colonel. Vuylsteke died at Ixelles on 21 May 1950.

	1918		HD					
1*	1 Nov	balloon	#68	11	Kaprijke	12.00	DES

* Gefr Hermann Wagner, Feld.Luftschiffer Abt. 47, born 26/8/1891, kia.

WAROUX Fernand Armand Joseph Hubert   1er Sergent Major   11

Born at Liège on 20 October 1894, Waroux was a volunteer, reaching the Centre d'Instruction on 1 April 1915 from where he was posted to the 2me Régt Grenadiers on 28 July. He was hospitalised from 25 June 1916 until 7 November and on 8 November Waroux was posted to the 1er Régt Grenadiers. Here he stayed till 20 December 1917 and joined the Aviation Militaire next day, qualifying at Etampes on 22 February 1918 and receiving his wings on 31 July. He was posted to the 11me Escadrille de Chasse on 8 September. The first flights were flown on the 13th and the following day saw the first offensive patrol in the pouring rain as a wingman to Lt E.Wouters. Waroux flew 42 sorties in which he was involved in eight aerial fights.

Waroux was decorated with the Ordre de la Couronne with Palme d'Or, Chevalier de l'Ordre de Leopold II, Croix Militaire 1ère & 2me classe, Croix de Guerre with Palme, Croix du Feu, Croix Civique 1ère classe, Médaille du Volontaire Combattant 1914-18, Médaille de la Victoire, Médaille Commémorative 1914-18, and the Serbian Silver Medal for Valour. He was demobilised as an Adjudant on 8 March 1919 and became a Medical delegate after he had worked with SABCA (Belgian aircraft construction company). A devoted tennis player, he also liked long walks with his dog into the beautiful countryside around his home.
He died at Uccle, Brussels, on 22 September 1977 of a cardiac arrest when his pace maker failed. Waroux left a small, unreadable, diary of his WWI feats to the Brussels Army Museum.

WEEKERS Edmond Isabelle   Adjudant   5,10

Born at Malines (Province of Antwerp) on 30 March 1886, Weekers was a surveyor, owning his own company. When war swept over Europe in August 1914, he volunteered at the Réserve Motor Pool and became a motorbike driver where he was promoted a Sergent. He obtained a transfer to the Aviation Militaire on 27 February 1917 and he qualified on 26 June at Etampes. Three months later he was assigned to the 5me Escadrille de Chasse where he was promoted to 1er Sergent Major in January 1918. His first OP was flown on 29 September and the first combat occurred on 31 October, together with Adjt A.de Meulemeester and 1Sgt Maj G.Kervyn de Lettenhove versus 6 Albatros scouts. His second attack was made on 13 November. This time he attacked a Gotha bomber and on the fourth attack, the bomber fell out of control over Nieuport. Weekers finally reached the rank of Adjudant on 26 March. Edmond Weekers scored another two probable victories, the first of these on 23 May 1918 with S/Lt J.Goethals when a two-seater was forced to land. For the second, one week later, together with Adjt Georges Medaets, he attacked an observation balloon. Weekers dived behind Medaets and when he started to fire, the balloon began to burn. However, it was concluded that Medaets had set the balloon on fire, so Weekers was not credited. When he was out on a lone sortie on 12 June, he was surprised by five Albatros scouts over Dixmude. Bearing in mind that attack was the best defence, Weekers turned his Spad and attacked one of his opponents. Disappointingly the Germans quickly abandoned the scene. Twice he fired at a runaway balloon, the first time on 26 June at 5,100 m altitude and secondly on 1 September. This British balloon was set on fire at 4,500 m. On the Belgian national holiday, 21 July, Weekers flew over the German lines from Ypres, over Roulers and Ghistelles to Ostende dropping some 2,000 photographs of the Belgian King and Queen. Adjt Weekers was severely wounded on 9 October, hit by a bullet fired from the ground, whilst attacking a two-seater at very low altitude and did not see further action. He had flown 243 sorties and participated in 37 aerial combats.

Adjt E.Weekers was made a Chevalier de l'Ordre de Leopold, Chevalier de l'Ordre de la Couronne, Chevalier de l'Ordre de Leopold II and was decorated with the Croix de Guerre with Palme, Médaille de l'Yser, Médaille du Volontaire Combattant 1914-18, Médaille de la Victoire, Médaille Commémorative 1914-18, eight Chevrons de front and one Chevrons de blessure, as well as the French Médaille Militaire and Croix de Guerre. He was commissioned onto the Reserve list on 29 December 1920 and finally reached the rank of Major. He was also a British Merchant Naval Officer on foreign trade routes.

During the 1940 Campaign, Major E.Weekers commanded the 3/I/3 (reconnaissance and bombing) Squadron. After the capitulation he took up civilian life again but was arrested at Liège on 19 May 1942. He was liberated, however, due to his age (57), on 19 October 1943.

	1917							
_*	13 Nov	Gotha	Spad	5	Nieuport	10.10-11.55	OOC
	1918							
_**	23 May	C	Spad	10	Houthulst	07.40	FTL
_***	30 May	balloon	Spad	10	—	15.20	DES

* Kampfgeschwader 1, Staffel IV lost Uffz Franz Jordan on this day. ** with S/Lt J.Goethals. This was possibly Flg Max Thomas/Ltn dR Rudolf Giesecke of Bomb.Geschw. 5, Staffel 6, kia. *** only credited to Adjt G.Medaets.

WOUTERS Jean Armand Charles   Adjudant   5,10

Charles as he was known, and brother of Louis (see below) was born at Antwerp on 27 April 1895 and became a professional soldier on 5 August 1913, joining the Artillerie de Fortresse at his hometown. Four months later he was posted to the Artillerie de Fortresse at Liège, being promoted to Brigadier (Caporal) on 26 March 1914 and, on the day of the German invasion, to Maréchal-des-Logis. He was one of the lucky few to survive the siege guns and took part in the withdrawal of the Belgian Army. He was, however, interned in Holland on 10 October, but managed to escape to rejoin his unit, 4me Régt Chasseurs à Pied, now on the Yser front, on 22 March 1915. One month later he was wounded in action and hospitalised at Cherbourg. He was posted to the 39me Batterie, 3me Régt Artillerie, 3me Division d'Armée on 22 April 1916 and in December he was again wounded in action, hit by shrapnel splinters at Dixmude, for which he obtained a Chevron de blessure. On 2 May 1917 he was made a soldier at his own request and two days later was sent to the Aviation Militaire. Wouters qualified as a pilot at Etampes on 24 May 1917 and received his wings on 27 July being promoted to Caporal four days later. On 13 December he was assigned to the Parc d'Aviation in Calais and on the 23rd he was promoted to Sergent. He was posted to the 5me Escadrille on 7 January 1918 and the first OP was flown three days later. Promotion to 1er Sergent occurred on 24 February and to 1er Sergent Major on 21 April. Meanwhile he crashed his Spad on 12 April at Oostduynkerke due to engine failure and later in the day was engaged in his first aerial combat when he was attacked by two Fokkers over Tervaete without success. On 23 April he flew a ground-strafing mission between Clercken and Woumen. Promotion to Adjudant occurred on 23 June. On 6 October, day J+6 of the Belgian Liberation Offensive, he was hit by shrapnel fire but was able to land his Spad safe behind Allied lines. Wouters too was involved in the biggest dogfight of the Aviation Militaire Belge; on 15 October when eight Belgian fighters met 15 Fokkers, probably belonging to the

Marinefeld-Jagdgruppe. Three days later he flew his last sortie. Altogether, Wouters was engaged in six combats during 132 OP's.

Charles Wouters was made a Chevalier de l'Ordre de la Couronne with Palme, Chevalier de l'Ordre de Leopold II and received the Décoration Militaire 1ère classe, Croix de Guerre, Médaille de la Victoire, Médaille Commémorative 1914-18 and obtained seven Chevrons de front.

On 8 August 1919 he engaged for another year and rose to the rank of Lieutenant in the Réserves. Wouters was a Capitaine de Réserve at the outbreak of World War II, being captured after the capitulation on 28 May 1940 and recalled to duty on 27 January 1945 at the Mission Militaire Belge. Eight months later he was promoted a Capitaine-Commandant. Wouters was pensioned out of the service on 17 January 1946 and promoted to Major de Réserve in 1947.

WOUTERS Louis François Emile   Lieutenant   I,3,11

Born at Antwerp on 30 August 1892 and brother of Charles, Emile as he was known, volunteered for a military career on 22 September 1911 and was assigned to the 1er Régiment Chasseurs à Cheval, where he was made a Maréchal-des-Logis on 1 March 1913. Due to a reorganisation, Wouters was posted to the 4me Régiment Chasseurs à Cheval on 16 December. He went to war with this unit and was commissioned an Officier Auxiliaire de Cavalerie on 27 October 1914, during the Battle of the Yser. Wouters, however, managed a transfer to the Aviation Militaire in 1915 and teamed up with Capt Jules Jaumotte. This team became famous with the Allied armies for their successful photo-operations and the quality of their pictures. For these feats both were awarded the Croix de Guerre and made a Chevalier de la Légion d'Honneur. Wouters saw his first aerial combat with Lt Fernand Jacquet on 6 November 1915. It was against four hostile aircraft. Although they could only attack one enemy, their own Farman was riddled with bullets. Late 1916, October 15th, Wouters moved to the 3me Escadrille, together with his team-mate Capt Jaumotte. As an observer, Wouters had flown 14 OP's and was involved in five aerial combats. Early 1918, he was sent to Juvisy as a student pilot and after qualifying, he was assigned to the 11me Escadrille in July flying his first OP on the 16th. On 3 August he was engaged in his first combat as a scout pilot but was attacked by two Fokkers at 09.10 over Nieuport at 4,000 m. After spinning to 700 m the attack was countered. Wouters mostly took the air with either Cdt Hiernaux, Adjt Lamarche or Sgts Cremers and Declercq and flew 66 OP's. Ten combats were fought and one of them was a seven vs seven situation south of Ursel on 22 October, at 10.30. On one occasion his guns jammed during an attack.

Lt Wouters was made a Chevalier de l'Ordre de la Couronne and received a supplementary Palme to his Croix de Guerre, Médaille de l'Yser, eight Chevrons de fronts, together with the French Croix de Guerre with Palme. Italy made him a Chevalier de l'Ordre de la Couronne and he was also decorated with the British Military Cross.

After hostilities, Wouters was assigned to the Inter-Allied Control Mission in occupied Germany on 7 January 1920 and was demobilised on 8 June 1921, being promoted a Capitaine a year later. He went to the Réserves and reached the rank of Major on 26 December 1931. Two years later, Wouters became the successor of Capt Willy Coppens de Houthulst as the Military Attaché in London, a post he held until the armistice of the Second World War. By then he had attained the rank of Air Commodore (Brigade General), CB, CBE, MC.

For his military career he was made a Commandeur de l'Ordre de la Couronne, Commandeur de l'Ordre de Leopold II, Officier de l'Ordre Leopold and was decorated with the Croix Militaire 1ère classe and 2me classe, Croix du Feu, Médaille Commémorative du Centenaire. From other countries he was made an Officier de l'Ordre de la Légion d'Honneur and was decorated with the Commemoration Medal of the Coronation of King Georges IV and Queen Elizabeth II, CBE (Commander of the Order of the British Empire), CB (Commander of the Most Honourable Order of the Bath), Commandeur de l'Ordre de la Couronne de Chêne and Croix de Guerre 1940 Luxembourgoise. Wouters retired after the war and died on 26 December 1964, aged 72.

APPENDIX I

THE STRUCTURE OF THE AVIATION MILITAIRE BELGE IN AUGUST 1914

Escadrille	Airfield	CO	Aircraft
I	Ans(Liège)	Lt A.Demanet	four M.Farman
II	Belgrade (Namur)	Lt J.Soumoy	four M.Farman
III	Louvain	Capt F.Deschamps	four M.Farman
IV	Wilryck	Cdt T.Wahis	four M.Farman

REORGANIZATION OF THE AVIATION MILITAIRE BELGE IN FEBRUARY 1915

Escadrille	Airfield	CO	Aircraft
I	Coxyde	Lt A.Demanet	M.Farman
II	Coxyde	Lt F.Isserentant	M.Farman
III	Coxyde	Cdt R.Dhanis	Voisin 3 LB
IV	Houthem	Capt J.Hagemans	M.Farman
V	Houthem	Lt E.Moulin	M.Farman

SITUATION IN JUNE 1915

Escadrille	Airfield	CO	Aircraft
I	Coxyde	Capt A.Demanet	five M.Farman & one Nieuport N10
II	Coxyde	Lt F.Isserentant	four M.Farman & two Nieuport N10
III	Coxyde	Cdt R.Dhanis	six Voisin 3 LB
IV	Houthem	Capt J.Hagemans	four M.Farman & one Nieuport N10
V	Houthem	Lt E.Moulin	five M.Farman
hydravions	Calais	Capt A.De Bueger	one M.Farman

FROM FEBRUARY 1916

Escadrille	Airfield	CO	Aircraft
1	Les Moeres	Capt F.Jacquet	Nieuport
2	Coxyde	Cdt F.Isserentant	M.Farman
3	Coxyde	Cdt R.Dhanis	M.Farman
4	Houthem	Capt J.Hagemans	M.Farman
5	Houthem	Cdt E.Moulin	M.Farman
6	Houthem	Capt R.Hedo	BE2c

REORGANIZATION MARCH 1918

Escadrille	Airfield	Duty	CO	Aircraft
1	Houthem	maintenance	Cdt Michaux	none
2	Les Moeres	observation	Cdt F.Isserentant	Bréguet XIV
3	Les Moeres	observation	Cdt R.Dhanis	Bréguet XIV
4	Hondschoote (France)	observation	Cdt P.Richard	Spad XI
5	Houthem	observation	Cdt S.Hugon	Spad XI

6	Houthem	observation	Cdt R.Desmet	Spad XI
7	Houthem	photo-recce	Cdt J.Jaumotte	Spad XI
8	Coudekerke (France)	bombing & night recce	??	Farman & Sopw. Strutter
9	Les Moeres	pursuit	Capt W.Gallez	Hanriot
10	Les Moeres	pursuit	Cdt J.Dony	Spad VII-XIII
11	Les Moeres	pursuit	Cdt P.Hiernaux	Camel
hydravions	Calais	observation	Cdt A.De Bueger	FBA Mod H

APPENDIX II

TOP THREE PILOTS FLYING OFFENSIVE PATROLS BY THE END OF EACH MONTH FEBRUARY 1915 — NOVEMBER 1918

The numbers between brackets are the total number of OP's during the month. Note that the number of sorties during 1915 are not only OP's, but enumerate most of the other patrols as well.

1915

Month	Rank	Name	Esc	Number
February (28)	Lt	Fernand Jacquet	esc I	13
	Lt	Paul Hiernaux	esc I	8
	Lt	Paul Hanciau	esc I	3
March (103)	Lt	Fernand Jacquet	esc I	18
	Lt	Jules Dony	esc V	13
	S/Lt	Louis Robin	esc II	12
April (a total of 332 sorties)	Sgt	Pierre Braun	esc V	19
	S/Lt	Louis Robin	esc II	19
	Lt	Jules Dony	esc V	18
May (32 OP's out of 356 sorties)	Lt	Fernand Jacquet	esc I	33
	S/Lt	Romeo Verhaegen	esc I	22
	Adjt	Aimé Behaeghe	esc I	21
June (127)	S/Lt	Henri Crombez	esc IV	17
	Lt	Fernand Jacquet	esc I	17
	Lt	Leon Stellingwerff	esc II	16
July (95)	Lt	Fernand Jacquet	esc I	9
	Lt	Gustave Declercq	esc IV	6
	Sgt	Charles Kervyn	esc IV	6
August (69)	Adjt	Aimé Behaeghe	esc I	14
	Capt	Arsène Demanet	esc I	8
	Lt	Romeo Verhaegen	esc I	7
September (138)	S/Lt	Jean Olieslagers	esc II	24
	S/Lt	Roger Castiau	esc II	21
	Adjt	Aimé Behaeghe	esc I	28
October (63)	S/Lt	Henri Crombez	esc IV	17
	S/Lt	Jean Olieslagers	esc II	9
	Adjt	Aimé Behaeghe	esc I	7
November (61)	S/Lt	Jean Olieslagers	esc II	13
	S/Lt	Jules Tyck	esc III	13
	Adjt	Aimé Behaeghe	esc I	6

December	S/Lt	Jean Olieslagers	esc II	10
(68)	S/Lt	Jules Tyck	esc III	10
	Lt	Paul Hanciau	esc I	8

1916

January	S/Lt	Jules Tyck	esc III	13
(113)	S/Lt	Jean Olieslagers	esc II	11
	Adjt	Abel De Neef	esc I	10
February	S/Lt	Jules Tyck	1 esc	19
(104)	Adjt	Abel De Neef	1 esc	16
	S/Lt	Jean Olieslagers	1 esc	12
March	S/Lt	Jean Olieslagers	1 esc	21
(159)	1Sgt	Jacques Goethals	1 esc	18
	Capt	Fernand Jacquet	1 esc	17
April	S/Lt	Jean Olieslagers	1 esc	26
(118)	Sgt	Albert Van Cotthem	1 esc	21
	Capt	Fernand Jacquet	1 esc	10
May	S/Lt	Jean Olieslagers	1 esc	34
(194)	Lt	Louis Robin	1 esc	31
	Capt	Fernand Jacquet	1 esc	27
June	S/Lt	Jean Olieslagers	1 esc	17
(117)	Adjt	Egide Roobaert	1 esc	16
	Adjt	Abel De Neef	1 esc	15
July	Capt	Fernand Jacquet	1 esc	22
(166)	Lt	Louis Robin	1 esc	22
	1SgtMaj	Max Orban	1 esc	20
August	S/Lt	Jean Olieslagers	1 esc	19
(96)	Capt	Fernand Jacquet	1 esc	9
	Lt	Louis Robin	1 esc	9
September	S/Lt	Jean Olieslagers	1 esc	19
(207)	Adjt	Egide Roobaert	1 esc	18
	1SgtMaj	Charles de Munck	1 esc	15
October	Adjt	Abel De Neef	1 esc	12
(105)	Adjt	Jacques Goethals	1 esc	11
	Sgt	Andre de Meulemeester	1 esc	8
November	1SgtMaj	Pierre de Chestret	5 esc	9
(112)	1Sgt	Maurice Franchomme	5 esc	9
	Adjt	Egide Roobaert	1 esc	9

December	Sgt	Andre de Meulemeester	1 esc	11
(75)	Adjt	Abel De Neef	1 esc	10
	Capt	Paul Hiernaux	1 esc	8

1917

January	1Sgt	Andre de Meulemeester	1 esc	14
(96)	Adjt	Abel De Neef	1 esc	10
	Adjt	Charles de Munck	1 esc	9
February	1Sgt	Andre de Meulemeester	1 esc	17
(162)	Sgt	Fernand de Woot	1 esc	14
	Adjt	Edmond Thieffry	5 esc	13
March	Sgt	Gustave de Mevius	5 esc	15
(101)	1Sgt	Andre de Meulemeester	1 esc	14
	Adjt	Edmond Thieffry	5 esc	12
April	1Sgt	Andre de Meulemeester	1 esc	20
(260)	Adjt	Edmond Thieffry	5 esc	18
	Sgt	Gustave de Mevius	5 esc	17
May	1Sgt	Andre de Meulemeester	1 esc	39
(404)	Adjt	Max Orban	5 esc	28
	1Sgt	Fernand de Woot	1 esc	25
June	Adjt	Andre de Meulemeester	1 esc	23
(309)	1SgtMaj	Gusto de Mevius	1 esc	18
	Adjt	Maurice Franchomme	5 esc	18
July	1SgtMaj	Andre de Meulemeester	1 esc	29
(353)	1Sgt	Georges Kervyn	1 esc	28
	Sgt	Carlos Verbessem	1 esc	19
August	1SgtMaj	Georges Kervyn	1 esc	24
(318)	Adjt	Andre de Meulemeester	1 esc	22
	S/Lt	Edmond Thieffry	5 esc	21
September	1SgtMaj	Georges Kervyn	1 esc	25
(453)	S/Lt	Edmond Desclée	5 esc	24
	S/Lt	Max Orban	5 esc	23
October	Adjt	Andre de Meulemeester	1 esc	37
(404)	1SgtMaj	Georges Kervyn	1 esc	22
	Sgt	Edmond Weekers	5 esc	20
November	1Sgt	Leon Gerard	1 esc	23
(291)	Sgt	Edmond Weekers	5 esc	22
	Adjt	Willy Coppens	1 esc	21
December	Adjt	Georges Kervyn	1 esc	17
(187)	Sgt	Edmond Weekers	5 esc	16

	Adjt	Gusto de Mevius	1 esc	14

1918

January (286)	Adjt	Andre de Meulemeester	1 esc	29
	Sgt	Charles de Montigny	5 esc	29
	Adjt	Georges Kervyn	1 esc	23
February (238)	Adjt	Andre de Meulemeester	1 esc	20
	Adjt	Georges Kervyn	1 esc	18
	1Sgt	Gilbert Ory	1 esc	18
March (482)	Adjt	Georges Kervyn	9 esc	32
	Adjt	Andre de Meulemeester	9 esc	25
	Sgt	Charles de Montigny	10 esc	25
April (504*)	Adjt	Andre de Meulemeester	9 esc	29
	Adjt	Georges Kervyn	9 esc	22
	Lt	Louis Robin	7 esc	21
May (896**)	Lt	Louis Robin	7 esc	49
	S/Lt	Andre de Meulemeester	9 esc	37
	Adjt	Georges Kervyn	9 esc	37
June (638)	Adjt	Edmond Weekers	10 esc	35
	Adjt	Robert Rondeau	11 esc	30
	Adjt	Jacques Lamarche	11 esc	29
July (575)	1SgtMaj	Charles de Montigny	10 esc	35
	Sgt	Maurice Jamar	9 esc	31
	Adjt	Edmond Weekers	10 esc	31
August (501)	S/Lt	Andre de Meulemeester	9 esc	27
	Adjt	Charles de Montigny	10 esc	27
	Adjt	Robert Rondeau	10 esc	26
September (492)	Adjt	Charles de Montigny	10 esc	23
	S/Lt	Robert De Leener	10 esc	19
	S/Lt	Andre de Meulemeester	9 esc	19
October (754)	Adjt	Jacques Lamarche	11 esc	31
	S/Lt	Max Orban	10 esc	28
	Adjt	Robert Rondeau	11 esc	27
November (142)	Adjt	Leon Cremers	11 esc	10
	S/Lt	Robert De Leener	10 esc	7
	S/Lt	Andre de Meulemeester	9 esc	7

* 154 out of these patrols were flown by pilots from all the other units : 2me Escadrille were in possession of three scouts, 3me Escadrille and 4me Escadrille had four, 6me Escadrille had three Sopwith Camels and 7me Escadrille eight! Lt L.Robin of this latter Escadrille flew more offensive patrols than many of the real fighter pilots of the Groupe de Chasse. ** 253 OP's by recce pilots.

APPENDIX III

TOP THREE PILOTS ENGAGED IN COMBATS BY THE END OF EACH MONTH
FEBRUARY 1915 — NOVEMBER 1918

The number between brackets are the total number of combats during the month

1915

February	Adjt	Henri Crombez	esc IV	2
(14)	Sgt	Tony Orta	esc III	2
	Lt	Lucien Poot	esc III	2
March (7)	Lt	Fernand Jacquet	esc I	2
April	Lt	Florent Noirsain	esc III	4
(35)	Adjt	Tony Orta	esc III	4
	Sgt	Roger Castiau	esc II	3
May	S/Lt	Romeo Verhaegen	esc I	8
(42)	Sgt	Aimé Behaeghe	esc I	6
	Adjt	Roger Castiau	esc II	4
June	Lt	Fernand Jacquet	esc I	6
(34)	Adjt	Aimé Behaeghe	esc I	4
	S/Lt	Leon Colignon	esc I	4
July	Lt	Fernand Jacquet	esc I	3
(25)	S/Lt	Jean Olieslagers	esc II	3
August	Adjt	Aimé Behaeghe	esc I	2
(16)	Adjt	Willy de Roy	esc II	2
	Lt	Paul Hiernaux	esc I	2
September	Lt	Fernand Jacquet	esc I	6
(31)	S/Lt	Jean Olieslagers	esc II	6
	S/Lt	José Orta	esc III	3
October	Adjt	Willy de Roy	esc II	3
(25)	1Sgt	Jacques Goethals	esc V	3
	Lt	Fernand Jacquet	esc I	3
November	Lt	Fernand Jacquet	esc I	4
(22)	S/Lt	Jean Olieslagers	esc II	4
	S/Lt	Jules Tyck	esc III	4
December (7)	seven pilots with one combat			

1916

January	S/Lt	Jules Tyck	esc III	4

(32)	Sgt	Jacques Goethals	esc V	3
	Lt	Charles Coomans	esc IV	2
February	S/Lt	Jean Olieslagers	1 esc	3
(23)	S/Lt	Jules Tyck	1 esc	3
	Lt	Charles Coomans	4 esc	2
March	S/Lt	Jean Olieslagers	1 esc	6
(47)	Capt	Fernand Jacquet	1 esc	5
	Lt	Louis Robin	1 esc	4
April (8)	S/Lt	Jean Olieslagers	1 esc	2
May	Capt	Fernand Jacquet	1 esc	26
(72)	Lt	Louis Robin	1 esc	25
	1Sgt	Charles de Munck	1 esc	2
June	Capt	Fernand Jacquet	1 esc	9
(36)	Lt	Louis Robin	1 esc	9
	S/Lt	Jean Olieslagers	1 esc	5
July	Capt	Fernand Jacquet	1 esc	20
(86)	Lt	Louis Robin	1 esc	18
	S/Lt	Jean Olieslagers	1 esc	12
August	S/Lt	Jean Olieslagers	1 esc	11
(27)	Capt	Fernand Jacquet	1 esc	5
	Lt	Louis Robin	1 esc	5
September	Capt	Fernand Jacquet	1 esc	5
(20)	S/Lt	Jean Olieslagers	1 esc	5
	Lt	Louis Robin	1 esc	5
October (5)	five pilots with one combat			
November (14)	S/Lt	Jean Olieslagers	1 esc	2
December	Sgt	Andre de Meulemeester	1 esc	2
(6)	S/Lt	Jean Olieslagers	1 esc	2

1917

January (9)	1Sgt	Andre de Meulemeester	1 esc	4
February	S/Lt	Jean Olieslagers	1 esc	5
(19)	1Sgt	Andre de Meulemeester	1 esc	4
	Adjt	Charles de Munck	1 esc	2
March	1Sgt	Andre de Meulemeester	1 esc	5
(19)	Adjt	Edmond Thieffry	5 esc	4
	Sgt	Gustave de Mevius	5 esc	2

April	Adjt	Edmond Thieffry	5 esc	8
(63)	S/Lt	Edmond Desclée	5 esc	6
	Adjt	Maurice Franchomme	5 esc	6
May	1Sgt	Andre de Meulemeester	1 esc	15
(60)	Adjt	Max Orban	5 esc	5
	Adjt	Pierre de Chestret	5 esc	5
June	Adjt	Edmond Thieffry	5 esc	12
(90)	Adjt	Andre de Meulemeester	1 esc	11
	S/Lt	Max Orban	5 esc	11
July	1SgtMaj	Andre de Meulemeester	1 esc	16
(87)	S/Lt	Jacques Goethals	5 esc	10
	S/Lt	Charles Ciselet	5 esc	7
August	Adjt	Andre de Meulemeester	1 esc	14
(85)	S/Lt	Edmond Thieffry	5 esc	10
	1SgtMaj	Georges Kervyn	1 esc	7
September	S/Lt	Max Orban	5 esc	7
(69)	S/Lt	Edmond Desclée	5 esc	6
	1SgtMaj	Carlo Verbessem	1 esc	6
October	Adjt	Andre de Meulemeester	1 esc	23
(108)	Adjt	Willy Coppens	1 esc	9
	1SgtMaj	Georges Kervyn	1 esc	7
November	Adjt	Georges Kervyn	1 esc	21
(124)	Adjt	Willy Coppens	1 esc	13
	Adjt	Andre de Meulemeester	1 esc	13
December	Adjt	Georges Kervyn	1 esc	7
(26)	Adjt	Andre de Meulemeester	1 esc	4
	Adjt	Gusto de Mevius	1 esc	2

1918

January	Adjt	Andre de Meulemeester	1 esc	22
(76)	Adjt	Georges Kervyn	1 esc	18
	Adjt	Gusto de Mevius	1 esc	8
February	Adjt	Andre de Meulemeester	1 esc	10
(39)	Adjt	Georges Kervyn	1 esc	8
	Adjt	Willy Coppens	1 esc	3
March	Adjt	Andre de Meulemeester	9 esc	15
(50)	Adjt	Georges Kervyn	9 esc	8
	S/Lt	Edmond Desclée	10 esc	4

April (42)	Adjt	Andre de Meulemeester	9 esc	5
	Adjt	Georges Kervyn	9 esc	5
	S/Lt	Gusto de Mevius	9 esc	4
May (136)	S/Lt	Andre de Meulemeester	9 esc	13
	Adjt	Georges Kervyn	9 esc	13
	S/Lt	Jacques Goethals	10 esc	12
June (110)	Adjt.	Willy Coppens	9 esc	11
	Adjt	Georges Kervyn	9 esc	8
	S/Lt	Jacques Goethals	10 esc	7
July (44)	S/Lt	Willy Coppens	9 esc	7
	1SgtMaj	Charles de Montigny	10 esc	5
	Adjt	Edmond Weekers	10 esc	5
August (89)	S/Lt	Willy Coppens	9 esc	10
	S/Lt	Andre de Meulemeester	9 esc	10
	Adjt	Georges Kervyn	9 esc	10
September (62)	S/Lt	Willy Coppens	9 esc	5
	Cdt	Jules Dony	10 esc	5
	Adjt	Robert Rondeau	11 esc	5
October (198)	Adjt	Robert Rondeau	11 esc	17
	Adjt	Jean van der Voordt	11 esc	17
	Adjt	Jacques Lamarche	11 esc	11
November (30)	Lt	Louis Robin	10 esc	6
	1SgtMaj	Joseph Vuylsteke	9 esc	4
	S/Lt	Bob De Leener	10 esc	3

APPENDIX IV

THE OFFICIAL CLAIMS OF THE AVIATION MILITAIRE BELGE

1915

17 Apr	F.Jacquet/ H.Vindevoghel	1 1 }	Albatros C	Roulers	DES(f)
12 Sep	J.Olieslagers	1	Aviatik C	Oud-Stuyvekenskerke	DES

1916

20 May	F.Jacquet/ L.Robin	2 1 }	Hydravion	Nieuport	DES
17 Jun	J.Olieslagers	2	Fok DII	Pypegaele	DES
23 Jun	F.Jacquet/ L.Robin	3 2 }	Fok DII	Couckelaere	DES
30 Jul	F.Jacquet/ L.Robin	4 3 }	LVG C	Houthulst	DES
17 Nov	L de Chestret	1	Fok	—	FTL

1917

1 Feb	F.Jacquet/ L.Robin	5 4 }	Rumpler C	Lombartzijde	OOC
15 Mar	E.Thieffry	1	C	—	DES
23 Mar	E.Thieffry	2	C	Ghistelles	DES
30 Apr	A.de Meulemeester	1	C	Leke	DES
12 May	E.Thieffry	3	C	Houthulst Forest	DES
9 Jun	C.Ciselet P. de Chestret	1 1 }	Alb DIII	Bixschoote	DES
12 Jun	A.de Meulemeester G.Kervyn	2 1 }	C	Vladsloo	DES
14 Jun	J.Olieslagers	3	EA	Schoore	DES
14 Jun	E.Thieffry	4	Alb DIII	Westende	DES
15 Jun	J.Olieslagers	4	D	Keyem	DES(f)
24 Jun	J.Orta/ L.de Burlet	1 1 }	D	Zevecoote	DES
3 Jul	E.Thieffry	5	Alb DIII	n Dixmude	DES
3 Jul	E.Thieffry	6	Alb DIII	n Dixmude	DES
8 Jul	J.de Meeus/ C.Kervyn	1 1 }	EA	—	DES
10 Jul	A.de Meulemeester	3	C	Nieuport	DES
20 Jul	A.de Meulemeester	4	C	20-21 km - post of Yser river	DES
27 Jul	M.Medaeets	1	C	Pilckem	DES
16 Aug	E.Thieffry	7	Alb C	Gheluvelt	DES
20 Aug	P.Braun	1	D	Beerst	DES
21 Aug	A.de Meulemeester	5	C	Slype	DES
21 Aug	C.Kervyn	2	EA	—	DES
22 Aug	E.Thieffry	8	D	Beerst	DES
26 Aug	E.Thieffry	9	EA	Slype	DES

4 Sep	Manseron/ J.Toussaint	1 } 1	D	n Tervaete	OOC
11 Sep	M.Medaets	2	EA	Grognies	DES
16 Oct	E.Thieffry	10	D	Merckem	DES
22 Oct	G.Lallemand/ H.Cornelius	1 } 1	D	Dixmude	DES
4 Nov	A.de Meulemeester	6	Alb	Kloosterhoek	DES(f)
5 Dec	P.Braun	2	EA	Nieuport	DES

1918

21 Feb	A.de Meulemeester Capt. H.Symons (65 Sqdn)	7 } 	Alb DV	Dixmude	DES
12 Mar	P.Dubois	1	C	St-Georges	DES
17 Mar	A.de Meulemeester	8	C	Dixmude	DES
18 Mar	A.Van Cotthem	1	Rumpler C	—	CAPT
25 Apr	G.de Mevius G.Kervyn	1 } 3	Pfalz DIII	Boitshoucke	DES
25 Apr	W.Coppens W.Gallez	1 } 1	D	St-Georges	DES
3 May	A.de Meulemeester G.Kervyn	9 } 4	D	Schoorbakke	DES
3 May	J.Olieslagers	5	Fok DVII	Westende	ABG
8 May	W.Coppens	2	balloon	Zarren	DES(f)
8 May	M.Siraut	1	DFW C	Linde	DES
8 May	W.Coppens	3	balloon	Houthulst	DES(f)
15 May	W.Coppens	4	balloon	Houthulst	DES(f)
17 May	A.de Meulemeester	10	C	Houthulst	DES
19 May	W.Coppens	5	balloon	Houthulst	DES(f)
19 May	J.Olieslagers	6	Alb DV	Woumen	DES(f)
30 May	C.de Montigny	1	balloon	Leffinghe	DES(f)
30 May	G.Medaets	1	balloon	Kortewilde	DES
5 Jun	W.Coppens	6	balloon	Houthulst	DES
9 Jun	W.Coppens	7	balloon	Zonnebeke	DES
10 Jun	W.Coppens	8	balloon	Ploegsteert	DES
24 Jun	W.Coppens	9	balloon	Warneton	DES
24 Jun	W.Coppens	10	Hannover C	Ploegsteert	DES
30 Jun	W.Coppens	11	balloon	Bovekerke	DES
30 Jun	W.Coppens	12	balloon	Gheluvelt	DES
30 Jun	W.Coppens	13	balloon	Passchendaele	DES
10 Jul	M.Jamar	1	balloon	Leffinghe	DES
14 Jul	W.Coppens	14	balloon	Passchendaele	DES
16 Jul	W.Coppens	15	balloon	Bovekerke	DES
19 Jul	W.Coppens	16	balloon	Ruyterhoek	DES
20 Jul	W.Coppens	17	balloon	Houthulst	DES
22 Jul	W.Coppens	18	balloon	Gheluwe	DES
22 Jul	W.Coppens	19	balloon	Wervicq	DES
22 Jul	W.Coppens	20	balloon	Comines	DES
23 Jul	G.Medaets	2	balloon	Zarren	DES
24 Jul	W.Coppens	21	balloon	Ruyterhoek	DES
3 Aug	W.Coppens	22	balloon	Reutel	DES

10 Aug	W.Coppens	23	balloon	Leffinghe	DES
10 Aug	W.Coppens	24	balloon	Ruyterhoek	DES
10 Aug	W.Coppens	25	balloon	Leffinghe	DES
21 Aug	J.Ledure	1	balloon	Staden	DES
24 Aug	W.Coppens	26	balloon	Ploegsteert	DES
24 Aug	W.Coppens	27	balloon	Warneton	DES
31 Aug	J.Ledure	2	balloon	s Clercken	DES
3 Sep	W.Coppens	28	balloon	Ten Brielen	DES
4 Sep	W.Coppens	29	balloon	Wercken	DES
16 Sep	B.De Leener	1	balloon	Zarren	DES
27 Sep	W.Coppens	30	balloon	Leffinghe	DES
27 Sep	W.Coppens	31	balloon	Leffinghe	DES
27 Sep	R.Rondeau	1	balloon	Clercken	DES
29 Sep	E.Hage	1	balloon	Armentières	DES
29 Sep	W.Coppens	32	balloon	Leffinghe	DES
2 Oct	E.Hage	2	balloon	Quesnoy	DES
3 Oct	R.Declercq	1	C	Lichtervelde	DES
3 Oct	W.Coppens	33	balloon	Leffinghe	DES
3 Oct	A.Gisseleire/ M.Roland	1 } 1	D	—	DES
4 Oct	F.Jacquet/ M.de Crombrugghe	6 } 1	Rumpler C	Gits	DES
5 Oct	A.de Meulemeester	11	balloon	Thourout	DES
5 Oct	W.Coppens	34	balloon	Lendeleede	DES
5 Oct	W.Coppens	35	balloon	Cruypenaerde	DES
7 Oct	J.Goethals	1	C	n Dixmude	DES
9 Oct	J.Goethals	2	C	Hazewind	DES
9 Oct	R.Rondeau	2	Halb C	Cortemarck	DES
14 Oct	W.Coppens	36	balloon	Praat Bosch	DES
14 Oct	W.Coppens	37	balloon	Thourout	DES
14 Oct	E.Hage	3	balloon	Houthulst	DES
14 Oct	H.Crombez/ du Roy de Blicquy	1 } 1	Fok DVII	Snelleghem	DES
15 Oct	J.van der Voordt	1	Fok DVII	n Roulers	DES
15 Oct	C.de Montigny	2	Fok DVII	Roulers	DES
15 Oct	L.Guillon	1	Fok DVII	Sleijhaege	DES
26 Oct	L.Guillon	2	balloon	Asseneede	DES
1 Nov	J.Vuylsteke	1	balloon	Caprijke	DES
6 Nov	F.Jacquet/ M.de Crombrugghe	7 } 2	C	e Ghent	DES

Sous-officier Jean Bastin was also credited with a victory in the latter part of 1918; but unfortunately combat records of this victory are lost, so the date cannot be found.

APPENDIX V

LIST OF PROBABLE/UNCONFIRMED VICTORIES

1914

25 Sep	A.'de' Petrowski/ G.Benselin	}	Taube	St-Agatha-Berchem	FTL

1915

26 Mar	A.De Bueger/ Boschmans	}	Alb C	Woumen	FTL
20 Jun	F.Jacquet/ L.Colignon	}	EA	—	OOC
26 Jul	F.Jacquet/ L.Colignon	}	Aviatik C	Gits	FTL
7 Sep	W.de Roy/ Dreyfus	}	Aviatik C	Middelkerke	DES
22 Sep	Mallet/ Walkenaer	}	Aviatik C	Ypres/Courtrai	OOC
22 Sep	J.Olieslagers		C	Avecapelle	OOC
30 Nov	J.Olieslagers J.Tyck C.Kervyn/ R.d'Hendecourt	}	Alb C	Furnes	FTL

1916

14 Mar	J.Olieslagers		EA	Dixmude	OOC
30 Mar	J.Olieslagers		EA	Praat Bosch	OOC
21 May	C.de Munck		EA	Beerst	OOC
25 May	C.Ciselet/ A.Rolin J.de Roest/ R.d'Hendecourt	}	LVG C	Dixmude	OOC
26 May	F.Jacquet/ L.Robin	}	Aviatik C	Thourout	OOC
27 May	F.Jacquet/ L.Robin	}	Aviatik C	Couckelaere	FTL
17 Jun	C.Kervyn/ R.d'Hendecourt	}	Fok DII	Poelcapelle	OOC
22 Jun	F.Jacquet/ L.Robin	}	LVG C	Staden	FTL
25 Jun	J.Olieslagers		LVG C	Nieuwcapelle	OOC
25 Jun	J.Olieslagers		Fok DII	Dixmude	OOC
30 Jun	F.Jacquet/ L.Robin	}	Aviatik C	Handzaeme	FTL
1 Jul	A.De Neef		EA	Houthulst	FTL
1 Jul	J.Orta/ L.de Burlet	}	EA	Westende	OOC

Date	Pilot	Aircraft	Location	Result
8 Jul	F.Jacquet/ L.Robin	LVG C	Middelkerke	OOC
28 Jul	J.Olieslagers	LVG C	Handzaeme	FTL
30 Jul	J.Olieslagers	LVG C	Houthulst Forest	FTL
30 Jul	F.Jacquet/ L.Robin	LVG C	Houthulst Forest	OOC
31 Jul	J.Olieslagers	LVG C	Houthulst Forest	OOC
3 Aug	J.Olieslagers	EA	Ghistelles	FTL
28 Sep	J.Olieslagers	Alb C	Slype	FTL
13 Nov	P.de Chestret	EA	Eesen	FTL

1917

Date	Pilot	Aircraft	Location	Result
1 Feb	A.de Meulemeester	Rumpler C	Lombartzijde	FTL
7 Feb	J.Olieslagers	LVG C	Steenstraete	FTL
8 Feb	J.Olieslagers	LVG C	St-Jacques-Capelle	FTL
8 Apr	J.Callant/ A.Glibert	Alb D	Bovekerke	FTL
24 Apr	E.Thieffry	C	Nieuport	DES
26 Apr	E.Thieffry	Alb DIII	Houthulst Forest	OOC
2 May	A.de Meulemeester G.de Mevius F.de Woot J.Goethals	C	Schoore	FTL
24 May	P.de Chestret	C	Clercken	FTL
1 Jun	J.de Roest/ A.Rolin	SS DIII	Gits	OOC
14 Jun	G.Kervyn	EA	Schoore	DES
15 Jun	A.de Meulemeester C.Verbessem	D	Keyem	DES
2 Jul	J.de Roest/ L.Robin	C	Ypres	OOC
7 Jul	W.Coppens/ R.Declercq	C	Middelkerke	OOC
10 Jul	E.Thieffry	Gotha	Houthulst Forest	DES
23 Jul	A.de Meulemeester	D	Kortewilde	OOC
27 Jul	P.Braun G.Medaets	EA	s Clercken	DES
27 Jul	J.Goethals	D	Dixmude	OOC
5 Aug	A.de Meulemeester G.Kervyn	D	Tervaete	OOC
18 Aug	E.Thieffry	C	Westende	DES
19 Aug	A.de Meulemeester	D	Dixmude	OOC
19 Aug	A.de Meulemeester	D	Slype	OOC
24 Sep	P.Dubois	C	Fme Bien Acquis	OOC
24 Sep	G.Kervyn	C	Fme Bien Acquis	OOC
27 Sep	J.Goethals	Alb DV	Tervaete	OOC
30 Sep	W.Coppens A.de Meulemeester	C	Roulers	FTL

30 Sep	G.de Mevius/ R.d'Hendecourt }	D	Tervaete	OOC
1 Oct	J.Olieslagers A.de Meulemeester W.Coppens J.Goossens }	C	Beerst	OOC
18 Oct	A.de Meulemeester M.Orban }	Alb	Tervaete	OOC
18 Oct	de Robiano/ R.Verhaegen }	Alb DIII	e Woumen	FTL
22 Oct	G.Lallemand/ H.Cornelius }	D	e Dixmude	DES
28 Oct	A.de Meulemeester	D	s Keyem	OOC
4 Nov	G.Kervyn	Alb DIII	Kloosterhoek	DES
9 Nov	E.Thieffry	C	Oostkerke	OOC
13 Nov	E.Weekers	Gotha	Nieuport	OOC
17 Nov	A.de Meulemeester	Alb	Leke	OOC

1918

16 Feb	A.de Meulemeester	LVG C	Pervyse	OOC
21 Feb	A.de Meulemeester G.de Mevius G.Kervyn }	C	Clercken	OOC
21 Feb	G.Kervyn	Alb	Dixmude	DES
26 Mar	A.de Meulemeester G.de Mevius G.Kervyn }	Pfalz DIII	Dixmude	DES
11 Apr	A.de Meulemeester	C	Schoore	OOC
12 Apr	M.Siraut	C	Merckem	OOC
21 Apr	J.Goossens	Rumpler C	Lampernisse	FTL
3 May	J.Olieslagers	Fok DVII	Dixmude	OOC
3 May	G.Ory	Fok DVII	Westende	DES
9 May	A.de Meulemeester G.de Mevius }	C	Handeghem	FTL
19 May	G.Ory	Alb DV	Woumen	DES
23 May	J.Goethals E.Weekers }	C	Houthulst	FTL
30 May	E.Weekers	Balloon	Kortewilde	DES
1 Jun	B.De Leener E.Desclée M.Siraut }	C	Houthulst	FTL
5 Jun	F.Jacquet/ M.de Crombrugghe }	Fok DrI	Houthulst	OOC
9 Jul	G.de Mevius G.Kervyn }	C	Menin	OOC
18 Jul	C.de Montigny	Balloon	Blanckaert Lake	DES
11 Aug	P.de Chestret P.Dubois W.Gallez }	Fok DVII	Tervaete	FTL
11 Aug	J.Lamarche	D	Staden	OOC

14 Aug	C.de Montigny	D	—	OOC
15 Aug	M.Jamar	Fok DVII	Ypres	DES
25 Aug	A.de Meulemeester			
	G.de Mevius }	C	Houthulst	OOC
	G.Kervyn			
23 Sep	M.Martin			
	R.Rondeau }	C	Middelkerke	OOC
	J.van der Voordt			
2 Oct	W.Coppens }	C	Handzaeme	OOC
	E.Hage			
2 Oct	A.de Meulemeester }	Halb C	Beveren/Lys	OOC
	G.de Mevius			
3 Oct	W.Coppens }	C	Menin	DES
	E.Hage			
7 Oct	C.de Montigny	C	n Dixmude	DES
8 Oct	W.Gallez			
	E.Hage			
	G.Kervyn de M }	C	Gits	FTL
	J.Lemaire			
	J.Olieslagers			
14 Oct	J.Lamarche	Fok DVII	Houthulst	OOC
3 Nov	L.Robin	C	Selzaete	FTL

APPENDIX VI

The following is a fictitious claim list of Belgian airmen, including probables etc. I am fully aware it is a chauvinistic claim list, but considering many of these probable victories would have been credited in other belligerent nations, Belgian authorities, if not so strict in their crediting, could have boosted the tally of our aces a little bit.

		c		u/c		total
S/Lt	Willy Coppens	37	+	6	=	43
S/Lt	Andre de Meulemeester	11	+	19	=	30
Lt	Jan Olieslagers	6	+	16	=	22
Cdt	Fernand Jacquet	7	+	9	=	16
S/Lt	Edmond Thieffry	10	+	5	=	15
S/Lt	Georges Kervyn	4	+	9	=	13
Lt	Louis Robin	4	+	8	=	12
S/Lt	Gusto de Mevius	1	+	7	=	8
S/Lt	Jacques Goethals	2	+	4	=	6
Sgt	Etienne Hage	3	+	3	=	6
Adjt	Charles de Montigny	2	+	3	=	5
S/Lt	Pierre de Chestret	1	+	3	=	4
Cdt	Roger d'Hendecourt (obs)	-	+	4	=	4
Cdt	Walter Gallez	1	+	3	=	4
S/Lt	Pierre Braun	2	+	1	=	3
Lt	Marcel de Crombrugghe	2	+	1	=	3
S/Lt	John de Roest d'Alkemade	-	+	3	=	3
Adjt	Pierre Dubois	1	+	2	=	3
Adjt	Georges Medaets	2	+	1	=	3
Adjt	Robert Rondeau	2	+	1	=	3
Adjt	Maurice Siraut	1	+	2	=	3
Adjt	Edmond Weekers	-	+	3	=	3

APPENDIX VII

The following is a list of Belgian fighter pilots who flew more than 200 offensive patrols during the conflict.

Lt	Jan Olieslagers	9 esc	518
S/Lt	Andre de Meulemeester	9 esc	511
S/Lt	Georges Kervyn	9 esc	402
Cdt	Fernand Jacquet	GdC	328
Lt	Louis Robin	10 esc	326
S/Lt	Jacques Goethals	10 esc	302
Capt	Walter Gallez	9 esc	287
S/Lt	Bob De Leener	10 esc	260
S/Lt	Gusto de Mevius	9 esc	260
S/Lt	Max Orban	10 esc	251
Adjt	Maurice Siraut	10 esc	244
Adjt	Edmond Weekers	10 esc	243
Lt	Edmond Desclée	10 esc	234
Lt	Willy Coppens	9 esc	228
S/Lt	Pierre Dubois	9 esc	223
Adjt	Charles de Montigny	10 esc	215
Lt	Abel De Neef	9 esc	209

APPENDIX VIII

Pilots listed who were engaged in more than 40 aerial combats during the Great War.

S/Lt	Andre de Meulemeester	9 esc	185
S/Lt	Georges Kervyn	9 esc	137
Cdt	Fernand Jacquet	GdC	124
Lt	Louis Robin	10 esc	117
Lt	Jan Olieslagers	9 esc	97
Lt	Willy Coppens	9 esc	94
S/Lt	Jacques Goethals	10 esc	75
S/Lt	Edmond Thieffry	5 esc	51
S/Lt	Max Orban	10 esc	47
S/Lt	Gusto de Mevius	9 esc	46

APPENDIX IX

The list of Orders that could be awarded during the Great War or in the course of their careers to any soldier. The Belgian Orders have several ranks (lowest to highest: Chevalier (Knight); Officier (Officer); Commandeur (Commander); Grand-Officier (Grand Officer)). The most important Order is mentioned first.

Grand-Officier de l'Ordre de Leopold II
1 Sgt Maj J.Vulysteke

Commandeur de l'Ordre de Leopold
S/Lt M.Franchomme

Commandeur de l'Ordre de la Couronne
Lts F.de Woelmont & L.Wouters; S/Lts M.Franchomme & G.Kervyn de Lettenhove

Commandeur de l'Ordre de Leopold II
Cdt P.Hiernaux; Lts F.de Woelmont & L.Wouters; S/Lts M.Franchomme & G.Kervyn de Lettenhove; Adjt J.Lamarche; Sgt E.Hage

Officier de l'Ordre de Leopold
Lts W.Coppens, F.de Woelmont & L.Wouters; S/Lts G.Kervyn de Lettenhove, J.Ledure & E.Thieffry

Officier de l'Ordre de la Couronne
Cdts W.Gallez & F.Jacquet; Lts W.Coppens, H.Crombez & L.Robin; S/Lts J.Ledure & M.Medaets; Adjts J.Lamarche & G.Medaets; 1 Sgt V.Benoidt

Officier de l'Ordre de Leopold II
S/Lt J.Ledure; 1 Sgt Maj J.Vuylsteke; 1 Sgt V.Benoidt

Chevalier de l'Ordre de Leopold
Cdts J.Dony & F.Jacquet; Capt L.Colignon; Lts H.Crombez & J.Olieslagers; S/Lts P.Braun, C.Ciselet, R.Lagrange & E.Thieffry; Adjts L.Cremers & M.Siraut; 1 Sgt Maj J.Vuylsteke; 1 Sgts V.Benoidt; R.Ciselet, L.de Maelcamp d'Opstaele & R.Verhoustraeten

Chevalier de l'Ordre de l'Etoile Africaine
Capt L.Colignon; Lts A.Behaeghe & R.Castiau

Chevalier de l'Ordre de la Couronne
Cdts J.Dony & P.Hiernaux; Capt L.Colignon; Lts R.Castiau, M.de Crombrugghe de Looringhe, E.Desclée, J.Goethals & L.Wouters; S/Lts P.Braun, C.Ciselet, L.de Chestret de Haneffe, P.de Chestret de Haneffe, B.De Leener, G.de Mevius, P.Dubois, C.Gordinne, M.Medaets, M.Orban & A.Van Cotthem; Adjts G.Coppens d'Eeckenbrugge, C.de Montigny, M.Jamar, G.Medaets, R.Rondeau, E.Roobaert, M.Siraut, E.Weekers & C.Wouters; 1 Sgt Maj J.Vuylsteke; Sgt L.Guillon

Chevalier de l'Ordre de Leopold II
Cdts A.Demanet, W.Gallez & P.Hiernaux; Lts R.Castiau, E.Desclée & A.Petrowski; S/Lts C.Ciselet, P.de Chestret de Haneffe, B.De Leener, A.de Meulemeester; M.Medaets, J.Tyck; Adjts M.Jamar, E.Weekers & C.Wouters; 1 Sgt Majs C.Verbessem, F.Waroux; 1 Sgt F.de Woot de Trixhe; Sgts G.De Ruyter, L.Lhermitte & M.Martin

Médaille d'argent de l'Ordre de l'Etoile Africaine
Lt R.Castiau

APPENDIX X

Hierarchical list of Medals awarded during the Great War to the fighter pilots.

Décoration Militaire — Acte de courage
Adjt C.Wouters

Croix de Guerre 1914-18
Every pilot mentioned in the previous biographies was decorated with the Croix de Guerre

Médaille — Croix de l'Yser
Cdts A.Demanet, W.Gallez & P.Hiernaux; Lts H.Crombez, M.de Crombrugghe de Looringhe, F.de Woelmont, L.Robin & L.Wouters; S/Lts L.de Chestret de Haneffe, P.de Chestret de Haneffe, B.De Leener, G.de Mevius, M.Franchomme, C.Gordinne, M.Orban & A.Van Cotthem; Adjts G.Coppens d'Eeckenbrugge, L.Cremers, A.Delaunoit, W.Heyvaert, J.Lamarche, G.Ory, R.Rondeau, M.Siraut, J.van der Voordt & E.Weekers; 1 Sgt Majs C.Verbessem & J.Vuylsteke; 1 Sgt F.de Woot de Trixhe; Sgts G.De Ruyter, L.Guillon & J.Lemaire

Croix du Feu
Cdt P.Hiernaux; Lts F.de Woelmont, J.Olieslagers, L.Robin & L.Wouters; S/Lts M.Franchomme, J.Goossens-Bara, G.Kervyn de Lettenhove, J.Ledure, M.Medaets & M.Orban; Adjts J.Lamarche & G.Medaets; 1 Sgt Majs C.Verbessem, J.Vuylsteke & F.Waroux; 1 Sgt V.Benoidt; Sgts F.Dallemagne & E.Hage

Décoration Civique 1914-18
1 Sgt V.Benoidt

Médaille du Combattant-Volontaire 1914-18
Lt J.Olieslagers; S/Lts C.de Munck & G.Kervyn de Lettenhove; Adjts J.van der Voordt, G.Kervyn de Meerendre, J.Lamarche, G.Medaets & E.Weekers; 1 Sgt Majs R.De Clercq, J.Vuylsteke & F.Waroux; 1 Sgt V.Benoidt; Sgts F.Dallemagne, L.Guillon, E.Hage & J.Lemaire

Médaille de la Victoire &
Médaille Commémorative de la Guerre 1914-18
Cdts W.Gallez, P.Hiernaux & F.Jacquet; Lts R.Castiau, H.Crombez, M.de Crombrugghe de Looringhe, A.De Neef, F.de Woelmont, J.Goossens-Bara, J.Olieslagers, L.Robin & L.Wouters; S/Lts C.Ciselet, L.de Chestret de Haneffe, B.De Leener, G.de Mevius, C.de Munck, E.Desclée, T.Franchomme, J.Goethals, C.Gordinne, G.Kervyn de Lettenhove, J.Ledure, G.Medaets, M.Medaets, M.Orban & A.Van Cotthem; Adjts G.Coppens d'Eeckenbrugge, A.Delaunoit, L.Gerard, R.Gordinne, M.Jamar, G.Kervyn de Meerendré, J.Lamarche, E.Leonard, R.Mulders, G.Ory, R.Rondeau, M.Siraut &E.Weekers; 1 Sgt Maj J.Vuylsteke & F.Waroux; 1 Sgt V.Benoidt; Sgts F.Dallemagne & J.Lemaire

Croix Commémorative de la Maison du Roi Albert
Lt F.de Woelmont

Croix Militaire, ancienneté
Cdt P.Hiernaux; Lts F.de Woelmont & L.Wouters; S/Lts M.Franchomme & G.Kervyn de Lettenhove; 1 Sgt Maj F.Waroux; Sgt L.Lhermitte

Médaille de Liège 1914
S/Lt M.Franchomme

APPENDIX XI

FOREIGN HONOURS AND AWARDS

British
Empire

Distinguished Flying Cross
Cdt F.Jacquet

Distinguished Service Order
Lt W.Coppens

Military Cross
Lts W.Coppens, H.Crombez and L.Wouters

Distinguished Conduct Medal
Lt J.Goossens-Bara

Distinguished Flying Medal
1 Sgt Maj J.Vuylsteke

Military Medal
Cdt W.Gallez

Ethiopia

Chevalier de l'Ordre de l'Etoile
Cdt P.Hiernaux & Lt H.Crombez

France

Chevalier de la Légion d'Honneur
Cdts A.Demanet, J.Dony & F.Jacquet; Capt L.Colignon; Lts H.Crombez, J.
Olieslagers & L.Wouters and 1 Sgt Maj J.Vuylsteke

Croix de Guerre
Cdts A.Demanet, J.Dony, P.Hiernaux & F.Jaquet; Lts A.de Meulemeester,
E.Desclée, L.Robin & L.Wouters; S/Lts G.de Mevius, J.Ledure, G.Medaets,
M.Medaets & M.Orban; Adj R.Mulders, R.Rondeau, M.Siraut, J.van der
Voordt & E.Weekers, Sgts L.Guillon & E.Hage

Médaille Militaire
S/Lt B.De Leener; Adjt E.Weekers; Sgts F.Dallemagne & E.Hage

Etoile de Service
Cdt P.Hiernaux

Etoile de Bronze
Adjt M.Siraut

Greece

Croix de Guerre, 3rd Class
Adjt G.Kervyn de Meerendré

Italy   *Chevalier de l'Ordre de la Couronne*
Lt L.Wouters

Medaglio d'Argento al Valore Militare
Cdt P.Hiernaux; S/Lts A.de Meulemeester & J.Ledure

Croix de Guerre
S/Lt J.Ledure

Jerusalem   *Commander of the Order of the Holy Heart*
Sgt E.Hage

Russia   *Order of St-Stanislaus, 3rd Class*
Cdt J.Dony; Lts J.Olieslagers & L.Robin

Order of St-Anna, 3rd Class
Cdts W.Gallez & F.Jacquet

Serbia   *Order of the White Eagle*
Lt W.Coppens

Golden Medal of Kara Georges
Sgt L.Lhermitte

Golden Medal of Merit
Lt J.Olieslagers & Adjt G.Ory

Silver Medal of Merit
Adjt L.Cremers & J.Lamarche; 1 Sgt Maj F.Waroux

Sweden   *Commander in the Order of the Swords*
Lt F.de Woelmont

APPENDIX XII

BELGIAN LOSSES DUE TO ENEMY FIRE, EITHER FROM THE GROUND OR FROM A HOSTILE AIRCRAFT

1915

On 1 June the first Belgian aircraft fell to the guns of the accurate German AA fire. A Farman two-seater, manned by Escadrille I's Lt Jean Petit and S/Lt Maurice Benselin, started for a recce-mission in the late afternoon. At 17.50 they were hit by AA fire and fell between Martjevaart and the Canal d'Ieperlee. Both crew were made a prisoner of war. Benselin, born in 1878, was interned due to his age, to Switzerland in December 1917 from where he was repatriated in July 1918. He again went to war and was commissioned on 30 September.

1916

The next victim fell on 13 March. 4me Escadrille's 1Sgt Maj Charles Ciselet with his observer Lt André Smits took off for an observation patrol. The Farman seemed to suffer engine trouble and Ciselet crash-landed into the sea, killing his observer and being severely injured himself.

One week later, 20 March, another observer of the 4me Escadrille was killed. Lt Pierre Rigaux took off for a bombing mission to Houttave airfield in the Farman flown by 1Sgt Raymond Rondeau, brother to the fighter pilot Robert. Whilst Rigaux was watching the result of his efforts, the Farman was attacked from the rear by a 'Fokker' (all German scouts at this stage were called Fokker by the Belgian pilots). Rigaux took to his gun but was then hit in the chest, being mortally wounded. Rondeau, however, managed to shake off his opponent and landed as close as he could to the Military Hospital, but his observer was dead.

Yet another 4me Escadrille observer fell victim, this time Lt Joseph Gilles mortally wounded on 2 July. His pilot, 1Sgt Maj Charles 'Sidi' Ciselet, hardly recovered from his first wound, was wounded yet again, but managed to land safely behind the Belgian lines. His Farman, however, was demolished.

1917

The first victim of this year fell on 7 April. Lt Richard Fanning, observer to the Escadrille Franco/Belge (Esc. C74) was mortally wounded by a piece of shrapnel during an observation sortie. His pilot, French Lieutenant Manseron, was unhurt.

Next day 6me Escadrille's BE2c two-seaters took off for an observation sortie to Bruges. On the way back, the BE, manned by Adjt Armand Glibert and S/Lt Jules Callant was attacked by three scouts. Ltn Alfred Träger and Ltn Walter Göttsch, Jasta 8, both attacked the same BE. Whilst Träger broke off the fight and hastily landed at Ghistelles airfield (being severely wounded), Göttsch went on and shot down the BE for his 8th of an eventual 20 victories. This fight was witnessed by Lts Walter Gallez/Marcel de Crombrugghe and Adjt Willy Coppens/Lt Gustave Declercq, both in two other 6me Esc. BE's. Both Gallez and Coppens were too far separated from the fight to be able to help. Lt Alexandre Petrowski and Adjts Pierre de Chestret and Edmond Thieffry, who came to the rescue in their Nieuports, were also too late to stop Göttsch's fatal attack.

On 1 May, the next Farman F40 was shot down in flames. 3me Escadrille's French born Sgt Jean Pauli and Lt Jean de Bersaques came down near Dixmude. Either Jasta 28's Karl Schäfer or Marinefeld Jasta I's Obltn zur See Gotthard Sachsenberg was the victor. Both men claimed a Belgian Farman although only one was actually lost on this day.

Another 3me Esc. Farman was lost on 12 May. Sgt Paul de Goussencourt and Lt Leon De Cubber were claimed by AA battery 711. The aircraft fell in flames close to Dixmude, killing its crew.

The next Farman, this time a 4me Escadrille machine, was lost on 15 July. S/Lts Charles Kervyn de Lettenhove and Jacques de Meeus were killed when they were attacked by two Jasta 7 pilots. Ltn Schäfer claimed his first and only victory over Vlasdloo as the fight pushed the Farman further and further behind the German lines. Due to the wind, the Farman could not dash for home and was doomed to be shot down. Both Belgians were renowned observation pilots and both had the aggressive spirit needed to be fighter pilots. Both men, however, were always refused a transfer to the 1ère Escadrille de Chasse although they had asked repeatedly to be transferred. Comte Jacques de Meeus arrived at the front on 21 June 1915 and saw his first combat on 14 December. Flying with Lt Charles Coomans in the observer's seat, they were attacked by three scouts. Coomans started to fire, but found his gun jammed. Whilst de Meeus was trying to avoid the German bullets, Coomans started to fire with his Verey Pistol, whereupon the Germans abandoned the fight. On 6 September 1916, de Meeus and Coomans flew an evening sortie to Brussels, throwing three bombs on the Zeppelin sheds at Etterbeek. De Meeus was also the first Belgian to fly an evening offensive patrol, together with Adjt John de Roest d'Alkemade, on 5 April 1917. During a photo-operation patrol de Meeus, again with Coomans as his observer, on 9 June, was attacked by three Halberstadt fighters. Protected by Adjts Pierre de Chestret and Charles Ciselet, all three were involved in a 'dogfight'. De Meeus, in his obsolete Farman was attacked by an all-red Halberstadt and his aircraft was riddled with bullets. De Chestret, seeing his companion and good friend in trouble, broke off his own fight and threw himself between the Farman and the Halberstadt. In this action de Chestret was severely wounded himself, but this action allowed de Meeus to dive to safety. He crash-landed his Farman behind the Belgian lines. The Farman was beyond repair, but the photographic plates were saved. Then in July, on the 6th, de Meeus was honoured in flying King Albert over the front. Two days later, with S/Lt Charles Kervyn de Lettenhove, they attacked and shot down an enemy aircraft for both pilots' only credited victory. Charles Kervyn, born in October 1892, was the older brother of Georges Kervyn, the highly praised fighter pilot. He was a volunteer who arrived at the front on the same day as Jacques de Meeus. With his usual observer Capt Roger le Sergeant d'Hendecourt, he claimed a probable victory in 1915 and another in 1916.

Another obsolete Farman (3me Escadrille) was shot down on 27 July. 1Sgt Max Vilain XIIII and his observer Lt Van Sprang were lost on this date, claimed by Flakzug 513 under the command of Ltn Hübner. Both Belgians were taken prisoner for the fourth victory of Flak 513. Ltn Jakob Wolff, a Jasta 17 pilot, was credited in shooting down a Farman south-west of Dixmude at 16.35 for his fourth victory. Location and time are the same as the 3me Esc.'s loss. Probably this is a double claim.

23 September saw the third and last severe wounds of S/Lt Charles Ciselet. He was not claimed by a Jasta pilot, but nevertheless 'Sidi' Ciselet was wounded in an aerial combat on that evening. Unfortunately, every detail of the combat is missing.

The first fighter pilot killed in action fell on 30 September. Lt Paul Hanciau took off together with Adjt Jules Goossens for the afternoon sortie. Separated from one another, Hanciau suddenly found himself surrounded by ten scouts and was attacked immediately. Mortally wounded, Hanciau broke off the fight at 14.45 east of Dixmude and headed for his lines. He nearly managed to land safe near Alveringhem, but must have been dead by this time, and crashed to the ground. He was apparently not claimed.

The first Belgian RE8 was lost on 23 October. 1Sgt Edouard Herman and his observer S/Lt Henri Van Geel were shot down by Vfw Hans Fritzsche, Jasta 29 for his third and final victory over St-Jacques-Capelle at 16.35. Although Ltn Fritz Kieckhäfer claimed a Belgian BE on the same day, ten minutes later, for his fifth victory, no other two-seaters were lost.

20 November saw the third demise of a fighter pilot. 1Sgt Robert Ciselet, brother to Charles, fell victim to Ltn Erwin Böhme, Staffelführer of Jasta 'Boelcke' for the latter's 23rd of an eventual 24 victories. The Nieuport fell at Caeskerke.

Another three fighter pilots were to be killed in December. First there was the demise of S/Lt Pierre Braun on the 5th. Two days later 1Sgt Armand Verhoustraeten was killed and on the 19th, 1Sgt Carlos Verbessem fell to his death (see their biographies for further details).

1918

The first victim in the last year of the war was non other than the renowned ace S/Lt Edmond Thieffry on 23 February, claimed by a two-seater and taken prisoner.

On 11 May Sgt M.De Grauw, a novice pilot belonging to the 2me Escadrille, took off in a Camel for a protection flight. This turned out to be the pilot's first and only war flight for he landed safely in an open field, but unfortunately on the wrong side of the lines!

Seven days later, another of the Ciselet brothers was killed in action. Sgt Marcel Ciselet, born May 1890, was a volunteer who, during the opening battles and the siege of Liège, back in August 1914, found himself surrounded and was taken prisoner. He managed to escape, reach Belgian lines and his unit, then transferring to the Aviation Militaire, like his three brothers. He flew his first war flight on 9 April 1918 in a 4me Escadrille Nieuport scout and flew 18 protection flights before he fought his first and only combat. No details are known and no Jasta pilot claimed a scout over Pierkenshoek at 14.50 on 18 May 1918. However, this is the last time and place he was seen and Ciselet is presumed to be shot down in a combat.

The following day another Camel was lost. This time a relatively new pilot, 1Sgt Pageot, belonging to the 2me Escadrille was lost during a protection flight. He was taken prisoner of war, but the reason he landed at the 'wrong side' is unknown.

Yet another fighter pilot was lost on 12 June. S/Lt Louis de Chestret was obliged to crash-land his Spad in 'Hun land' due to fuel shortage (see his biography).

On 28 September, on the opening day of the Belgian liberation offensive, two two-seaters were lost. The first was a Bréguet XIV, manned by Adjt R.Cajot and Lt A.Bricoult. Both 2me Escadrille crew were taken prisoner after Cajot had brought his burning machine down close to Cortemarck. They were claimed by Ltn z S Theo Osterkamp for his 28th of an eventual 32 victories. Cajot had been assigned to the 2me Escadrille in March where he immediately teamed up with Bricoult.

The other two-seater lost was the 7me Escadrille Spad XI, manned by two famous aircrew, S/Lt John de Roest d'Alkemade and Lt Charles Coomans. Coomans was the main observer to S/Lt Jacques de Meeus from 1915 until the latter's death in action in 1917. The bombing of the Zeppelin sheds at Etterbeek on 6 September 1916 was Coomans' 205th war flight! On one occasion, Coomans, on a photo-mission, was surprised by an attacking scout. Not at all impressed, Coomans first took a photograph of the oncoming danger and then took to his gun! Two other brothers (Jean and Constant) were observers as well. John de Roest, born in March 1894, arrived at the front as a pilot on 14 December 1915 and flew many OP's in 1916. He was also engaged in many night bombing sorties and on 7 December 1916, with his observer S/Lt Alberique Rolin and accompanied by two scouts flown by Adjts Edmond Desclée and Max Orban, occupied Ghent and Antwerp were 'visited'. 125 newspapers and banners and flags were thrown to the surprised people. As mentioned earlier, de Roest was the first to fly a night-fighter patrol with Jacques de Meeus. He was also the first to be engaged in a night combat on the night of 1-2 October 1917. With observer

Lt Louis Robin, two Gotha bombers were engaged without result. On 13 November, with Rolin in the observer's seat, flying a Sopwith 1½ Strutter, he was attacked by an Albatros two-seater. He was however rescued by Flight Commander Joseph Fall, 9 (Naval) Sqdn, RNAS, who shot down the two-seater. When in 1918, German troops tried to break through the Belgian front-lines at Merckem on 18 April, the recce-pilots of the Belgian army saved the day by flying many ground-strafing missions. Five two-seaters, including de Roest, flew at a height of only 50 metres emptying their guns and dropping a few bombs at the overwhelming German front-line trenches. On 28 September, however, de Roest and Coomans were attacked over Houthulst Forest and crashed. The Spad was not completely wrecked, but the two men were killed. They were possibly the victim of Ltn dR Hermann Bargmann, MFJII, for his first and only victory. Bargmann, however, claimed a DH9 but this might have been the Belgian Spad XI.

The next Spad XI was lost on 3 October. 6me Escadrille lost S/Lt André Gisseleire and observer Lt Max Roland in # Sp11 during a combat with 11 Fokkers. Gisseleire was another two-seater pilot who was engaged in ground-strafing missions on 17 and 18 April during the battle of Merckem. During their last fight, Roland managed to shoot down an adversary (Ltn z S Meyer, MFJ IV ?) before their own demise.

On the same day, 9me Escadrille's Adjt Maurice Jamar was shot down in his Hanriot by AA fire and became a prisoner of war. Next day Sgt Max Martin was killed in action in a fight with Jasta 56 (see each pilot's biographies).

The demise of both 10me Escadrille pilots S/Lt Jacques Goethals and Adjt Charles de Montigny is also narrated in their biographies.

A Spad XI, manned by Wittewrongel/Van Thorenburg, 6me Escadrille was forced to land at Zandvoorde on 17 October, but apparently not claimed. The same Escadrille lost Adjt René Gerard (brother to Léon, the fighter pilot) and Capt. Biver on the 22nd. They were taken prisoner of war, but it is not known whether they were shot down or not. Ltn Karl Plauth, Jasta 51, scored a victory that day north of Deynze, claiming a Bréguet XIV for his 16th of an eventual 17 victories.

APPENDIX XIII

OTHER BELGIANS SERVING WITH THE AVIATION MILITAIRE WHO DIED DURING THE GREAT WAR

SOUMOY Jules D, Lieutenant, Escadrille II. Killed at Buc (Seine et Oise) in an accident, flying a H.Farman 20, on 5 September 1914. Aged 28.

DECHAMP François E.N., Capitaine, Escadrille III. Killed at Ghyvelde when a bomb exploded whilst being taken off the H.Farman 20 on 21 December 1914. Fifteen casualties were counted among the ground personnel. Aged 29.

BUSSY Léopold A., Lieutenant, Escadrille III. Killed by accident in a Voisin two-seater at Villacoublay on 7 May 1915. Aged 25.

TACCOEN Robert, Caporal, Pilot School. Crashed his M.Farman while landing at Etampes on 21 June 1915. Aged 28.

MICHAUX Henri J., Caporal, Pilot School. Killed during a test flight at Etampes on 1 February 1916. Aged 24.

EVRARD Marcel, Caporal, Pilot School. Killed whilst flying a M.Farman at Etampes on 21 September 1916. Aged 19.

DEPROOST Robert, Soldat, IIIme Section des Aérostiers (Balloon nr.3). Killed when his balloon was set on fire by Ltn Alfred Ulmer, Jasta 8. Deproost jumped but his parachute caught fire and he fell to his death at Eikhoek, Oostvleteren on 1 October 1916. Aged 23.

DUPONT Jules J., Caporal, Pilot School. Killed in a crash at Etampes, flying a M.Farman XI on 20 August, 1917. Aged 22.

HALLET Lucien V., Sergent, 2me Escadrille. Killed during a test flight with 1er Sergent L.de Maelcamp d'Opstaele in a Farman 40 on 22 August, 1917. Aged 22.

de MEULEMEESTER Jacques L, Caporal, Pilot School. Brother to Andre de Meulemeester, the renowned fighter pilot, he died of illness at Etampes on 5 December 1917, aged 24.

VERTONGEN René, Sous-Lieutenant, Parc d'Aviation. Got lost in a gale over the sea, flying the mail of HM King Albert to England on 1 February 1918 in a Hanriot. His body was found off Oye (France) on 14 April. Aged 40.

de MELOTTE de LAVAUX Paul, Sergent, Parc d'Aviation. Killed whilst flying a Nieuport N23 at Beau-Marais, Calais, on 11 March 1918. Aged 21.

ARTAN de SAINT-MARTIN Louis C.F.M.M., Caporal, Pilot School. Killed whilst flying an RE8 at Juvisy on 24 April 1918. Aged 24.

PRINGIERS Fritz, Sergent, 2me Escadrille. Killed with his passenger, mécanicien Benjamin Meurisse, flying a test flight in a Sopwith 1½ Strutter at Coxyde on 9 May 1918, aged 23.

VAN STAPPEN Victor, Sergent, 4me Escadrille. Killed when his Sopwith 1½ Strutter suddenly caught fire and crashed on 19 May 1918 at Houthem airfield. Aged 20.

VLIECKX René, Sergent, 3me Escadrille. Killed with his observer Sous-Lieutenant Cornesse, when the former crashed his Sopwith 1½ Strutter at Les Moeres airfield on 21 May 1918. Aged 21.

CORNESSE William, Sous-Lieutenant, 3me Escadrille. Killed when his pilot, Sgt Vlieckx crashed his Sopwith 1½ Strutter at Les Moeres airfield on 21 May 1918, aged 28.

VAN DYCK Léon, Caporal, Pilot School. A student pilot who crashed his M.Farman XI at Juvisy. Mortally wounded, he died at the Hôpital St-Charles on 23 May 1918. Aged 22.

MALHERBE Didier, 1er Sergent, 4me Escadrille. Crashed his Sopwith Camel whilst taking off at his airfield (Houthem) on 4 June 1918. Aged 21.

GALLER Robert, Sous-Lieutenant, Pilot School. Killed when his Sopwith 1½ Strutter crashed at Juvisy on 2 July 1918. He was heading for the front to deliver a new propeller for S/Lt Willy Coppens' Hanriot. Aged 30.

BOEL Gaston, Sergent, 6me Escadrille. Killed whilst taking off in a Sopwith Camel at Houthem airfield on 7 August, 1918, aged 23.

KASEL Gabriel, Caporal, Pilot School. A student pilot who crashed his Farman 40 at Athis-Mons (France) on 4 September 1918. Aged 21.

ECKSTEIN Serge, Capitaine-Commandant, Ière Section des Aérostiers. Killed by a shell at Passchendaele on 5 October 1918, whilst leaving a pill box. Aged 41.

DEMOT Jean, Sous-Lieutenant, Ière Section des Aérostiers. Killed by the same shell that had killed Cdt Eckstein at Passchendaele on 5 October 1918. Aged 42.

GRUBER Servais, Sous-Lieutenant, Observer, 4me Escadrille. Died of illness at Cabour Military Hospital on 20 October 1918. Aged 24.

GILSON Arthur, Sergent, Pilot School. Died of illness at Calais on 26 October 1918, aged 35.

JONNIAU Fernand, Adjudant observer, IIme Compagnie des Aérostiers. Died of illness at the Military Hospital at Bruges on 30 October 1918. Aged 28.

LEBON Pierre, Capitaine-Commandant, Commanding Officer of the Technical Service at Calais. Died as a victim of influenza at the Military Hospital Roi Albert at Paris on 8 November 1918. Aged 30.

GROUND STAFF WHO DIED DURING THE WAR

BERRESSE Jules, Soldat, died 12 September 1914, aged 21.

BISIAU Ferdinand, Soldat, Escadrille III, died in the same explosion that had put an end to Cdt Dechamp at Ghyvelde, 21 December 1914. Aged 22.

SANTERMANS Albert J., chauffeur, Escadrille III. Mortally wounded when a bomb, attached to an aircraft, exploded at Noorenberghe farm, Ghyvelde on 21 December 1914. Transferred to Dunkerque, he died three days later, aged 28.

DELORY René G.J., Soldat, Cie des Aviateurs, died at Furnes 23 January 1915, aged 20.

LAMBLOTTE Gerard, Sergent. Hospitalized due to illness at St-Pol-sur-Mer on 19 January 1915 and died 2 February aged 30.

BOSCHMANS Fernand L.M.O., aviateur, died at Coxyde 17 May 1915, aged 18.

SARTIAUX Narcisse, Soldat, 3me Escadrille. Killed in a car accident at Etampes, 10 June 1915, aged 23.

THONUS François J., Soldat, 2me Escadrille, Chevalier de l'Ordre de Leopold II. Mortally wounded (fracture of the skull) at Coxyde, 8 February 1917 and died two days later, aged 29.

DAPSENS Henri A.A.G., chauffeur, 3me Escadrille, mortally wounded in a car accident on 25 February 1917, died the same day at l'Océan Military Hospital, aged 25.

DUBOIS Isidore, Soldat, Parc d'Essence de l'Aviation at Calais. Died of illness at Calais, 20 May 1917, aged 39.

VERHELLE Victor, Soldat, Parc d'Aviation, Calais. Succumbed to illness 7 September 1917, aged 30.

DENECKER Joseph B.H., chauffeur, 4me Escadrille, mortally wounded during a bombing raid and died at Dunkerque 11 September 1917. Aged 23.

TROCH Emile E., Soldat, Parc d'Aviation at Calais. Drowned off Calais 8 January 1918, aged 41.

DURIEUX Jules, Soldat, 10me Escadrille. Accidentally shot through the head and died of his injuries on 21 March 1918, aged 33.

MARY Léon L.G., Caporal-mécanicien, Parc d'Aviation at Calais. Went ill and died at Calais, 24 April 1918.

MEURISSE Benjamin E., 1ère mécanicien, 2me Escadrille. Died when his pilot, Sgt Pringiers, crashed his Sopwith 1½ Strutter at Coxyde, 9 May 1918. Aged 26.

CORNELISSIS Stanislas R., Soldat, 3me Escadrille, mortally wounded during a bombing raid on Les Moeres airfield on 6 June 1918, aged 23.

DEBUYSER Adolphe J., Soldat, 3me Escadrille. Mortally wounded during a bombing raid on Les Moeres airfield on 6 June 1918, aged 20.

PRÉAT Alfred J., Soldat, 3me Escadrille. Mortally wounded during a bombing raid on Les Moeres airfield on 6 June 1918, aged 20.

VERMEULEN Gustave F.M., Soldat, 3me Escadrille. Mortally wounded during the bombing raid on Les Moeres airfield, 6 June 1918, aged 25.

DE LISSNYDER Ernest A., Soldat, Pilot School, died of pneumonia at Juvisy, 4 August 1918, aged 33.

DEVILERS Telesphore, A., Soldat, 2me Escadrille. Hospitalized at Cabour 28 August 1918 and died three days later of illness, aged 28.

KLANT Louis, Soldat, 2me Escadrille. Went ill and was hospitalized at Cabour, 23 August 1918. Died 3 September aged 21.

MARCHAND Alfred B., Caporal, 2me Escadrille. Hospitalized at Cabour, 31 August 1918 and died 4 September aged 24.

DUPONCHEEL Cyrille, Soldat. Hospitalized as an endocarditis patient from which he died at Calais on 6 September 1918, aged 38.

MEERT Jean B., Soldat, 8me Escadrille. Accidentally wounded at Kwaadrijke 15 September 1918 and died the same day, aged 29.

DE VOGELAERE Leon, Soldat, 8me Escadrille. Died of illness at Bourbourg, France on 16 September 1918, aged 30.

VERSTRAETE Gustave, Soldat, aérostiers, 3me Cie. Mortally wounded by a piece of shrapnel in the abdomen and died at Langemarck, 30 September 1918, aged 29.

NOÉ Pierre J., Soldat, 6me Escadrille. Hospitalized with bronchopneumonia at Cabour and died 24 October 1918. Aged 36.

GOBERT Armand A.C., Adjudant, 6me Escadrille. Victim of the influenza epidemic, hospitalized at Cabour on 24 October 1918 and died two days later, aged 35.

MUTSAARS Jean L.C., Soldat-mécanicien. Another victim of the influenza epidemic, he was hospitalized at Cabour 23 October and died on the 29th, aged 28.

VAN de WEYER Antoine H., Adjudant, 3me Escadrille. Victim of the influenza epidemic, hospitalized at Cabour 27 October 1918 and died four days later, aged 26.

VLAEMINCK Hector J., 1er Sergent Major, 2me Escadrille. An influenza victim, he died at Calais, 29 October 1918, aged 32.

DAUWEN André C., Brigadier-chauffeur. Hospitalized at Gravelines, 26 October 1918 and died four days later. Aged 32.

HELLEN Leon P., Soldat, 6me Escadrille. Hospitalized (illness) at St-Michel Hospital at Bruges, 13 October 1918 and died 1 November aged 26.

BAAR Maurice L.A.H.J., Caporal, 3me Escadrille, died at Bruges St-Michel Hospital 4 November 1918, aged 26.

COLLARD Nicolas J., Sergent, 5me Escadrille. Hospitalized on 1 October 1918 as an influenza victim and died at Calais, 2 December 1918, aged 26.

GELDHOF Jean E., Soldat. Demised at Rosendael, France, 29 January 1919. Aged 20.

FESTRAETS Henri L., Soldat. Died of illness contracted during active service at Cabour Military Hospital 16 August 1919, aged 25.

APPENDIX XIV

The insignias of the Aviation Militaire Belge:

2me Escadrille d'Observation:

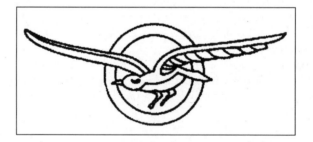

3me Escadrille d'Observation:

4me Escadrille d'Observation: zebra:

5me Escadrille d'Observation:

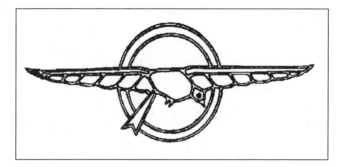

6me Escadrille d'Observation:

7me Escadrille d'Observation Photographique:

8me Escadrille de Bombardement et de Reconnaissance de Nuit:

9me Escadrille de Chasse:

10me Escadrille de Chasse:

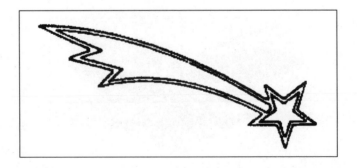

11me Escadrille de Chasse:

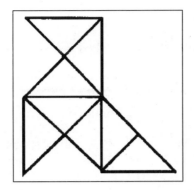

SOURCES

Archives
Ordre Journalières du Grand Quartier General, Ière Section, Aviation Militaire Belge, Carnet de Vols, Groupe de Chasse. Both at CHD, Evere

Books
COPPENS de HOUTHULST (Willy O.F.J.) *Jours Envolés* :
COPPENS de HOUTHULST (Willy O.F.J.) *Reclassement, hélice en croix — Genève* 1945
COPPENS de HOUTHULST (Willy O.F.J.) *Reclassement, vue cavaliere — Genève* 1947
COPPENS de HOUTHULST (Willy O.F.J.) *Un homme volant: Jan Olieslagers*
FRANKS (Norman L.R.); BAILEY (Frank), *Over the Front, A complete Record of the Fighter Aces and Units of the United States and French Air Services 1914-1918.* - London : Grub Street, 1992
FRANKS (Norman L.R.); GUEST (Russell); BAILEY (Frank), *Above the Lines. A complete Record of the Fighter Aces of the German Air Service, Naval Air Service and Flanders Marine Corps 1914-1918.* — London : Grub Street 1993
FRANKS (Norman L.R.); BAILEY (Frank); DUIVEN (Rick), *The Jasta Pilots . Detailed listings and histories, August 1916 - November 1918* — London : Grub Street 1996
FRANKS (Norman L.R.), *Who downed the Aces in WWI ? Facts, figures and photos on the fate of over 300 top pilots flying over the Western Front.* — London : Grub Street 1996
LYR (René), *Nos Héros, Morts pour la Patrie.* - Bruxelles : Societé Anonyme Belge d'Imprimerie 1923
ROBERTSON (Bruce), *Air Aces of the 1914-1918 War.* — Letchworth : Harleyford Publications Ltd 1959
Guldenboek der Vuurkaart — Brussel : J.Rozez, 1937
SHORES (Christopher); FRANKS (Norman L.R.); GUEST (Russell), *Above the Trenches. A Complete Record of the Fighter Aces and the Units of the British Empire Air Forces 1915-1920.* — London : Grub Street 1990

Magazines
La Conquête de l'Air;
La Guerre Aériennes Illustrée;
Le Courier de l'Armée Belge

Photographs
Aviation Society of Antwerp (heritage of the late Mr E.Rerren); Baron de Crombrugghe de Looringhe; Baron de Woelmont; Brussels Air Museum; Centre de Documentation Historique de l'Armée Belge, Evere; La Guerre Aériennes Illustrée; Mr G.Lecomte; Mrs M. Olieslagers; Mr J. van der Voordt

Apart from the above mentioned sources, several persons helped and sustained me during the research, the build-up and the finalising of this history, so I want to make a special tribute to Mr D.Buytaert at ASA, Deurne Airport, Antwerp; Mr P.Dallemagne; Baron de Chestret de Haneffe; Baron E.de Crombrugghe de Looringhe; Dr J.de Moor, PhD; Mr G.Destrebecq; Baron H.de Woelmont; Lt-Col SBH M.Emonts-Gast; Mr Notary B.Hage-Goetbloets; Mr J.Huyghelier, Centre Historique at Evere; Mr Y.Lamarche; Lt-Col G.Leclercq, Centre Historique, Evere; Mr G.Lecomte; Mrs M.Olieslagers; Mr J.J.Orban; Mr Ch.Pieters; Mr A.Rely; Mr E.Reunis (Brussels Air Museum); Mr R.Schuermans; Lt-Col SBH Terlinden;

Mr M.Traute; Mr Van Belleghem at ASA, Deurne Airport, Antwerp; Mrs K.Van den Berghe (Radio 2); Mr J.van der Voordt and Lt-Col C.Wouters and all other persons I might have forgotten in the list.

Very special thanks to Norman Franks, Cdt Guy De Win at the Centre Historique & last but not least my wife Hilde and children Jana, Raf & Katrien for their patience.

NOTES

NOTES

NOTES

NOTES

NOTES